STRANGE LEADERSHIP

40 WAYS TO LEAD AN INNOVATIVE ORGANIZATION

{Revised & Updated}

GREG ATKINSON

Foreword by

MARK BATTERSON

New York Times Bestselling Author

Cover design by Chuck Scoggins
Interior design by Bob Sharpe – Two Stone Lions Press

Published in the United States of America by Two Stone Lions Press
ISBN: 978-1-62390-062-5
1. Religion / Christian Church / Leadership
2. Business & Economics / Leadership 14.02.14

STRANGE LEADERSHIP

GREG ATKINSON

Foreword by

MARK BATTERSON

New York Times Bestselling Author

Dedication

This book is dedicated to my wife, Chrissy. Only you know how much this book means to me and the years of research, traveling, speaking (my blood, sweat, and tears) that I've put into this work. Thank you for supporting me, believing in me, and encouraging me. Thank you for reading through my manuscript numerous times, looking for errors and correcting my grammar. You are a blessing and a treasure. I love our life together. I am stronger with you by my side.

Acknowledgements

I'd like to thank the people who helped me research this book and process through the ways innovation can be birthed. I'd like to thank the many pastors who gave me ideas. I'd like to thank the bold people that had the courage to come up to me after one of my conferences on innovation and say, "What about" and share with me a new way innovation can come about.

I'd like to thank my family, friends, and peers for believing in me and allowing me to live out my dream of equipping church leaders. I'd like to thank Henry and Richard Blackaby and Claude King for their amazing work *Experiencing God*, which was foundational in my life. I went through it for the first time when I was twenty years old, and I've gone back through it numerous times over the last two decades.

I'd like to thank all those who encouraged me to release a Second Edition and my friend who helped me make it possible. May God bless you all.

Lastly, I'd like to thank my Savior, Jesus Christ, for His work in my life and how He chooses to use the weak to lead the strong.

Praise for *Strange Leadership*

Innovation is imperative in today's leadership culture. *Strange Leadership* reminds us all that innovation is about doing a whole new thing, that ultimately flows from God, the Chief Innovator. Thanks Greg for pointing us back to our true source for innovation and inspiration.

—Brad Lomenick, author and Former President of Catalyst

Because leadership in Jesus' upside-down Kingdom is so different and distinct from the world, it is "strange leadership." In his book, Greg offers practical and helpful thoughts on leading others as one under the rule of God.

—Eric Geiger, author and Vice President LifeWay Christian Resources

It's one thing to say to ourselves "let go and let God"—it's a whole different level when, without realizing it we say, "I've got it now, God. You can let go of me. I'll be fine." Those words and this book is a great call back to know Who's we are and to have a desperate dependency on the One true source for positive change within our ranks. Greg's quoting of the word brings root to the seeds that he is helping each reader plant in their ministry. This book stirred me and reminded me that it's not so much about letting go as much as it is about holding on with a healthy desperation that will catapult you into new levels of God's "marvelous and wonderful things" for you, your ministry and your leaders.

—Todd Rhoades, Director—Leadership Network

To be effective, church leaders must be open to innovation. We have to be willing to allow something new to happen in our churches as we seek God's leading; we have to stay on the cutting edge, so we can be relevant in the world we are trying to reach. One of the best ways to stay innovative is to listen to and learn from those who model biblical innovation every day, like my friend Greg Atkinson.

—Nelson Searcy, Founder and Lead Pastor of The Journey Church, author and founder of www.ChurchLeaderInsights.com

Strange Leadership is an engrossing and enchanting collection of probes into the emerging field of innovation studies. It is filled with firecrackers, and sometimes even fireworks.

—Leonard Sweet, best-selling author, professor (Drew University, George Fox University), Chief Contributor to sermons.com

I'm not sure most of us would aspire to be called a strange leader . . . until I read Greg Atkinson's book and caught a vision of the rich meaning of that word, "strange." I applaud Greg's call for leaders who are prayerful listeners to the often-risky voice of the Holy Spirit, and courageous enough to act on those whispers.

—Nancy Beach, Leadership Coach, SlingShot Group and author of An Hour on Sunday and Gifted to Lead

So many people are fascinated with being innovative these days. Greg reminds us that our focus should rest in Christ and in joining where God is at work. This is a great Biblical view of innovation and something I hope church leaders will cherish for years to come.

—Dr. Johnny Hunt, Senior Pastor First Baptist Woodstock, former President of the Southern Baptist Convention

Everyone wants to be the first to discover the next big thing. We are obsessed with new ideas and products; we love innovation, but Greg reminds us that God is the Great Innovator and listening to His voice is the first step in learning to innovate ourselves. I hope you'll check out *Strange Leadership*, because when we make following Jesus our goal, innovation will come naturally.

—Greg Surratt, Founding Pastor of Seacoast Church, Founder and President of ARC

Innovation is not a secular concept. At its core, it's a spiritual concept. And for the Christian leader, it's in an understanding that our God is the creator God who is still breathing new vision and insights into his people through the Holy Spirit and the mind that he gave us. will help you think through your unique situation and the unique triggers and circumstances that God may be using to lead you and your team into the next stage of innovation and growth.

—Larry Osborne, author and pastor, North Coast Church, Vista, CA

If you throw a rock in the 21st century, you'll likely hit a self-appointed leadership guru. They seem to be everywhere, and they've written a library of books with enough strategies and steps to make one dizzy. Luckily, Greg is not just another guru who has written another leadership book. He sinks his feet into the rich soil of Scripture and keeps his eyes on Christ as he discusses this important topic. In a leadership-saturated age, that is something strange indeed!

—Jonathan Merritt, author of Jesus is Better than You Imagined; Senior Columnist for Religion News Service

Everything that happens is a result of leadership and decision making by human beings serving God on mission. However, where the strength and power of that leadership comes from makes all the difference. We can be making decisions and leading from human philosophy and our own strength or we can turn to the One who gives us wisdom, strength and the ability to lead. Greg helps us see that although it may seem "strange" to lead this way, it is the only way leaders serving Jesus should lead. Lord help us if we aren't "strange" in this way.

—Dan Kimball, Founding Pastor of Vintage Faith Church, author of They Like Jesus but Not the Church

For the Christian leader to find success, he or she cannot lead apart from God's Spirit. Leave it to my innovative friend to innovatively connect the two . . . Christian leadership and God's Spirit. Of course. We cannot separate the two. Thank you, Greg, for making us better leaders.

—Ron Edmondson, Pastor, Blogger and Church Consultant

It's not a coincidence that God chose to introduce himself in the first verse of the Bible as a "Creator." I believe God puts a far higher value on creativity and innovation than most people believe. That's why I'm thrilled with Greg's new book. It's a wake-up call to the Church and a powerful reminder that change is here whether we're ready or not, and whether we like it or not. Leaders—dismiss this book at your peril.

—Phil Cooke, Ph.D. Filmmaker, Media Consultant, and author of Unique: Telling Your Story in the Age of Brands and Social Media

Innovation for the sake of innovation is never a good idea—it must be led by the Holy Spirit. And often this makes us appear strange. In this book Greg shares how this type of innovation takes place.

—Bill Easum, Author and Senior Consultant, 21st Century Strategies

Innovation isn't just for Disney and mad scientists. With a strong foundation of Scripture, Greg Atkinson leads us through thoughts on using innovation in the church, using stories from various churches to illustrate. Whether working through everyday situations, frustrations or desperation, leaders are encouraged to color outside the lines of normal, being intentional in seeking God's best for His church. Be prepared to roll up your sleeves as you put the book into practice . . . innovation isn't always pretty!

—Dr. David R. Fletcher, Founder of XPastor, Executive Pastor of EvFree Fullerton

I like innovative thinkers, but I love innovative do-ers. Greg is an innovative local church do-er. He is in the trenches every day of pastoral ministry. He's been there, done that and still doing it. Every generation of church leaders has to deliver the timeless Gospel in timely ways. It takes intentional innovation from strange leaders who are willing to step outside the box, take risks and endure criticism to change the world. Greg's book will goad and inspire you and your team to be pioneer practitioners but will also give you practical steps on how to innovatively get 'r done.

—Jim Tomberlin, Founder & Chief Strategist, MultiSite Solutions, author of 125 Tips for Multisite Churches and Better Together: Making Church Mergers Work

Greg's *Strange Leadership* is strange only because the general populace knows so little of God's ways. Brimmed full of wisdom from God's word, this volume presents the way to genuine success.

—Dr. Paige Patterson, President, Southwestern Baptist Theological Seminary

Strange Leadership provides leadership help to teach you how innovation can come about in your life and organization by keeping

God at the center and will equip you with practical thoughts to lead with integrity.

—Pete Wilson, author of Plan B and Let Hope In

While the message and the mission of the Gospel never changes, churches today have to start thinking more like missionaries on a foreign field instead of being comfortable with the status quo of bygone days. Through tons of conversations with pastors who are actually engaging this culture with the life-giving message of Christ, Greg's *Strange Leadership* holds that careful balance of timeless truth and godly innovation. A good read to learn what is going on out there.

—Dr. George M. Hillman, Chair and Associate Professor of Educational Ministries and Leadership at Dallas Theological Seminary

Greg knows church and you can learn about good church leadership here. But more important, Greg knows Jesus and the power of the Holy Spirit. If you want to learn about Spirit-led innovation, this book should be prayerfully read, internalized, and acted upon. You and your ministry will never be the same.

—Dr. John Jackson, President of William Jessup University and author

The foundation of leadership is trust. Greg's book is based on biblical and innovative ideas that are Spirit-led. Strange leaders find direction, wisdom and courage in discovering where God is working and joining Him in bringing about positive change which is essential for effective leadership during challenging times. This book is an excellent resource for Leadership Development that is documented with biblical references and illustrations.

—Dr. Jairy C. Hunter, Jr., President, Charleston Southern University

I've had the privilege to work with many brilliant ministry leaders and church teams as they seek innovative ways to build God's Kingdom. Human innovation and leadership alone won't get the job done. Greg's book, *Strange Leadership*, adds the "missing ingredient"—connecting with the heart and Spirit of God. Leaders from all life domains will benefit from reading this book and applying the timeless principles Greg has written for us.

—Linda Stanley, Team Leader—Leadership Network

What Greg has put together for us in this work is a theology of leadership; a way of leading that begins and ends with God's desires and the Gospel. More leaders should form their leadership this way! Greg shows us how. Read this!

—Shawn Lovejoy, Directional Leader, Mountain Lake Church and Churchplanters.com; author of The Measure of Our Success: An Impassioned Plea to Pastors

Oftentimes, when we hear the word "innovate" connected to the church, the response is not always positive. Greg's *Strange Leadership* teaches us, in a very compelling, but practical way, that innovation that helps to produce true life change, can only originate from the heart and mind of the Chief Innovator Himself.

—Brian Bloye, Senior Pastor, West Ridge Church, author of It's Personal

This book deals with one of the biggest issues in the church today . . . How can our church be innovative and Spirit-led at the same time? Are you kidding, the more Spirit-led you are, the more innovative you will be! Greg helps us get back to the core of where life changing innovation really comes from . . . the presence of God. I pray that God will use this book to raise up a generation of Kingdom Leaders who are both deeply spiritual AND strategic. You don't have to be one without the other.

—Scott Wilson, Senior Pastor of The Oaks, author of Ready, Set, Grow

One of the things I love about Greg is his passion for helping churches. I love the message of *Strange Leadership* because you can't follow God by "copy and paste". Instead, we need His revelation in our lives. This book challenges us to do that!

—Bob Franquiz, Senior Pastor of Calvary Fellowship, author, and founder of ChurchNinja.com

Many people agree with the concept of innovation, but limit it to a small part of what they do. In *Strange Leadership*, Greg teaches us to stretch innovation to touch every area of our lives. The idea isn't new—which is why Greg points us back to Scripture over and over to learn from the Greatest Innovator.

—Tim Stevens, Executive Pastor of Granger Community Church, author of Vision: Lost and Found

True innovation comes straight from God. Greg reminds us of great innovators throughout Scripture and history, and points to the fact that being led by the Spirit is the most "cutting-edge" thing we can do. Follow hard after God and you'll be innovative.

—Steve Stroope, Senior Pastor, Lake Pointe Church

Innovation is like breakfast for leaders—skip it for long and you feel the difference. Greg has written a great book taking a biblically sound spiritual approach to innovation and leadership. I love the short and quickly accessible chapters—each is packed with insights that will stand the test of time.

—Dan Reiland, Executive Pastor, 12Stone Church, author of Amplified Leadership

Innovation is no longer an option in our world today. We have to innovate. *Strange Leadership* is a timely reminder of God's heart for innovation and his desire to lead us in it.

—Charles Lee, CEO of Ideation & author of Good Idea. Now What?

What's innovation? The act of injecting "newness" into something. Especially into something you thought could never change. In *Strange Leadership*, Greg makes the profound point that Jesus is the Chief Innovation Officer—because through Him, God is always doing something new. *Strange Leadership* delivers wisdom in fast-acting, bite-sized nuggets that will fuel your drive to innovate.

—Scott Williams, Church Growth Consultant and Strategist at Next Level Solutions. author of Church Diversity and Go Big

There are so many great models of 'how' to do ministry in America and the world today and yet—the Church is still losing! God-inspired innovation is absolutely required to turn the tide. This book that will help any leader find the unique ways God wants to innovate through them and lead into the future.

—Ashley Wooldridge, Senior Pastor, Christ Church of the Valley

Strange Leadership will hook, provoke and entertain any leader looking who has a desire to grow and change. At the same time, Greg brings in the "yes but" is this what the Lord would have me pursue. Each chapter is a fast, conversational provocation to look at Scripture in a new light and look at yourself. Greg's book is well researched and supported by insights from many Christian leaders. As a futurist and Senior Partner for an international consulting firm innovation and change is our trade and focus. We work with corporations, governments, denominations and churches. I felt renewed in my own passion and Biblical grounding for the subject of innovation as I go out and serve our clients. Greg captured my attention in the very first pages with a quote from Henry Blackaby, "When you recognize where God is working, you can join in what He is doing." That to me, friends, is at the very core of being innovative." Exactly!

—Rex Miller, Senior Partner for TAG Consulting, author of The Millennium Matrix

Some books have the power to motivate a person, or a tribe, or a church to do something differently that ultimately charts a new course for the future. Greg's wisdom about innovation in the church will not only motivate but will act as a guide. I can see this book in the hands of a church staff, a team of volunteers, or a gathering of pastors. What I can't see is that group of people remaining stuck in the same place for very long. Buy this book and move forward!

—Brandon Cox, Pastor at Grace Hills Church and Editor at Pastors.com

Are you called to be a leader? To lead something? One thing I know about leadership is that it implies taking people somewhere. And taking people somewhere almost always implies moving from the status quo to a new place, a preferred future. To do that, to lead people to a preferred future, almost all of us need a guide or guidebook to keep us moving in the right direction. I think you'll find that kind of resource in Greg's *Strange Leadership*.

—Mark C. Howell, Pastor of Communities, Canyon Ridge Christian Church, Small Groups Specialist at LifeWay, Blogger at MarkHowellLive.com

When I think of innovation, I think of creative leadership. Who is more creative than God himself? To walk in the power of the Holy

Spirit is to allow his creativity, wisdom and love to flow through us. *Strange Leadership* offers a fresh perspective on leading by letting the Holy Spirit have his way. If you've felt stale lately, Greg will get you ready for newness!

—Tom Harper, publisher of ChurchCentral.com and author of Leading from the Lions' Den: Leadership Principles from Every Book of the Bible

Good leaders are open to new ideas from the innovators in their lives; great leaders seek to implement new ideas from the greatest Innovator, God himself. In *Strange Leadership*, Greg shares a vision for cultivating Spirit-led innovation in your church or organization. Full of both inspiration and practical advice, this book is a good read for any leader or team with a desire to be part of creating something new.

—Justin Lathrop, Strategic Relations, Kingdom Connector, author

In *Strange Leadership* Greg unfolds the many critical aspects of what it takes to be an innovative leader. The pungent mix of practical daily life applications, corresponding biblical examples and personal life experiences makes this a book that is easily absorbed by both novice and veteran leaders. The included action steps make this a book that is a genuine practical guide for those who aspire to be innovative leaders.

—Allen Ratta—CEO SpiritualProgress.com and author of Making Spiritual Progress

Created in the image of the Creator, following a Rabbi who claimed to be making all things news, and filled with the dynamic and ever-active Spirit of God, how can we who lead justify simply continuing to do the same things the same way we always have? Greg Atkinson, veteran innovator and leader, shows us through the revelation of Scripture and the practical lessons of his own extensive experience what it looks like to follow the Spirit's lead as we lead others. If you want to be part of the "strange" new things God is doing in his Kingdom today, read this book!

—Bob Rognlien, Lead Pastor, author of Experiential Worship, and Communicator for 3 Dimensional Ministries (weare3dm.com)

Contents

Foreword

I've known Greg for over a decade and he is a strange leader. Of course, I mean that as a compliment. After all, who wants to be normal? Greg seeks to love, live and follow the leading of the Holy Spirit in his life and ministry. As a matter of fact, years ago when Greg was traveling the country teaching on innovation, one of his stops was right here in Washington DC, where he spoke at our coffeehouse on Capitol Hill, Ebenezers.

The thing that gets me up early in the morning and keeps me up late at night is this simple conviction: there are ways of doing church that people have not thought of yet. I know that creative impulse is the motivation behind Greg's book. If we're going to reach new people, we have to find new ways to doing church. The message never changes, but our methodologies must. The way we put it at National Community Church is this: we're orthodox in belief, but unorthodox in practice. You could even say we're strange. But that is part of embracing our unique church print.

As you read Greg's book, *Strange Leadership*, it will challenge your status quo. And we all have one. I hope the net result isn't just good ideas or new ideas. I'd rather have one God idea than a thousand good ideas! I pray that God gives them to you as you read this book.

—Mark Batterson, New York Times bestselling author of The Circle Maker and Lead Pastor of National Community Church

Preface

Let me say up front this book is full of Scripture. You might get tired of all the biblical references or verses I share in each chapter, but my heart from the start was to teach on a biblical view of innovation. As I travel, teaching on innovation, I always say up front our lens for the discussion will be the Bible.

I believe God is extremely innovative. He is the Chief Innovator. It is He who is doing a new thing, as we'll discuss later. I believe some of the people mentioned in Scripture are some of the most innovative (and strange) people to have ever lived.

You may also notice that I spell Church with a capital *C*. This is referring to the universal Church (the body of Christ). If I have a lowercase *c*, then I'm talking about a local church.

This book is a six-year project and is the result of much travel, discussion with thousands of leaders and pastors, and much thoughtful prayer and reflection. Through traveling North America extensively and a couple of third-world countries teaching on and discussing innovation and leadership, I came up with ways that innovation can be birthed. This book is a true collaboration project and the fruit of the conversations and ideas of the Body of Christ.

What are you getting yourself into? In the Fall of 2013, I spoke at the TurnAround20/20 Conference in Nashville, TN and got to meet and talk with Dr. Bob Whitesel, Professor of Christian Ministry and Missional Leadership at Wesley Seminary in Indiana. Dr. Bob (as I call him) told me a story of John Wesley that he discovered in the research for his forthcoming book. The story was about how Wesley kept sending pastors to Sheffield and not to Manchester because he sensed God was at work in Sheffield. Sensing God's hand of blessing and favor on Sheffield, he continued to send that city pastor after pastor. This is the essence of strange leadership—following where the Spirit leads you and joining God where He's at work. I thank Dr. Whitesel for adding fuel to my fire as I was in the editing stages of this book.

Lastly, please know that I offer no magic pill or formula for innovation. The chapters contained in this book are nothing more than ways that innovation can be birthed. The forty ways are to help you be alert to God's activity around you, your team and your church or ministry. The key is to follow the leading of the Holy Spirit, not my instructions or human thoughts. So, with that said: buckle up. It's going to be an adventure. Let's begin!

"Innovation is not absolutely necessary, but then neither is survival."
—Andrew Papageorge

"The best ways of ministry have yet to be discovered."
—Ron Martoia

"I used to think anyone doing anything weird was weird. Now I know it is the people that call others weird that are weird."
—Paul McCartney

"Live life fully while you're here. Experience everything. Take care of yourself and your friends. Have fun, be crazy, be weird. Go out and screw up! You're going to anyway, so you might as well enjoy the process. Take the opportunity to learn from your mistakes: find the cause of your problem and eliminate it. Don't try to be perfect; just be an excellent example of being human."
—Anthony Robbins

"Be yourself; everyone else is already taken."
—Oscar Wilde

"I love strange choices. I'm always interested in people who depart from what is expected of them and go into new territory."
—Cate Blanchett

Introduction

Setting the table

Innovation—it's a popular buzz word now and a sought after topic of discussion in conferences, and in both the business and ministry world. Whether the topic is outreach, leadership, worship, technology, or ministry in general, how to be innovative is a desire most Church leaders share.

The dictionary defines innovation as "something new or different introduced" and "the act of innovating; introduction of new things or methods." Some people say the goal of innovation is positive change, to make someone or something better. I think we'd all agree we want to introduce positive change and see our churches and ministries become better.

Forget about what's happened; don't keep going over old history. Be alert, be present.

I'm about to do something brand-new. It's bursting out! Don't you see it?
—Isaiah 43:18–19 (MSG)

I was chewing on the whole concept of doing something brand-new and decided to look up "new" in the thesaurus. One of the words the thesaurus listed as a synonym for "new" was "strange"—especially when referring to a new approach to doing something. I started thinking about innovators over the years (both in the Bible and not) were often thought of as strange. Many people thought Noah was "strange"—especially when referring to a new approach to doing something. I started thinking about how innovators over the years (both in the Bible and not) were often thought of as strange. Many people thought Noah was strange for building a boat before it had ever rained. Many people thought Jesus, Peter, and Paul were strange. After thinking about it for a while, I discovered innovative leaders are often considered strange and so this book is for you, the strange leaders of the world.

Please know up front, I approach innovation a little differently and try my best to look at it through a biblical lens. Innovation, as we just defined, is the act of introducing something new. God tells us in Isaiah 43:19 it is God who is doing new things. He's the Chief Innovator. Something foundational in my own life was studying Henry Blackaby's *Experiencing God*. In the book, Blackaby teaches when you recognize where God is working, you can join in what He is doing. To me, friends, this is at the very core of being innovative—to be so in tune with God; His dreams become your dreams.

Is it wrong to want to be an innovative leader or lead an innovative church? I don't think so, especially if your goal of being innovative is to follow where God leads. We just need to check out motives and heart here early in this journey. One of my favorite tweets is from March 8, 2010. Pastor Matt Chandler of The Village Church in Dallas, TX wrote, "Jesus is not a means to an end . . . he's the goal or you're an idolater." Wow! What a sobering exhortation. Innovation cannot be the goal.

This book isn't how to manipulate Jesus to make you more innovative. This book is about being in sync with Jesus, listening to Him and following Him. It just so happens if you do, you'll be innovative. See the difference? Tony Morgan, when writing about "America's Most Innovative Churches" for *Outreach* magazine (Jan/ Feb 2008) said, "If it's just innovation for innovation sake, it really has no value in the Church. If the end result is life-transformation through Christ, then the Church needs to be more innovative." I agree. what does being innovative require?

> *Watch what God does and then you do it.*
> *—Ephesians 5:1 (MSG)*

Innovation requires a couple of things: First, we must grasp onto this concept of joining God in His mission. Henry Blackaby likes to say, "God's activity is far greater than anything we could aspire to do for him." (*7 Truths from Experiencing God* p. 1) Let this one sink in a little bit. For some of you, it may be painful. For some it may be a relief. So, a first step in being truly innovative is listening to the Spirit of God and looking for where He's moving. It requires our innovation antennas to be up and seeking God moments leading to breakthroughs in our ministries.

Another step in being truly innovative is walking with God and being men and women of integrity. Genesis 6:9 teaches us Noah "was a righteous man, blameless in his time; Noah walked with God." What did Noah do? Only one of the most innovative and unprecedented acts in all of human history. He built an ark to protect himself, his family, and many animals from a flood before it had ever rained—this is innovative (doing something new) and at the time, was strange.

Let me state something up front I've said as I've traveled and spoken on this subject all over: There is no shortcut to innovation. *You cannot bypass prayer*. Stacy Spencer (senior pastor of New Direction Christian Church in Memphis, TN), in his keynote address at the Leadership Network Innovation 3 Conference in 2009 said,

"The main thing is to be pure and praying." He was talking about his church and how he leads them. I've stated, "You cannot bypass prayer," because everywhere I go, a church leader will ask, "How can we be an innovative church?" When I talk about prayer, they say, "Yeah. Yeah. What's next?" To me, prayer is not how you just open the meeting—it's the meeting.

Prayer has got to be the hub of your church's wheel, not a spoke in it. Obviously, Christ is the Head of the Church. I'm just talking about our praying to and seeking Him in all things. In 2009, I got to attend a Highlands Up-Close two-day workshop with Chris Hodges (Senior Pastor at Church of the Highlands in Birmingham, AL). In one of this sessions on leadership, he said in passing, "*You can't delegate prayer*." I wrote it down quickly and devoured it. I thought it was a huge golden nugget from a leader who has been seeing God do unbelievable things in their midst.

> *Since we are living by the Spirit, let us follow the Spirit's leading in every part of our lives.*
> *—Galatians 5:25 (NLT)*

Who is this book for?

Okay, so now you get the background, the premise, and we're starting from the same foundation. Now, whom am I writing to? Simply put: you. If you felt the desire to pick up this book (and I don't think this was by accident), then I'm writing to you. Young, old, male, female, black, white, Asian, Hispanic, volunteer, and paid staff. I'm writing to you. Whether you're on staff at a local church, a ministry leader in a parachurch organization or run a nonprofit, this book has application to your life and work. Whether you pastor a booming church over ten thousand and have multisite campuses or you're in a dead and declining church of less than a hundred, there is a word (or two) in this book for you.

The principles contained in this book are universal, not

necessarily "one size fits all" but universal. This book contains several ways innovation can come about and applies to you regardless of your organization's size, budget, and number of staff.

The book is also purposefully based on timeless principles and truths and should not get outdated. Many books on innovation have a shelf life of a year or two. My prayer is you can pick this back up five or ten years from now and still be encouraged, challenged, and inspired to lead a strange and innovative organization.

What's unique about this book? Like Tim Stevens and Tony Morgan's *Simply Strategic* series of books, these chapters are brief (I think the longest chapter is twelve pages), and they can stand alone. Some chapters are extremely short and can be read in a couple of minutes. I would love for you to start at the beginning and work your way through the book (as this is how the book is intended—each chapter builds on top of the previous chapters), but I realize this may not be the case. You may see a chapter title and know this is something you need to read right away. Feel free to. This book is designed in such a way for you to skip around. I hope you read it all, but how you do is up to you.

Sometimes, I'll print out a Scripture for you to read. Sometimes, I'll simply quote Scripture or refer to something in Scripture and put the verse in parentheses. I encourage you to read through this book with your Bible handy. Check up on me. Look up verses I mention and reflect on them. They will bring context and meat to what I, a simple human being, am saying. Even though this book is about innovation, I don't think this book offers any new concepts in it. I'm just going to share some ideas and principles I've learned and many of which were shared with me.

This book has evolved over time. This is due in large part to the body of Christ. Almost every city I shared my thoughts on innovation with, I would walk away with new ways innovation can happen that were shared with me by one of the people in the audience. This is truly a work forged through the thoughts, words, insights, and wisdom of far more people than just me. I am simply taking all the ideas God has shown me, mixed with the words and insights of others I've met during my travels and putting them into book form. Again, nothing is really new or groundbreaking, this will simply give you a framework for how to approach the subject of innovation.

I encourage you to wrestle and meditate on each chapter. Take your time. To go along with each chapter, we have produced a study guide for use with your team or staff containing questions for discussion and reflection. My friend Scott Wilson has told me he gets far more out of reading books if he takes a little time to wrestle with the issues. This book is meant to be read by your whole team. No matter what type of job or role you find yourself in, this book has something for you and your entire team. Maybe you'll want to take your board of elders or deacons through this. The questions in the study guide are meant to be used as a discussion guide for your team meetings. These are available as a free resource for you. To find out where to get the study guide, simply go to the book's website (www.StrangeLeadership.com) or my personal website (GregAtkinson.com). There are forty chapters, forty ways innovation can come about. In this Second Edition, I've added a new chapter at the end on reconciliation as a bonus chapter.

Take one chapter per meeting or one chapter a month and wrestle and discuss these with your team. The chapters are brief, so many of you can do one chapter a week and have this knocked out in under a year. If you take this extra step, I think you'll see great fruit from it.

Not many books come with a guarantee. I offer a guarantee with this book. In this work are principles and ideas—biblical, practical, and innovative ideas, which, if you allow them, can change the way you operate and live. If you wrestle with, grasp, and live out these principles, I feel confident you will lead an innovative organization or church. You may not make the *Outreach* magazine's most innovative church list, and it may not look like what you thought or imagined, but if you're following the leading of the Holy Spirit, you'll be innovative.

In *Jesus for President: Politics for Ordinary Radicals* (p. 165), Shane Claiborne said, "Christianity is at its best when it is peculiar, marginalized, suffering, and it is at its worst when it is popular, credible, triumphal, and powerful." Have you been called peculiar? Have you ever been marginalized? Are you ready to suffer for the cause of Christ? Then you might just be a strange leader!

"The greatest enemy to human souls is the self-righteous spirit, which makes men look to themselves for salvation."

—Charles Spurgeon

"Salvation is found in no one else, for there is no other name under heaven given to mankind by which we must be saved."

—Acts 4:12 (NIV)

Salvation

First things first

As I said before, innovation is "the act of doing or introducing something new." Before we can do new things in ministry and for the kingdom, we must first become new ourselves.

> *Therefore, if anyone is in Christ, he is a new creation. The old has passed away; behold, the new has come. —2 Corinthians 5:17 (ESV)*

I was a child when my eyes were opened to the gospel and my need for a Savior. Maybe you have a more dramatic or exciting salvation story. For some, maybe you still need to accept Christ into your hearts. For all of us, this is the starting part, but it is not the ending point.

Salvation is simple and deep at the same time. It's simple enough, I, as a young boy, could grasp it and pray to receive Christ. My daughter, Grace, and my son, Tommy, both prayed to receive Christ into their hearts at the age of seven. My youngest, Katie, recently prayed to receive Christ at the age of seven as well. I had the privilege of baptizing all three of my kids. Now, as a pastor, I have the opportunity to lead men, women, boys, and girls to Christ and see them grow in their faith. I love how the gospel can penetrate hearts, both old and young.

Salvation is also deep and daily. The Bible tells us to work out our own salvation "with fear and trembling" (Phil 2:12). We are saved (from hell and the wrath of God) and at the same time we are in the process of being saved (sanctification). It's a beautiful mystery like many of God's ways. This sanctification is a process, not something that occurs instantaneously at our conversation. It is a gradual process done by the Holy Spirit over the course of our entire life. Justification, however, happens at the moment of conversion. We are forever "right" with and cleansed before a Holy God. I recently read *Jesus + Nothing = Everything* by Tullian Tchividjian and The Explicit Gospel by Matt Chandler. Both books cover this topic far better than I ever could and really drive home our justification in Christ.

Moving on . . . .

How do we come upon salvation? By hearing and receiving the gospel (good news). I like how Bill Hybels of Willow Creek says other religions spell salvation "do." Christianity spells salvation "done." We trust in the finished work of Christ on the cross for our sins.

Though I believe once one prays to receive Christ as the forgiver and leader of their life and has a true conversion, they cannot lose their salvation, I also am learning the gospel (good news) is something we should live and preach continually. I'm thankful to our Acts 29 friends for their constant exhortations to preach the gospel. I got to hear Darrin Patrick's thoughts on preaching the gospel to Christians, not just the lost, and it deeply resonated with my spirit. Check this out:

That is why I am so eager to preach the gospel also to you who are in Rome. For I am not ashamed of the gospel, because it is the power of God that brings salvation to everyone who believes: first to the Jew, then to the Gentile. For in the gospel the righteousness of God is revealed—a righteousness that is by faith from first to last, just as it is written: "The righteous will live by faith" - Romans 1:15–17 (NIV).

Wait a second! Who is Paul talking to? He's "so eager to preach the gospel" to those in Rome. He's talking to the Church—the Church in Rome. Get this: Paul couldn't wait to preach the gospel to the Church. Why? Because we must continually be repenting and believing, repenting and believing. This was the message of John the Baptist; it was the message of Christ. It is still our message today: repent and believe!

Do you want to see God do something new in your church and the lives of the people who attend your worship gatherings? Preach the gospel to them. If you're leading an older, established congregation with a majority of believers present, it will revitalize them and refocus their priorities, reminding them of their need to repent and believe. It will soften their hearts and remind them of the good news they once received and why it is life to those friends, family, and coworkers they love and don't yet know Christ. To the church that is young and reaching mainly those far from God, preaching the gospel will be like water to someone dying of thirst in the desert. It is your partnering with the Holy Spirit who is the reason they are even there. Remember no one seeks God on their own. If you have lost people in your congregation, God is already at work, drawing them to himself.

Most church leaders want to see their church alive and vibrant with new people, new ideas, new dreams, and new innovations of doing ministry. Preach the unchanging truth of the gospel and new things (innovation) will be a natural byproduct. Remember:

> *Therefore, if anyone is in Christ, he is a new creation. The old has passed away; behold, the new has come.*
> *—2 Corinthians 5:17 (ESV)*

I know some of you leaders and pastors roll your eyes or groan inwardly, yearning for your church to once again be full of life. Maybe it's been so long since anything associated with your church would be considered new or innovative. There is hope! Just as Paul was eager to preach the gospel to the church in Rome, God the Father, Jesus Christ, and the Holy Spirit are eager for you to preach the gospel (good news) to your local fellowship of believers. My prayer for you is this:

> *Restore to me the joy of your salvation and grant me a willing spirit, to sustain me.*
> *—Psalm 51:12 (NIV)*

These next forty ways innovation can happen are not just plug-and-play magic tricks. They are pieces of my heart and soul and I believe gifts from our heavenly Father. They won't mean much to you if you don't first try to grasp and live courageously in the "joy of your salvation"

For some of you, maybe most of you, the best starting place on this journey of being an innovative church and innovative leader is a simple acknowledgement and remembrance of your own story. Take a moment to reflect back on your personal testimony. Remember your salvation story. Remember what Christ did for you on the cross. If you don't have a story, start now. Pray God would forgive you of your sins and come into your heart as the Savior of your soul and leader and Lord of your life. Thank Jesus for the cross, what it represents, and the good news the gospel truly is.

Three keys to consider

At the heart of what I hope to share in this book is true innovation comes from God. This is a supernatural thing—something we can't take credit for. Thus, your understanding of salvation and the gospel become crucial here at the start. Maybe a verse I shared earlier looked at in *The Message* says what I'm trying to say better:

What I'm getting at, friends, is that you should simply keep on doing what you've done from the beginning. When I was living among you, you lived in responsive obedience. Now that I'm separated from you, keep it up. Better yet, redouble your efforts.

> *Be energetic in your life of salvation, reverent and sensitive before God.*
> *—Philippians 2:12 (MSG)*

Before we dive into any spiritual or practical ways innovation can happen, I think it's wise to do what *The Message* encourages us to: "Be energetic in your life of salvation, reverent, and sensitive before God."

Being "energetic in your life of salvation" is what I've been alluding to—remembering your own salvation story, remembering the good news for everyone (Jesus died once for all), and living out the gospel daily (repenting and believing). I like how *The Message* says to "be energetic". This won't happen by accident folks; it takes intentionality. You have to make an effort—an energetic one indeed!

Philippians 2:12 goes on to say be "reverent". To me, this gets to the very root of our motivation. Why did you pick up this book? What is leading you to want to be innovative? What drives you? Are you wanting to be innovative because it's a cool thing to be these days and you want to make it onto the *Outreach* Magazine "Top Innovative Churches" in the country list or are you so in love with Jesus and so living a life of reverence, respect, awe, and wonder at your own salvation and the grace you've been shown your only desire is to go where God leads? Again, being innovative is being Spirit-led; this has got to be our sole motivation. Believe me, I know this is easier said than done, but it's our goal. Be reverent.

Lastly, be "sensitive before God." This is the most crucial part of all I have to share with you, friends. If you're not sensitive and able to hear God's still, small voice, you won't turn when He turns. You won't duck when He ducks. You won't jump when He jumps. Remember it is God who said,

> *"I'm about to do something brand new."*
> *—Isa 43:19 (MSG)*

If we are going to be innovative and do new things, we must hear from the Holy Spirit. We must be "sensitive before God." This will lead us, guide us, focus us, keep us, and see we're always seeking to be innovative with a pure heart and right motive.

Do I want you to be an innovative leader? Absolutely. Do I want your church to be known as an innovative church? Yes. I just want to be clear: you must strive (again being intentional) to be energetic, reverent and sensitive before God.

Having a root in and grasp of your salvation story will help keep you grounded. Some of you have nice, neat, pretty salvation stories and this is okay (my coming to Christ was similar, though, I have uglier parts of my testimony). For some of you, you had a Damascus Road experience. For some of you, you were strung out, addicted, sick, and just plain dirty when Christ turned your life upside down. This is important to remember as we begin because being innovative isn't about having the best website or most creative Internet campus or most Disney-like children's facilities. Some stories I will share are downright ugly. Some churches and pastors I know are not afraid to get their hands dirty, and I consider them innovative.

> *And Jesus said to them, "Follow me, and I will make you become fishers of men."*
> *—Mark 1:17 (ESV)*

You only have to go fishing once to realize you get dirty. From dealing with bait (worms, crickets, chicken livers—gross) to taking the fish off the hook (slimy) to cleaning the fish (I've seen people faint while watching)—fishing is a fun but dirty sport. I think innovation is similar. Boy, can it be fun, but it can also get dirty and downright uncomfortable.

Jesus also told us to "love our neighbor" (Matt 22:39). Dave Gibbons, senior pastor of NewSong Church, says this is not someone we like (this would be easy). In his book *The Monkey and the Fish*, Dave suggests loving our neighbor is often someone we hate. If innovation for you and your church is loving the unlovable, the you've got to be rooted in the gospel, driven by love, have a reverence and sensitivity to the Holy Spirit, and full of the joy of your salvation—it's the only way you'll survive ministry.

So if you are a Christ-follower, be ready to get your hands dirty and love those who may hate you and then you're ready to discuss ways innovation can be birthed in your life and ministry. My encouragement to you again is to "be energetic in your life of salvation, reverent and sensitive before God." If this is the foundation you're building from, then you're ready to move ahead and look at the other ways innovation can happen in your ministry. Let's dive in!

"Whenever you see a successful business, someone once made a courageous decision."
—Peter Drucker

"The indispensable first step to getting the things you want out of life is this: decide what you want."
—Ben Stein

"Standing in the middle of the road is very dangerous; you get knocked down by the traffic from both sides."
—Margaret Thatcher

"When you have to make a choice and you don't make it, that itself is a choice."
—William James

"What you have to do and the way you have to do it is incredibly simple. Whether you are willing to do it is another matter."
—Peter F. Drucker

"Successful people make right decisions early and manage those decisions daily."
—John C. Maxwell

Decision

The point of no return

I can save you a lot of time right here at the beginning of this book by talking about this second way innovation happens. The second way innovation happens is by making an intentional and strategic decision to grow and be innovative. If you have no interest in becoming a healthy, growing, innovative church, then I'd strongly suggest you put this book down and walk away. Every other chapter will only bore you, frustrate you, or make you mad. At this point, I'd like to thank you for buying this book and encourage you to give it as a gift to a pastor who you think is interested in this sort of thing.

If you are up for some changes—changes in the way you think, changes in the way you lead, changes in the way your church does ministry, then I welcome you with open arms and look forward to the rest of this journey together. In this book, you will find many different ways innovation can happen. I offer no formulas or magic pills. I have not "arrived," and I'm no genius. I take the approach and mentality of a farmer. I have traveled, taught, studied, researched, discussed, and practiced innovative thinking and principles for years. What I've learned is innovation requires a certain mindset, environment and intentional atmosphere—let's call it a fertile soil. What I will attempt to do in this book is give you seeds, seeds that it's up to you to plant. It's up to you to provide the right type of soil. It's up to you to water. It's up to you to harvest when the time is right.

So why start with a decision? Obviously, you can't do a new thing in ministry without first becoming new yourself (on the inside). That's why we started with salvation. But to move forward with the ideas, suggestions, insights, and practical ways innovation can happen requires something on your part: a decision. Let's make a deal. I will promise to hold nothing back. I have put years of my life into this book, and I have a God-given desire to see you and your church lead an innovative ministry, but I will need your cooperation. I'll share what I've learned and you promise to act when appropriate. Deal?

While we're getting stuff out here in the beginning of this book, there's something you should know about me. I use the word "intentional" a ton! Think back to the first chapter and my saying, "This won't happen by accident folks, it takes intentionality. You have to make an effort—an energetic one indeed!" I won't go as far as to say "nothing happens by accident." The scary truth is bad things happen by accident—things you don't want to happen. Things you'd like to avoid and keep out of your church. So bear with me and get used to me encouraging you to be intentional often. Even the innovations which may come out of experimenting will happen because you made the choice to take a chance, take a risk, and try an experiment.

Intentionality is critical to being an innovative leader.
—@GregAtkinson

I stated in the introduction of this book I was writing to you regardless of your church's size. What's important to note is all of you, depending on your church's unique DNA and circumstances, have a decision to make. For large churches who struggle with rocking the boat, you will probably need to make the decision to change. Maybe you're technically a mega-church (by definition over two thousand in attendance), but your growth is in plateau. You will need to make an intentional decision to change the way you do things. What you change, I don't know. Maybe this God-insight will hit you between the eyes later in this book or maybe God will use one of the chapters to open your eyes to something that needs to be done differently. Stay tuned.

Maybe you're a church of less than five hundred people (which is the overwhelming majority of churches in America); you will have to make the intentional choice you want to grow. To some of you reading this, this seems like a no-brainer; something you settled long ago. For many of you reading this book, this decision is life or death. Rick Warren wrote about this in his article *How to Break through the 200-300 Barrier*. His first point on how to get past the two-hundred barrier is: "The church must decide if it really wants to grow." He goes on to say "that's the primary barrier right there. Do we really want to grow?"

Why is this important? Like many of my friends and peers who have written, taught or blogged about innovation and church growth, we have a God-given passion to see church health. Healthy organisms grow. Healthy organizations grow. Let me put it more bluntly: healthy churches grow. Yes, most churches in the US are under two-hundred people in attendance, but this doesn't mean they shouldn't strive to be healthy and thus grow. Diagnosis: We have too many sick churches in America. Now, why a church is sick is a discussion for another book, and a quite lengthy one I would imagine. I'll simply say we as the Church (big C Church) need to return to our first love (Rev 2:4), be led by leaders (again paid or volunteer) who are in love with Jesus and his Bride, and driven by His heart, His mission, and His desire none should perish (2 Pet 3:9). So, it is from this foundation I just laid and the desire of your church being first healthy, I even mention your church growing.

Church Growth Is Biblical

> *Those who accepted his message were baptized, and about three thousand were added to their number that day. —Acts 2:41 (NIV)*

The Bible seems to take great joy in seeing the local church grow and lives be changed for eternity. After all, it's about lives being changed and transformed, right? This is why we signed up for this in the first place. God so greatly and forever impacted our own lives so out of our love and worship of our Redeemer, we earnestly desire for others to experience this changed life. In this Acts 2 account, Peter preached and three thousand received Christ as Lord and Savior. In your church, maybe you communicate the gospel and one or two receive Christ—this is growth, and it's a beautiful thing.

Friends, don't be down on growth. There are too many haters of the Church. Frankly, I'm tired of it. Some teach and write about people my age, forty, and younger who don't like large churches or prefer to "walk on the beach" as our weekly worship. Not so. Many of my peers and I are passionate about the local church; we believe it's the hope of the world and Christ (who is the Head) is on the move and wants to change the world through the great invention of the Church. I will admit that when I refer to the church, I'm referring to the body of Christ and this has nothing to do with four walls and a building—just making sure we're on the same page. And this isn't about missional vs attractional. It's not either/or. If you read *On the Verge* by Alan Hirsch and Dave Ferguson, you'll hear of several great and large churches that are living on mission. Please don't be anti-church, my friends.

Christ said, "I will build my church." The growth I'm talking about comes about from Him and is a magnificent work of the Holy Spirit. Our task as leaders is to seek to be as healthy as we can as a local expression of the universal Church. "How do we do this?" you may ask. By being "energetic in your life of salvation, reverent, and sensitive before God." (Phil 2:12 remember?) This challenge I mentioned in the last chapter is the decision that lays before you right now, Christ-follower. Will you be "energetic in your life of salvation"? Will you be "reverent"? Will you be "sensitive before God"?

Mark Batterson is about my age, and he is very energetic in his life of salvation and his passion for the local church. In his article, *Postmodern Wells: Creating a Third Place*, he wrote, "I love the church. I believe in the church. And I've poured ten years of blood, sweat, and tears into the church I have the privilege of pastoring—National Community Church in Washington, DC. But the church needs to change! And change always starts with some honest self-reflection." So, I ask you: Are you ready to do some honest self-reflection that will lead to change? If so, it will start with a decision.

Throughout this book, I will share stories, ideas, examples of innovation and several Biblical illustrations of a particular principle being carried out. For decision, I can think of no better example than Jesus Christ—the Innovator. Just as all creativity flows straight from our Creator God, I believe innovation comes about by listening to and following the ultimate Innovator, Jesus.

When it comes to focus, intentional living, and making a decision to be obedient, have you ever come across a better example than Christ? He was about His "Father's business" (Luke 2:49 NKJV), and He wouldn't let anything deter Him from this. One day Jesus' disciples were encouraging him to eat something. Jesus replied, "My food . . . is to do the will of Him who sent me and to finish

His work" (John 4:31–34). Christ had made an intentional (there's this word again) decision to follow His Father's will, and he lived accordingly. I'd like to point out this decision guided Him even in His early days. The above quote about being about His "Father's business" was made by Christ at the age of twelve.

Charles Spurgeon was perhaps one of the greatest preachers in history, and he also had a lot to say about the way Christ followed suit. In a sermon delivered on March 4th, 1860 by Charles Spurgeon, he said, "Our Lord and Master had but one thought, but one wish, but one aim. He concentrated his whole soul, gathered up the vast floods of his mighty powers, and sent them in one channel, rushing toward one great end: "My meat is to do the will of him that sent me and to finish His work." Christ had made up His mind and lived according to the decision that drove Him—"to do the will of Him who sent Me."

Oh, the depth of the riches of the wisdom and knowledge of God! How unsearchable His judgments, and His paths beyond tracing out! "Who has known the mind of the Lord? Or who has been His counselor?" "Who has ever given to God, that God should repay him?"

> *For from Him and through Him and to Him are all things. To Him be the glory forever! Amen.*
> *—Romans 11:33–36 (NIV)*

Jesus was and is perfect so therefore He is not only our Redeemer, Savior, and Lord, He is our model for leadership. Picture this: Jesus is the Innovator.

> *("for from Him and through Him and to Him are all things"), the Holy Spirit is our guide, and God the Father said, "See, I am doing a new thing!"*
> *—Isa 43:19*

The decision to follow our triune God is a roller coaster of a ride. As we will see later in this book, it's not always pretty, easy, or glamorous. Some of your biggest breakthroughs in ministry (and innovation) may come about from a valley in your spiritual life or your church's history. Dave Browning said his leaders are well versed in the following phrase: "There is no growth without change, no change without loss, and no loss without pain." He goes on to say, "There are some extremely dedicated, disciplined leaders at CTK (his church) who have paid the price for those who are about to come." (*Deliberate Simplicity*, p. 12)

The Cost of Deciding

There are highs and lows, joys and sorrows in this decision to follow Christ. Make no mistake: it will cost you something. It might cost you everything.

> *Then Jesus told his disciples, "If anyone would come after me, let him deny himself and take up his cross and follow me.*
> *—Matthew 16:24 (ESV)*

Can we please put away the myth innovation is synonymous with sexy? If you decide to follow Christ wherever He leads . . . . If you decide to be a healthy church . . . . If you decide you want to grow and reach the lost in your community . . . . If you decide you want to try new and innovative means of ministry . . . it will cost you something. Maybe your pride. Maybe a dear friend will leave or betray you. Maybe you'll make the news and be seen as controversial. Maybe other pastors and church leaders will talk behind your back. Maybe you'll have to get your hands dirty and people will start attending your church who do not look like you, smell like you, or dress like you. Please hear me: if you have made up your mind—the decision has been made—you will follow Christ and do as He leads at all costs—this will sustain and keep you in the tough times, and there will be tough times. Remember, the Bible says in Matthew 4:1, Jesus was "led by the Spirit" into the desert to be tempted by the devil.

Here's where this decision I'm talking about comes full circle. First, you won't do anything significant or groundbreaking without making the decision to: follow Christ, be sensitive to the Holy Spirit, be healthy, grow, be innovative, etc. Second, you won't be able to stand up to the criticism, maintain the course, bear the burden and "carry your cross" (whatever this may be) without a foundation of a settled decision. Please read this last paragraph again, friends.

Christ made up His mind and set His resolve—he was going to do the Father's will, and this allowed him to literally carry the cross. Yes, He agonized and wrestled with the weight, pain, and suffering of this decision in the Garden of Gethsemane, but once He heard from the Father and made up His mind to do "not what I will, but what You will" (Mark 14:36), there was no stopping Him. He had passed the point of no return. After Gethsemane, we witness a drive, determination, focus, and decision-making process that led Christ straight to the cross and ultimately His death. If Jesus was wishy-washy on whether or not He was set to die for the sins of all mankind, I think He would have backed out somewhere along the Via Dolorosa if not before, during the scourging.

Remember the deal I mentioned in the beginning of this chapter? We're in this together. For some of you, this chapter will have one, if not two, different meanings. To a large group of you, you will need to read, soak in, and trust this whole decision thing. You realize things need to change and it all starts with a decision—a decision to try new or different things. Whether you're the church of sixty (and I've been there) or the church of five thousand (I've been there, too), you can't get started without a decision.

For others of you, you'll need to come back and reread this

chapter long after you've read this book. Maybe God uses this book in some way to spark something in your team and you decide to do something brand new—a true first for your church. Watch out! Get your shield ready because it's about to start raining fiery darts. Hear me friends, especially those of you reading this for the second or third time, there will always be consequences to your decisions. Now whether those consequences are deserved or not, I do not know. Sometimes, we as humans, make poor choices—bad decisions. If this is the case, you need to run to God, ask forgiveness and strive to get back on track.

But, to those of you who followed a God idea and made a decision to try something new based on your sensitivity to the Holy Spirit, this chapter is for you, too! Remember God's whisper. Remember the day, place, and circumstances that led you to make a significant decision to stick your neck out, risk it all, and go for it. Remember the first time you read this chapter and the initial decision you made to follow God at all costs. Remember your decision to be healthy, even if this means removing a longtime team member. Remember your decision to grow, even if outsiders or insiders question your motives. Remember your decision to be innovative, even if it means "we've never done it that way before". And finally, rest. Rest, beloved. Rest in your decision. Leadership is not for the faint of heart. It is for the weak! God uses broken and weak people all the time. Praise God. But, leadership is not for the faint of heart. It is for the tender-hearted.

One of the ways the dictionary defines faint is "lacking courage." My exhortation to you, my partners in the gospel ministry, is the same as Scripture and God's exhortation to you: "be strong and courageous" (Deut 31:6). I know this is easier said than done. The good news is you're not alone! Look around you. If you haven't already, give a copy of this book to each one of your team members. Devour this chapter together. This was not written to a lone ranger or solo artist. This was written to a coach, assistant coaches, players, and the entire orchestra—if you catch my drift.

I bring this up for a number of reasons. First, there's comfort in numbers. Once you make a tough decision to try something for the first time, you'd be wise to rest in the fact you made the decision as a team and this is something you all agreed on. Second, if you make a solo decision and it backfires, you could get in trouble or even get fired. This won't happen (or shouldn't happen) if it was a team decision. Lastly, you need to fit into the overall vision and mission of your local church. I don't want you to use this book and the principles in it to go off on your own initiatives and disregard what your pastor or leadership has said. My preference is you agree together on a new idea, goal, or initiative and even if it comes down to just you executing it, you have the full support of those above and around you.

Recently, one of my mentors (Lee Ross) said, "There's a gap between good intention and godly action." He suggested many of us have good intentions; we just fail to act on them. Andy Stanley's book The Principle of the Path (p. 15), talks about this as well. In his book, Andy says, "Your direction, not your intention, determines your destination." He suggests there's "often a tension between where we want to end up in life and the path we choose to get there. We fail to see that having good intentions is never good enough." You may have every intention to be a healthy church. You may have every intention to be a growing and vibrant church. You may have every intention of leading an innovative ministry, but this one truth is staring you dead in the face and keeping you from "godly action." You haven't made the decision to do it—no matter what the cost. I'm going to stop preaching for a bit and let you take the time you need. I think I've made my point. My encouragement to you is to take time before you go on to Chapter Three.

Chew on this. Mediate on the Scriptures I shared. Reflect on the life of Christ. Wrestle with what I've proposed in this chapter and when you're ready, make a decision. Remember, we made a deal. We're in this together. I'm ready when you are to explore more ways innovation can happen. When you are ready, join me in the next chapter!

The road to success leads through the valley of humility, and the path is up the ladder of patience and across the wide barren plains of perseverance. As yet, no short cut has been discovered.
—Joseph. J. Lamb

"Grant that I may not pray alone with the mouth; help me that I may pray from the depths of my heart."
—Martin Luther

"Get into the habit of saying, 'Speak, Lord,' and life will become a romance. Every time circumstances press in on you say, 'Speak, Lord,' and make time to listen. Chastening is more than a means of discipline—it is meant to bring me to the point of saying, 'Speak, Lord.' Think back to a time when God spoke to you. Do you remember what he said? As we listen, our ears become more sensitive, and like Jesus, we will hear God all the time."
—Oswald Chambers, My Utmost for His Highest

Inquisition

Welcome back!

I trust you've taken the time to make a decision in your heart. If so, you're ready to really dive into practical ways innovation happens. We've covered salvation (when God does a new work in you) and decision (when you make a conscious choice to follow God), now you're ready to prepare the soil for innovation.

This next way innovation can happen is so simple, so elementary and so obvious, I'm almost embarrassed to write about it. Almost, I said. It's praying and seeking God, and I actually take great joy in encouraging people to do it. As a father of three precious kids, this is one of my greatest joys in life. We pray and seek God every night as a family, and I'm hoping my kids grow up with an appreciation of how vital an active prayer life is. Just last week, I was teaching them about prayer and how it's a two-way conversation. We speak to God, and He speaks to us. I will talk more about this in the next chapter. For now, let's look at our speaking to God and presenting our requests before Him.

> *Then you will call upon me and come and pray to me, and I will hear you. You will seek me and find me, when you seek me with all your heart.*
> *—Jeremiah 29:12–13 (ESV)*

Here's the short premise of this whole chapter: just ask. If you want to lead an innovative church, ask God. You may now skip to the next chapter. Just kidding! Stay with me. If you've been on this Christian journey for a while, you know there's a little more to it than this. This inquisition takes humility, openness, patience, perseverance, a great deal of faith, and sensitivity to the Holy Spirit (the ability to hear God's whisper). We pray with faith believing God hears us and will answer. You may not like His answer, but eventually, He'll answer.

Please know I'm not talking about praying and asking God to make you an innovative church—this is the wrong motive. I'm talking about praying and asking God what He is up to, what He's already doing, and where He's already working so you can join Him. When this significant marriage happens (God's heart with your hands and feet), my, oh my, it is something to behold. I want to encourage you to wrestle with and finally grasp this; it's His heart, His goal, His plan, His dream, and His leading with your hands and feet. Remember Henry Blackaby, in his great work *Experiencing God*, said, "God's activity is far greater than anything we could aspire to do for Him"

I'm so tired of faulty teaching where we bring our plans to God and ask Him to bless them. I have labored to teach my kids God is not a genie. We don't just come to him with all our requests and poof! they magically appear. God is the Creator of the universe. He is all-knowing. We are to earnestly seek to have the mind of Christ in all matters of life.

> *For as the heavens are higher than the earth, so are my ways higher than your ways and my thoughts than your thoughts. — Isaiah 55:9 (ESV)*

This is where the humility I mentioned earlier comes in. Do you really believe God knows best? Do you really believe "every good and perfect gift is from above" (James 1:17)? I think we often settle for good ideas when God was ready to share with us a great, God idea. Humility means we get down on our knees (literally or figuratively) and we say, "God, Your ways are higher than my ways and Your thoughts are higher than my thoughts. I sincerely believe Your way is best and I trust in Your leading in this (and every) situation." Humility works hand in hand with openness.

> *"Humility is the only true wisdom by which we prepare our minds for all the possible changes of life."*
> *—George Arliss (Arliss was the first British actor to win an Academy Award.)*

How do you approach God?

When we pray, and seek God with a sense of openness, it means we acknowledge we don't have the answer. Most pastors and many church leaders are high D on the DISC personality profile. We have the spiritual gift of leadership. We're pioneers, trail blazers, adventurers, entrepreneurs, etc.; we're not used to stopping to ask for direction. Have you ever been in the car with a driver who was lost and refused to stop to ask for directions? It can be pretty funny or frustrating depending on your personality type. A lot of leaders bring God their great ideas and say, "Bless me, Lord". They never stop to wonder if God wanted to do something different. They don't come with an honest openness that reveals a heart of "whatever you want, God, I want too."

I've had the privilege of serving with some great people over my twenty-plus years in ministry. I remember the first time I heard a fellow staff member ask God something in her prayer. It threw me off guard. I had never heard anyone ask God a question. This may seem strange, but go with me here for a second. At this point of my Christian journey, I had spent about twenty years telling God things. "God, show me." "God, lead me." "God, give me." My fellow staff member, Beth, was leading us in prayer and she started a sentence with the word how. I had never, ever heard someone phrase their prayer like this. She asked God, "How can we . . . ." Did you notice the subtle difference in her approach to God?

I had spent my life praying prayers, like "God show us what to do in this situation." Not a bad prayer, but notice who's telling who what. I'm praying "God, show me." Beth prayed, "Father, how should we go about this?" I made a statement. She asked a question. Inquisition. Get it? It's the posture in which we approach God. How open are we to Him taking us in a direction? How open are we to doing things His way? How open are we to the fact of which the way we feel about something could be dead wrong and God wants to do something totally different?

> *Trust in the Lord with all your heart, and do not lean on your own understanding. In all your ways acknowledge him, and he will make straight your paths.*
> *—Proverbs 3:5–6 (ESV)*

This leaning not "on your own understanding" is what I mean by openness. Are there times when we boldly ask God for something (e.g., "Lord, please heal my mom.")? Yes. I believe in times of supplication—defined as a humble prayer and petition before our great God and King. What I'm humbly suggesting is inquisition—

defined as seeking facts, information, or knowledge, curious, and questioning. Now there's something! When was the last time you came to God curious? A.W. Tozer said, "What comes into your mind when you think about God is the most important thing about you." What I'm implying is your prayer life, your words and thoughts, the way you approach God, show (like it or not) what you really believe about God. If I put you in a room with Albert Einstein or today's world's smartest man, would you have a lot to say or would you inquire and listen?

The next way, I suggested we should come to God is with patience. Because God is not a genie, you may not get an answer right away. Some of you have been praying for something for years, probably in the area of supplication—maybe praying for the salvation of a loved one, neighbor or friend. When it comes to inquisition and inquiring with God about something it's usually not for very long. When you're praying for God's leading and direction for a certain decision you're facing, it probably won't take years, but it may require faithful prayer and maybe even fasting. When I mention patience, I'm again talking about the posture in which you approach God. Ever try to rush God? He usually doesn't play along. As we've all been reminded by faithful pastors and authors countless times, God cares more about the journey or the process than the destination. We come to God to inquire and seek His wisdom (which is good); He's just enjoying us being in His presence and drawing close to Him. As James 4:8 tells us, God comes close to us when we come close to him. So be patient. He's taking pleasure in it.

> *If you don't know what you're doing, pray to the Father. He loves to help. You'll get His help, and won't be condescended to when you ask for it.*
> *—James 1:5 (MSG)*

There lies such a wonderful hope and encouragement. When you don't know what to do, "pray to the Father." And surprise of all surprises: "He loves to help." Put simply: The Bible teaches us if you want wisdom, just ask for it (James 1:5). As a father, I love it when my kids come to me and ask me for my help. I love it when they ask me what I think about something. I feel I have a lot to offer them and have lived a little longer than them and thus have some wisdom they don't have, yet. So, I receive great joy in being able to lead them in the right direction. Imagine what our heavenly Father must think (who truly knows everything and is all-wise) when we come to Him and ask him for help and to guide us. I'm positive He delights in our inquisition and acknowledgment of our need for Him.

Keep holding on

> *And He said, "Let me go, for the day breaks." But he said, "I will not let you go unless you bless me!" —Genesis 32:26 (NKJV)*

The next way I suggested we pray is with perseverance. I can think of no better example of this than Jacob wrestling with God. When I taught my kids about perseverance in prayer, I taught them about Jacob and his astounding determination. My son used to end his prayer every night by saying, "And I won't let you go until you bless me. In Jesus' name. Amen." Maybe you're praying about a huge decision in your life or ministry. Maybe you're contemplating a building campaign, a new campus, a new staff hire, a new ministry or initiative or simply a different way of doing something you've done for a long time. You might need to "wrestle" with God over this for some time. Not years but for a while.

You might need to have a Gethsemane moment with God when

you cry out to Him, knowing he's asking you to do something huge, something painful, something significant, and you just need one final clarification this is truly the way He's leading—it will take perseverance. For many of you, friends, I've got to be completely honest with you. Your answer may not come until you are obedient to the Spirit's leading and have a dedicated time of prayer and fasting. Sometimes, I feel the weight of a decision or the unknown of what's next, and I'll tell my wife, "I need to fast." Mind you, I hate fasting, but I know there is power and clarification that comes from it. I have a good friend who used to fast for long periods of time, and he would fill his journal with words from God. Leader, you may never hear so clearly from God as when you fast and seek Him with perseverance.

> *Consider it pure joy, my brothers and sisters, whenever you face trials of many kinds, because you know the testing of your faith produces perseverance. Let perseverance finish its work so that you may be mature and complete, not lacking anything. If any of you lacks wisdom, you should ask God, who gives generously to all without finding fault, and it will be given to you. But when you ask, you must believe and not doubt, because the one who doubts is like a wave of the sea, blown and tossed by the wind. That person should not expect to receive anything from the Lord. Such a person is double-minded and unstable in all they do.*
> *—James 1:2–8 (NIV)*

Another way I suggested we pray and seek God is with a great deal of faith. I wanted us to look at this passage in James so you can see how everything I've been writing on this chapter is not new insight on my behalf; it's pulled straight from the pages of Scripture. Earlier, we talked about how "if any of you lacks wisdom, he should ask God". We also now see how the perseverance we talked about and our faith work hand in hand ("the testing of your faith develops perseverance"). I'd like us to zoom in on the verse about doubt, because this is key when we pray. The Bible teaches us "But when he asks, he must believe and not doubt". This does not contradict the openness I brought up earlier. We should always be open to whatever God says and however the Spirit leads, but we must approach God with a mindset and posture of supreme faith in God that knows He alone can provide, lead, and move.

Allow me to demonstrate. Each night, my family and I gather to have a time of devotion, maybe a Bible story and prayer. We pray each night for the healing of people who are on our radar. For example, we pray nightly for my wife's best friend Becky (who is waiting for a kidney transplant), Pastor Rick (Rick White of the People's Church in Franklin, TN), Pastor Matt (Matt Chandler of The Village in Dallas, TX), and we used to pray each night for Mr. Billy and Mrs. Charlene (Billy and Charlene Hornsby. Billy was the President of ARC—the Association of Related Churches).

So each night as we lift up "Becky, Pastor Rick, Pastor Matt, Mr. Billy and Mrs. Charlene, we come with both bold faith (we know God has the ability to heal them) and openness (we realize His answer may be to take them home with Him in Heaven).

Update: Since first writing this years ago, Billy and Charlene Hornsby have both gone to be with Jesus. Becky got her kidney transplant and is recovering. Pastor Rick and Pastor Matt are both doing great. As a matter of fact, I recently went to Nashville and got to spend some time with Pastor Rick who had just that day received a clear scan and is cancer free! We know God can heal, but we realize He doesn't always choose to. Make sense?

How we come to God

> *Let us then approach the throne of grace with confidence, so that we may receive mercy and find grace to help us in our time of need. —Hebrews 4:16 (NIV)*

So, as you're leading your area of ministry and seeking God's wisdom, you must have total faith God is sovereign, He's all-knowing, all-wise, and all-powerful. Nothing is impossible for God (Luke 1:37). Nothing! Therefore, we "approach the throne of grace with confidence, so that we may receive mercy and find grace to help us in our time of need." Do you need grace to help you in your "time of need"? I do. Each night in our family prayer time, I say this in my prayer because I hope the repetition of my kids hearing those words will sink in overtime, and they'll own those words for themselves. I want to encourage you, my brothers and sisters, to come before God and seek Him with bold faith, believing He knows best and where He leads is where you need to follow.

The final thing I suggest in your time of prayer is critical and pulls this all together. This last step is having sensitivity to the Holy Spirit. I'll touch on this a little in the next chapter, but this has to do with listening to the Holy Spirit. Hearing His still, small voice. Knowing when God whispers to your heart. All of this requires an intentional choice to listen. This means you don't do all the talking. You come to God with your inquisition and your supplications (and worship, praise and thanksgiving), but you also pause, reflect, sit, bow or lay and wait for God to speak. I will often pray a simple prayer to God that goes like this, "Speak to me, Lord. I long to hear from You." Can you imagine having an audience with the smartest and wisest person in the universe (who also knows the future, by the way) and you do all the talking? This sounds insane. I would sit there with a notebook, laptop, or my iPad and take notes furiously. I would hang on every word he had to say. In this case, this brilliant person happens to be deity and deserves to be worshiped and revered. Yes, I would hang on every word He had to say, but I'd also have times of intentional silence when I just was "still and know that He is God." (Ps 46:10)

> *Delight yourself in the Lord and He will give you the desires of your heart.*
> *—Psalm 37:4 (ESV)*

Early in this chapter, I talked of a significant marriage that happens when God's heart unites with your hands and feet. I realigned our aim and motives by saying it's His heart, His goal, His plan, His dream, and His leading with your hands and feet. Psalm 37:4 is a verse I've treasured and marveled at for years. As you know, this is not a genie-type passage that means God will give us whatever we want. It means when we are so in love with Jesus, so close in communion with Him, so sensitive to the Holy Spirit, and tuned in to what God is doing in our lives; when all this matches up, what we "desire" is actually what God wants us to desire. We have the mind of Christ and of course He wants to give us the desire of our heart (what He's leading us to want). Getting ourselves to this sacred place and position before God takes an enormous amount of intentionality and dedication. I admit I'm not always there. But the times I have been there are unforgettable and precious to me.

Now put all these things we've talked about in this chapter together in light of Blackaby's quote, "God's activity is far greater than anything we could aspire to do for Him." This is basic or elementary stuff, but it's healthy to be reminded of it from time to time. We come to God with a posture and mindset that believes He knows not only better, but best and we seek His wisdom. Again, we don't bring our man-made plans to God to bless, rather we join Him in what He is up to. Of course, this implies an acknowledgement of what we talked about in the introduction— God is at work, on the move, and doing new things all around us. We simply must join God where He is working. This is the message of Blackaby's *Experiencing God* and if you'll let it, it can change the direction of your life.

"Few people arise in the morning as hungry for God as they are for cornflakes or toast and eggs."
—Dallas Willard, Hearing God: Developing a Conversational Relationship with God

"Individually the disciple and friend of Jesus who has learned to work shoulder to shoulder with his or her Lord stands in this world as a point of contact between heaven and earth, a kind of Jacob's ladder by which the angels of God may ascend from and descend into human life. Thus the disciple stands as an envoy or a receiver by which the kingdom of God is conveyed into every quarter of human affairs."
—Dallas Willard, Hearing God: Developing a Conversational Relationship with God

"In many cases, our need to wonder about or be told what God wants in a certain situation is nothing short of a clear indication of how little we are engaged in His work."
—Dallas Willard, Hearing God: Developing a Conversational Relationship with God

"By definition, a God-ordained dream will always be beyond your ability and beyond your resources."
—Mark Batterson

"Our failure to hear His voice when we want to is due to the fact that we do not in general want to hear it, that we want it only when we think we need it."
—Dallas Willard, Hearing God: Developing a Conversational Relationship with God

"We are God's creation, designed to enjoy Him and for Him to enjoy us."
—Donald Miller, Storyline Conference 2013

Revelation

Hearing from God

Whereas in the inquisition concept or principle we go to God, in this chapter on revelation, we see God sometimes comes to us. For inquisition, we take the initiative. For revelation God takes the initiative and it's a marvelous thing. Can you imagine out of the seven billion (with a B) people on Earth, God would take the time, care, thought, and initiative to personally speak to you? To think He would reveal His thoughts, His plans and His agenda to you? Let this wash over you and accept how precious and special you are to your Heavenly Father and Creator. Not only did Christ die for you and make a way for you to spend eternity with Him, not only does He sit at the right hand of the Father and intercede on your behalf, but He's sent His Holy Spirit to be our Comforter, Guide and Revealer of truth.

For this chapter, I have moved outdoors. I'm sitting on my back porch on a rocking chair looking out across a lake, listening to birds chirp and squirrels dash around through the leaves. Today is the first warm day in what seems like forever. It's about seventy degrees outside, and I'm wearing a T-shirt and shorts. This is strange considering it was snowing last week. Nevertheless, I'm going to enjoy it and have urged my kids to go outside and play in this beautiful weather. I wanted to be close to and among nature for my inspiration for this chapter on God's revelation to us.

God speaks through a number of ways. One of the ways He speaks is through His creation. Have you ever been moved by a sunset? Or found yourself worshiping while spending time at a beach, on a mountain, or even at an aquarium or zoo? I have! Every time I take my kids to the aquarium (and's a lot—we have a season pass) or to the zoo, I am absolutely amazed at God's creativity. I look at fish of all sorts of colors, sizes and shapes and am blown away God would take the time to create something so spectacular.

In the last chapter, I talked about having a sensitivity to the Holy Spirit and seeking to listen to His still, small voice. Sometimes, I hear His whisper when I'm outdoors. Sometimes God speaks to me through my dreams—not often, but it's happened several times over the course of my life. Sometimes, God speaks through other people (which we'll look at in the "Conversation" chapter). Sometimes, God speaks through our circumstances (which we'll look at in the "Situation" chapter). God definitely speaks to us through prayer (which we just discussed in the "Inquisition" chapter). Most times, God speaks through His word (which we'll look at in the "Illumination" chapter).

Revelation is different from those. It's supernatural, and honestly, it's controversial. Please hear me up front: I'm not talking about a new revelation, which we take over the authority of Scripture in our lives. I believe God's word is the official authoritative voice from God and thus gives us the best insight into His heart and nature. It might be wise to emphasize God will never give a revelation contrary to what the word says—1 Cor 14, the tongue's chapter says to test the spirits, and make sure whatever is being presented as a word of revelation is consistent with His word. I want to make this clear. God's word and the gospel are paramount. Nothing supersedes Scripture.

The reality is, though, we serve a living God—a God who cannot be contained, covered up in a box, or told to be silent. Our living God still speaks to His children. As a matter of fact, he speaks and calls out to those who do not even believe in Him. I hope if you've learned or been reminded of anything so far in this book, it is our God is active, alive and well, and on the move. He is the God who pursues, and I love this about Him! God pursues me like crazy, and this is precious and humbling to me. As one of my favorite Hillsong United songs says, He's "relentless" in His pursuit of us.

When God interrupts

So let's take a closer look at this revelation from God. This is different from inquisition in which we are actively seeking God and intentionally asking His guidance. In this chapter on revelation, we are usually caught off guard. God surprises us. He decides to interrupt our lives and sometimes disturb us. Has God ever interrupted your life and your plans? Has God ever surprised you? And maybe a more sensitive question: Has God ever disturbed you? Just totally rocked your world and changed your heart about something, someone or a situation? Again, oftentimes, He does this through Scripture or prayer, but there are times where maybe He has to get our attention a different way.

Let me put it another way (this isn't a "one size fits all" statement, it's just a statement): if it were true all of us read our Bible daily—365 days a year—and spent quality time in prayer each and every day, God would probably regularly speak to you by His Holy Spirit, and you would live in close communion, knowing His heart (like we talked about in the last chapter) and letting His desires become your own desires.

For some of us, a consistent, daily, quality quiet time is a challenge and something we struggle to make a priority. Is God just supposed to sit back and wait for you to come seeking Him?

Maybe. Sometimes, this is the case. Sometimes, God seems distant and as Rick Warren says, "If God seems far away, guess who moved?"

Other times, though, God decides He wants to come to you, whether you like it or not and whether you asked for it or not. Remember He's relentless. He's God, and He can do whatever He pleases (Ps 115:3). In 1 Sam 3, we read of God calling to Samuel and waking him up in the night. I'll just share the end of the story:

> *The Lord came and stood there, calling as at the other times, "Samuel! Samuel!" Then Samuel said, "Speak, for your servant is listening." And the Lord said to Samuel: "See, I am about to do something in Israel that will make the ears of everyone who hears about it tingle.*
> *—1 Samuel 3:10–11 (NIV)*

Do you remember the first time God spoke to you? I do. I was five years old. I was actually just talking with my mom the other night, and she reminded me of this story. I was telling her of how I was teaching my kids one night in our family devotional about how God speaks to us, and I had told them about Samuel and the above passage of Scripture. My mom recalled how when I was five years old, and my brother was three, I prayed each night God would give me a baby sister. This was humorous to my mom each night because she had no plans to have another child and was making plans to get her tubes tied.

One night, we were saying our prayers as usual, and I mentioned nothing of a baby sister. My mom thought it was strange but didn't say anything. The next night, I prayed and again didn't mention anything about a baby sister. My mom asked me, "Greg, why didn't you pray for a baby sister?" She said I answered back very calmly and confidently, "God told me I didn't have to pray for a sister anymore—he was going to give me a baby sister." My mom's sense of humor about the whole thing quickly changed to wonder. She went into my parent's bedroom and said to my dad, "You will not believe what Greg just said to me." Two weeks later, the doctors confirmed my mom was expecting, and eight months later, my sister, Amy, was born. My sister is now married with four kids, and I still kid her and joke she owes her life to the perseverance of a five-year-old boy determined to have a baby sister.

Praying for a sister at the age of five was the first of many times God has spoken to me over my forty years. About five years ago God spoke to me through a vivid dream. I woke up at 3:00 a.m. (which is not like me), remembering the dream, and I heard God clearly whisper someone's name. His name is actually a name many of you would know, and I'm still trying to put all the pieces together of why he whispered this man's name so clearly. I have some idea as I ran into him recently and God spoke to me through him. Maybe God was wanting to make sure I paid attention? I don't know, but I heard His voice. Another time, God again spoke to me during the middle of the night and gave me a special vision for a new way of doing church. This revelation is the discussion for another book, though my close friends know what God shared with me.

The most recent two stories are significant because I'm a deep sleeper. As a matter of fact, I take medicine that puts me in a drug-induced sleep and keeps me asleep through the night. So the fact I was awakened in the middle of the night and both times heard from God clearly is huge for me. Again, I wasn't in the middle of a time of worship or Bible study. I was in a deep sleep and God took the initiative to come to me, wake me, and speak to me. This is our God who pursues!

There's a man in my church named Rick, who I led to Christ, baptized, and discipled. He has an amazing story of God, waking him up in the middle of the night and telling him he was going to get an invitation to church, and when he got it, he should go. He was then invited to our church by someone he knew, and he received one of our flyers in the mail. This story is special to me because this man was addicted to drugs and was a mean and hardcore man. God radically saved him.

No assistance needed

How does this tie into innovation? Years ago, when I awoke with a vision, a dream and a burden, they were all tied to an extremely innovative idea—as I mentioned before God first gave me this idea about four years ago, and it's an entirely new way of doing church based on changing the existing role of many senior pastors throughout the country. Again, this will hopefully one day be its own book, but the key is this was a new idea—an innovation—I didn't plan, dream up, brainstorm, or try to manufacture. This was innovation straight from God Himself.

Maybe you have a similar story. Maybe God has woken you up in the middle of the night before and disturbed you. I'd love to hear your story. If we run into each other at a conference sometime, please come up to me and share it. For some pastors I know, they've been driving through a city or traveled to a city and God spoke to their heart, gave them a burden for this particular city and they ended up planting a church there. For some they were driving around downtown, saw a homeless person and God whispered to them, "I needed clothes and you clothed me" (Matt 25:36) or "I died for him, too" or "I love him. Help him." Many of you have stories like these; you can remember the date, you remember where you were, what God said, and how it forever changed you. For some of you, what God said or revealed to you wasn't major or earth-shattering.

I had a dream one time when I was eighteen and serving my first church as minister of music and youth. It was the fall, and I had gone to the local Christian bookstore to choose a Christmas musical for the choir to do. I remember I had narrowed it down to two musicals I liked. I decided to leave, think about it longer, and come back another day. I had a dream where I was talking to an angel, and he said he knew I was doing the musical *Shepherds and Kings*. I replied, "Yes, that's one of the musicals I'm looking at doing." The angel again said, "You're doing *Shepherds and Kings*'." I immediately woke up. Guess which musical I went to the store and bought? Now this is not a huge revelation like the idea I have of doing church a totally different way. This was a seemingly small decision of which musical to purchase. Who knows though, maybe there was a song or a line in the drama that was impactful to someone in the audience, and I'll never know on this side of heaven what the reason was for the dream? Perhaps, it was an exercise in learning to hear from God.

Suffice to say: Sometimes, this revelation can be major. Sometimes, it can be minor. Sometimes, God speaks to you, and it will forever change the course of your life. Sometimes, He just wanted to let you know He cares and is involved in the details of your life. Having been a worship pastor and songwriter and the friend of many worship pastors and songwriters, I'm very aware of how God will often come to a songwriter with a new lyric for a song or a new melody in their head. I've woke up singing a new tune before. Maybe some of you can relate.

In Zeph 3:17, the Bible tells us God "rejoices over you with singing." I've had several times in which I've woke up with a song in my head that I hadn't heard in months. I had a strong sense God had been singing over me while I was sleeping. Many award-winning songwriters can share stories of God giving them a song and will tell how they really were just a vessel. God came to them and guided them in their songwriting, if not, initiated it to begin with.

You want to talk about an interruption and God taking the initiative? Let's talk about the Incarnation and the story of the birth of Christ. Now there is an example of a living God is still alive, still moving, still acting, still up to new things. Go reread the marvelous story of Christ's birth and see just how many times God used revelation to intervene and change things. Check out Matthew 1:19–20 and Matt 2:11–13, 19–23.

The repetition in this story is what jumps out at me. Did you notice how many times God came to someone in a dream? God, again, took the initiative and intervened. His action changed what the Magi and Joseph ended up doing. You also know from Luke 1:26–38, an angel came to Mary, which is also a part of the Christmas story.

Do you have a peace?

Another way God reveals His will to us is by giving or withholding His peace. Have you ever been trying to discern God's will for something and just not had a peace about a solution that was presented to you? Boy, I have. When I'm praying about a ministry position God may be leading me to, this is crucial. I will not go to a church unless God gives me a peace about it.

I was recently offered a good job as a worship professor at a Christian college. I've often thought about teaching at a college or seminary one day, so this seemed like a great opportunity. The problem? I didn't have peace about it. Maybe one day, I'll end up teaching (even if just on the side as an adjunct professor). Maybe not. But I knew this wasn't the right time, right opportunity, and right fit. All because God withheld His peace in this matter, and I couldn't move forward with them. On the opposite end, I've had times in life when I lived by faith and took some big risks and moved my family across the country, simply because God had given me and my wife a peace about the opportunity. I'm sure you can relate.

Aren't you glad God pursues, intervenes, gives His peace, withholds His peace and takes the initiative? I am. He's relentless! What if God hadn't intervened in the Christmas story we looked at earlier. What if God hadn't come to Noah and asked him to build the ark (Gen 6:13–22)? What if God didn't come to Moses as a burning bush (Exod 3)? Can you imagine if God hadn't blinded and confronted Saul on the Damascus road (Acts 9:1–19)? And what if God didn't call to Ananias in a vision and ask him to go to Saul, lay hands on him to restore his sight and be filled with the Holy Spirit? (Acts 9:10–19) Paul is such a crucial part of the Christian faith, having written the majority of our New Testament. What if God hadn't intervened there? And think of your salvation story. What if God hadn't come to Peter in a vision? Read Acts 11:4–10.

Are you Jewish? I'm not. Throughout most of the Bible, those who fell outside of God's covenant with Israel were considered spiritually impure and unclean. But in this, dare I say innovative, Scripture passage, God clearly stated his Gospel is for all people. Remember, innovation is the act of doing or introducing something new. I would say God speaking to Peter about the Gentiles was pretty innovative.

Perfect example of this chapter and principle in practical terms: On Monday of July 22, 2013, I woke up at 2:30 a.m. after having a vivid dream. In the dream, I dreamed of a speaker at a conference teaching with a new, creative, cool, innovative idea of teaching without notes in a TED-style conference. Is this a great idea that I'll use in the future? Yes. Is this something I'd take over the authority of Scripture? Absolutely not. It was simply an innovative and strange idea that came to me in my sleep. The key was I didn't brainstorm or try to think this up—it just came to me. Get it?

So, to wrap up this chapter, God has (as demonstrated through Scripture) clearly spoken to, and revealed His will to people through dreams, visions, and angels. This can also be attested by myself and countless other people over the years who have heard God's voice and answered His call. Here's the part that frustrates many leaders, especially those high D—driven leaders who are on the move. This is the only chapter in this book you don't control. Let this sink in. Driven leaders (to whom I can relate), please don't skip over this chapter. Be sure to submit to the leading of the Holy Spirit and stay open to God speaking to you in unconventional ways. And please know: I can tell you God still speaks, but I can't make Him do it.

I pray God wakes you, I pray He opens your eyes to something new, I pray He interrupts you and blows you away, but there's no magic formula for making it happen. You could try praying something like Samuel, "Speak Lord, for your servant is listening", but this is again you being proactive and fits in better with the last chapter. Don't worry though, if God wants to get your attention, He will. He is the God Who pursues and has no problem taking the initiative to come to you. You just have to be patient, alert and ready to listen when He speaks. But watch out! He's relentless in His pursuit of our hearts.

"God doesn't seek for golden vessels, and does not ask for silver ones, but He must have clean ones."
—Dwight L. Moody

"Give me one hundred preachers who fear nothing but sin and desire nothing but God, and I care not a straw whether they be clergymen or laymen, such alone will shake the gates of hell and set up the kingdom of God upon earth."
—John Wesley

"The way to preserve the peace of the church is to preserve its purity."
—Matthew Henry

Who may ascend the mountain of the Lord? Who may stand in his holy place? Those who have clean hands and a pure heart, who do not put their trust in an idol or swear by a false god. They will receive blessing from the Lord and vindication from God their Savior.
—Psalm 24:3–5

Blessed are the pure in heart, for they will see God.
—Matthew 5:8

Consecration

Cleansing the temple

In the last part on "Revelation," I stated it was the one thing you couldn't conjure up. If and when revelation happens, it will be because God took the initiative and came to you. For the remainder of ways innovation can happen, you are actively involved and proactive in preparing this fertile soil we talked about earlier.

This isn't a long chapter, but don't let this fool you—it's an extremely important one. Consecration or the act of consecrating means "dedication to the service and worship of a deity." We serve, lead, and minister from a place and posture of consecration. This is the prerequisite for God choosing to use us in His grand plan. The book of Exodus uses the word consecrate nineteen times.

The book of Leviticus uses it eleven times. It's used several more times throughout the Old Testament and a few times in the New Testament. Under the direction of king Hezekiah, the priests consecrated and purified the temple of the Lord, clearing out everything that was ritually unclean. Side note: You want to talk about innovation and creativity? Just look at all the work that went into building the temple. Wow.

> *"Go, consecrate the people. Tell them, 'Consecrate yourselves in preparation for tomorrow; for this is what the Lord, the God of Israel, says: There are devoted things among you, Israel. You cannot stand against your enemies until you remove them.*
> *—Joshua 7:13 (NIV)*

God tells Joshua to tell the people to consecrate themselves in preparation for a coming battle. He says they will not win unless they do it. I'm sure you've realized by now, we're in a war. I'm not talking about Iraq or Afghanistan or Syria, or whatever the current conflict is when you are reading this. I'm talking about the spiritual war we as ministers of the gospel are all engaged in. Ephesians 6:12 reminds us, "For our struggle is not against flesh and blood, but against the rulers, against the authorities, against the powers of this dark world and against the spiritual forces of evil in the heavenly realms."

If you want to see supernatural innovation in your life and ministry—something that can only be explained by the hand of God and changes people's lives for eternity, you must be a consecrated servant leader. I'm not talking about being perfect, for we know only One has lived a perfect life. I'm talking about striving for a life of personal purity and holiness and dedicating our whole being to the will of God. Then and only then, will you be able to "stand against your enemies." This is important because each of you, in your city and community, have strongholds and evil forces at work that are waging a war for the souls you so desperately long to reach. God may be wanting to do a "new thing" in your midst and shower you with the blessing of insight, knowledge, wisdom and discernment, but He is urging you (like He did Joshua) to "consecrate yourselves in preparation for tomorrow."

We recently moved into a new building at my church and when we were preparing for our first week in the new building, God gave me the following verse:

> *Then Joshua said to the people, 'Consecrate yourselves, for tomorrow the Lord will do wonders among you.'—Joshua 3:5 (NASB)*

I had an art piece made up and our entire congregation signed it with Josh 3:5 in the middle of the art piece. Many Saturday nights, I will post the Scripture on Facebook and ask people to pray for what God will do in the morning when we gather for worship.

Friends, don't miss this: consecration is required if you want to see God move. I'm talking about personal and/or corporate consecration. Let's take a quick look at what the Bible says to Noah:

> *This is the account of Noah. Noah was a righteous man, blameless among the people of his time, and he walked with God.*
> *—Genesis 6:9*

Noah was a man consecrated to God, and God used him to change history. Proverbs 3:32 tells us God "is intimate with the upright." To truly be led by the Spirit as we talked about in the introduction, one must be upright and live a life of daily consecration. Out of this can flow all sorts of new ways of ministry and innovation.

"It is in the process of being worshipped that God communicates His presence to men."
—Reflections on the Psalms, C.S. Lewis

"Expect great things from God; attempt great things for God."
—William Carey, who is called the father of modern missions

"Keep your dreams alive. Understand to achieve anything requires faith and belief in yourself, vision, hard work, determination, and dedication. Remember all things are possible for those who believe."
—Gail Devers

"You block your dream when you allow your fear to grow bigger than your faith."
—Mary Manin Morrissey

"What comes into your mind when you think about God is the most important thing about you."
—A.W. Tozer

"Faith is deliberate confidence in the character of God whose ways you may not understand at the time."
—Oswald Chambers

"Faith is expectancy. You do not receive what you pray for, nor even what you say you have faith in. You will always receive exactly what you expect."
—Eric Butterworth

Expectation

Believe the unbelievable

Expectation is the act or state of looking forward or anticipating; an expectant mental attitude. I'm putting this chapter and principle early in the book because it's important for you to grasp. The mindset and posture in which we should approach God is one of expectation. We expect God to show up, move, lead, and guide. If He doesn't then we are simply leading in the flesh and won't make an eternal difference. William Carey said, "Expect great things from God; attempt great things for God." This is the premise of this chapter. The innovative and strange leader expects great things from God. The innovative and strange leader leads by faith and is rooted in hope.

One of my favorite Christian artists, Steven Curtis Chapman, wrote a song entitled *Great Expectations*. Let's look at his lyrics to the chorus:

Believe the unbelievable
Receive the inconceivable
And see beyond my wildest imagination Lord,
I come with great expectations

Can we really "believe the unbelievable" and "receive the inconceivable?" A few years ago, I got to hear Joel Hunter preach at Buckhead Church in Atlanta. He taught on expectation and defined it as "a belief that is centered on the future." Joel said, "We can expect God to be: available, wise, gentle and tough, patient, comforting, strong, and relentless." Does your belief in God to be wise and strong effect how you lead and make decisions? If God truly knows what is best, do we trust Him no matter where He leads and no matter what He asks and requires of us?

> *I wait expectantly trusting God to help for He's promised.*
> *—Psalm 130:5 (LB)*

> *I pray to God—my life a prayer—and wait for what he'll say and do.*
> *—Psalm 130:5 (MSG)*

My friend, Steve Komanapalli, who used to be special assistant to Rick Warren and a pastor at Saddleback wrote a guest blog for me a while back. In it, he said, "A farmer doesn't plant some seeds and go to Hawaii for a year! He spends the time anticipating, expecting a harvest." He also encouraged my readers to check out James 5.

> *Be patient, then, brothers and sisters, until the Lord's coming. See how the farmer waits for the land to yield its valuable crop, patiently waiting for the autumn and spring rains. You too, be patient and stand firm, because the Lord's coming is near.*
> *—James 5:7*

Steve went on to say, "If I'm going to wait, I need to wait confidently. Micah 7:7 says, "I wait confidently for God." Rick Warren says,

"When the outlook is bad, you look up. That is what hope is." It's confident expectation. One of my favorite Bible stories is of Joshua. In Josh 1, Moses just died, and Joshua is now leading the Jewish people to a place they have never been. Do you think he was nervous? Remember what God told him?

> *Haven't I commanded you? Strength! Courage! Don't be timid; don't get discouraged. God, your God, is with you every step you take"—Joshua 1:9 (MSG)*

The God factor

To lead an innovative organization, you must lead from a place, posture, and mindset of faith mixed with hope in Christ. The difference between business innovation and ministry innovation is the supernatural factor. We seek to be led by the Holy Spirit and not just think up new ways of doing things. Once you've done your part of prayerfully seeking God (inquisition) and reflecting on his word (illumination and meditation), you must believe God will answer, lead, and direct you and your team. As you know, "without faith it is impossible to please God" (Heb 11:6).

> *In the morning, O Lord, You hear my voice; in the morning, I lay my requests before You and wait in expectation.*
> *—Psalm 5:3 (NIV)*

Psalm 5 is my encouragement to you, friends. Lay your requests before God and "wait in expectation." This does not mean to sit on your hands and do nothing until you hear the audible voice of God. Sometimes we act, move or lead in expectation and anticipation of something we believe God has said or promised He will do. If God has spoken to you through His word, His Spirit, or given you a vision for something, you should confidently expect God to move mountains on your behalf. Be humble and trust in God for the victory. Check out Ps 62:

> *I wait quietly before God, for my victory comes from Him.*
> *—Psalm 62:1 (NLT)*

Throughout this book, we'll look at the characteristics of an innovative leader and organization. An innovative leader is strange, prayerful, bold, courageous, decisive, a risk-taker, organized, motivated, commissioned, visionary, and on mission—as well as full of faith, hope, and an expectation God is going to show up and come through. It reminds me of the lyric from Delirious? band, *My Glorious*:"God will save the day and all will say my glorious!" Do you believe "God will save the day?" When you're backed into a corner, confused, scared, nervous, or just plain don't know what to do in a situation, where do you turn? Do you expect and anticipate God to answer your cry for help and lead you down a new trail of adventure? I do. I believe God has a plan for me, my life, my mission, and my ministry. I believe He is listening to my prayers and stands ready to answer and come to my rescue when I sincerely seek Him.

At the time of this most recent revision of this book, I've been the campus pastor at a multisite church for around three years. Ever since week one at my church, I close each service with Ephesians 3:20-21. Every week I stand before my congregation and I say "Let's pray this with a spirit of expectation!" We've seen God do some great things over the past three years, but I'm expecting Him to do so much more. I can't wait to update you years down the road of what God is up to in my city. Pray it with me and our church:

Now to Him who is able to do immeasurably more than all we ask or imagine, according to His power that is at work within us, to Him be glory in the church and in Christ Jesus throughout all generations, for ever and ever! Amen.
—Ephesians 3:20–21 (NIV)

"Great dancers aren't great because of their technique; they are great because of their passion."
—Anonymous

"Whatever your heart clings to and confides in, that is really your God."
—Martin Luther

"Passion, it lies in all of us, sleeping... waiting... and though unwanted... unbidden... it will stir... open its jaws and howl. It speaks to us... guides us... passion rules us all, and we obey. What other choice do we have? Passion is the source of our finest moments. The joy of love... the clarity of hatred... and the ecstasy of grief. It hurts sometimes more than we can bear. If we could live without passion maybe we'd know some kind of peace... but we would be hollow... Empty rooms shuttered and dank. Without passion, we'd be truly dead."
—Joss Whedon

"We cannot be sure of having something to live for unless we are willing to die for it."
—Che Guavara

"If there is no passion in your life, then have you really lived? Find your passion, whatever it may be. Become it, and let it become you and you will find great things happen for you, to you and because of you."
—T. Alan Armstrong

"Nothing great in the world has been accomplished without passion."
—Georg Wilhelm Friedrich Hege

Passion

What keeps you singing?

God has wired you uniquely and specially—your DNA and what makes you tick is different from mine and those around you. God has a personal plan for your life (Jer 29:11). Often, when God wants to use you for something significant, he will give you a passion for a cause or area of ministry. This is the H or "heart" in your SHAPE profile by Rick Warren. Mark Waltz of Granger Community Church says, "Every person has a fondness for a certain cause, need, or group of people. This is reflected in our conversations and is deeply tied to our emotions." (*First Impressions* p. 48) God will put his finger on something in your area of passion to use you for His cause.

> *Guard your heart above all else, for it determines the course of your life.*
> *—Proverbs 4:23 (NLT)*

The Bible instructs us to guard our heart. In the NLT, it goes on to say "for it determines the course of your life." Where you go next and what you do next may be directly tied to your heart and passion. This is key for the innovative and strange leader. In a blog post at www.9Marks.org, Kevin DeYoung encourages pastors:

> "Let your person constantly be refined by the spirit of God, and let the truth of God's word shine through your own personality." God is the one who gave you your unique personality and like it or not, He has a purpose and plan for it.

> *For we are God's handiwork, created in Christ Jesus to do good works, which God prepared in advance for us to do.*
> *—Ephesians 2:10 (NIV)*

In the next chapter, we'll look at the role vision plays in the life of the leader. Andy Stanley said, "Vision is always accompanied by strong emotion [or passion]. And the clearer the vision, the stronger the emotion." (*Visioneering* p. 10) Another -ion I could list as a way to lead an innovative organization is by conviction, but to me this is closely tied with passion so I'm combining them. I believe God gives you a passion, and this becomes a conviction for you. Like Christ, you won't let anything deter you from what you feel led to do, pursue, or change. Jeremiah had a similar passion and conviction about sharing God's word and speaking on His behalf. Look at this awesome verse:

> *But if I say, 'I will not mention Him or speak any more in His name,' His word is in my heart like a fire, a fire shut up in my bones. I am weary of holding it in; indeed, I cannot.*
> *—Jeremiah 20:9 (NIV)*

A heart check

Jeremiah, like so many of God's servants over the years was living a passionate life based on the conviction he needed to be obedient to God's call on his life. Jeremiah knew his shape, even though it wasn't called this then. Do you know your shape? I encourage you to take a SHAPE profile and read more about it in Rick Warren's best-selling book *The Purpose Driven Life*. Rick writes in his Ministry ToolBox:

"At Saddleback, we talk about the five different factors that make up a person's SHAPE: Spiritual gift(s), Heart, Abilities, Personalities, and Experiences. Why is this important? Why should we bother figuring out how God has shaped us? I'll give you five benefits." Warren then promises these five benefits from understanding your SHAPE: reduces stress, increases success, determines how you learn, deepens satisfaction, and builds self-esteem.

Rick Warren says, "The heart represents the core of your desires, hopes, interests, dreams, ambitions, and affections. The heart is the seat and source of all your intentions and motivations, what you love to do and care most about. Your heart is the real you, what you really are, not what others think you are or what circumstances pressure you to be. The heart determines why you say and do what you do, and feel the way you do about it. Just as each of us has a unique heartbeat, so God has given each of us a unique "Emotional Heartbeat" that signifies our passion in living."

"What you are passionate about reveals your emotional heartbeat—find your passion and you will find your heart. And God looks upon the heart. And God wants you to serve Him out of heartfelt passion, not duty. There are two basic characteristics that determine when you are serving God from your heart. First is enthusiasm: You will be working out of love and enjoyment. Second is effectiveness: When you do what God has shaped you to love doing, you will get good at it."

Throughout the course of human history, many have led from their heart and passion and many were thought to be strange—this goes with the territory. The beautiful thing about this concept to me is when you tap into your passion, the ministry, and service you do just flows out and you are less likely to burnout. Leading from passion is a secret to endurance and success in life and ministry. When God wants to do a new thing (innovation) through you, He may very well start with something near and dear to your heart. He may give you a passion for something He wants to change or be done differently. Follow your heart. Follow your passion and be obedient to God's call.

"Innovation distinguishes between a leader and a follower."
—Steve Jobs

"Throughout the centuries there were men who took first steps, down new roads, armed with nothing but their own vision."
—Ayn Rand

"The shepherd always tries to persuade the sheep that their interests and his own are the same."
—Henri B. Stendhal

"A true visionary is someone who's always thinking about the future and making it happen."
—Peter Jackson

"The very essence of leadership is that you have to have vision. You can't blow an uncertain trumpet."
—Theodore M. Hesburgh

"One reason so few of us achieve what we truly want is that we never direct our focus; we never concentrate our power. Most people dabble their way through life, never deciding to master anything in particular."
—Tony Robbins

"Someone's sitting in the shade today because someone planted a tree a long time ago."
—Warren Buffett

Vision

Seeing the future before it happens

Vision is different from the chapter on revelation because revelation is a God idea in which He may choose to whisper to you. Vision is a God-sized goal and dream for your organization God gives you to narrow your focus and keep you on a certain path in your leadership. God may choose to reveal something to you that is special but not a vision for which direction to lead your organization.

So first let's define vision. Bill Hybels at the Global Leadership Summit defined vision as "a picture of the future that produces a passion in the heart of people." Andy Stanley defines vision as "a clear mental picture of what could be, fueled by the conviction that it should be. Vision is a preferred future." Webster's 1970 edition of *The New World Dictionary* says vision is "the ability to foresee or perceive something not actually visible, as through mental acuteness." Lastly, Dawson Trotman, founder of Navigators said, "Vision is getting on your heart what God has on His." I resonate with this!

As we discussed in the Revelation chapter, God sometimes speaks through dreams. As Andy Stanley said, this is not what this chapter or concept is about—this is about a "clear mental picture of what could be."

In this chapter, I want to share with you what some senior pastors have said about vision. I'm a campus pastor at a multisite church (so I oversee my campus or congregation but not the entire church), but as I've never been a senior or lead pastor, I can't fully speak into having a vision for an entire church. I can speak into having a vision for my campus or a particular area of ministry in a church that supported the overall vision. I've coached pastors on how to go about crafting a vision statement for their church. I also helped start a company called WorshipHouse Media and remember our vision at the beginning. We envisioned a one-stop shop for media resources for the Church—where pastors and volunteers could save time by going to one central website to find all the media resources they would need. I also was given a vision for a different way of doing church ("a preferred future"), which I shared in the Revelation chapter. This was something that came about by revelation from God but is a specific vision for how church can be different. However, for the purposes of this book, we're going to talk about how vision relates to the organization.

> *Where there is no vision, the people perish.*
> *—Proverbs 29:18 (KJV)*

This same verse as told in *The Message* is the key to vision leading to innovation.

> *If people can't see what God is doing, they stumble all over themselves; But when they attend to what He reveals, they are most blessed*
> *—Proverbs 29:18 (MSG)*

Without vision, people "stumble all over themselves"—they're unhealthy, unfocused and naturally tend to drift. Adhering to a given vision will help guard against drift. When I think of great teaching on vision, I think of Andy Stanley who said, "Visions are born in the soul of a man or woman who is consumed with the tension between what is and what could be." He went on to say, "Nehemiah's vision didn't begin as a vision. It began as a concern, a burden. A burden for his nation and its people . . . ." (*Visioneering* p. 18) Craig Groeschel talks about vision being a "divine burden" and a "divine focus."

I was recently listening to *It* by Craig Groeschel as an audiobook. I was grabbed by those words and concept: a divine burden and divine focus. I love the word divine because it shows the supernatural nature of vision. This isn't something man-made or manufactured, it is given by God and thus should be taken seriously and "guarded by all," as my old pastor says.

In *7 Practices of Effective Ministry*, Andy Stanley has a whole chapter dedicated to "Narrow the Focus"—where he talks about things that will come up to take away from or distract you from your divine focus and divine burden for the organization you're a part of and the community you're called to serve. Stanley says, "Our world has been greatly impacted by men and women of almost single-minded determination whose contributions were defined by the passionate pursuit of excellence in a specific area. Somewhere in their personal journey, either by accident or on purpose, these few discovered the advantage of narrowing their focus." (*7 Practices of Effective Ministry* p. 99–100)

Seth Godin said, "Leaders communicate their vision of the future. Leaders commit to a vision and make decisions based on that commitment." (*Tribes* p. 126) We've talked about the importance of making healthy decisions—these decisions should be based on your commitment to the vision God has given you. If you're the leader of an organization, you should also prayerfully consider a vision or mission statement and work hard to make sure you and everyone on your team is aware of it and leads in light of it. You would not believe how many CEOs, college presidents, and others in leadership could not recite their organization's mission statement. This presents a number of problems.

If your vision is not clear, you can get tangled up in details that can completely throw you off your path. When you know your vision as an organization you keep from drifting and becoming weak, scattered, and ineffective. We all know staff and lay leaders aren't the only ones who sometimes get foggy about the vision for a church. I know pastors who don't know their church's vision. Scary!

Pursuing your vision

I remember many years ago at the C3 Conference hosted by Fellowship Church in Grapevine, Texas, hearing Pastor Ed Young say, "People don't give to need—they give to vision." Meaning they're not motivated to pay the electric bill, but they'll give to reach kids for Christ. It's hard to lead the charge in fundraising and taking on a new project or initiative as an organization if you can't clearly communicate the vision.

I asked Pastor Mark Cummins at Church of Hope in Ocala, FL, what his thoughts were on vision. Mark said, "Vision is the picture of a preferred future. Vision is seeing how life can be, when we go in this direction, make these sacrifices, partner together for a purpose bigger than we are individually . . . life will look like this. Vision must be cast with clarity and continually (Nehemiah cast the vision every twenty-five days). People will try to steal, adjust, dilute, change your vision—that's why you have to believe that the vision is given by God and must be guarded by all. Vision is not my agenda. Vision must be conceived in the leader from God's word . . . the leader must be convicted and convinced the vision is from God, giving him the courage to give his life to fulfill the vision for God's glory!"

Scott Wilson, senior pastor of the Oaks Fellowship, has some good thoughts on vision as a whole. He says, "In one sense, the purpose and vision of every local congregation on the planet, from Pentecost until today, is exactly the same: to fulfill the Great Commandment and the Great Commission. This global, universal vision statement won't change until the Lord returns, but every local body of believers has its own unique way of living out this God-sized vision. When God calls a pastor to lead a church, it's a holy calling." Scott goes on to say, "While learning from others is essential, each leader must do the hard work of pursuing God for their own vision." (*Steering Through Chaos* p. 45) This is how vision is different from revelation. In revelation, God pursues you and often takes you by surprise. For vision, you pursue God and beg him to give you a vision for your organization. See the difference?

> *Brothers, I do not consider that I have made it my own. But one thing I do: forgetting what lies behind and straining forward to what lies ahead, I press on toward the goal for the prize of the upward call of God in Christ Jesus*
> *—Philippians 3:13–14 (ESV)*

So how do you narrow the focus and hone in on your vision as an organization? Scott Wilson said, "As we asked God to clarify our vision, I asked our staff and board three questions: What do we do exceptionally well? What are we passionate about? What are the demographics of our community?" (*Steering Through Chaos* p. 48) As we discussed in the last chapter on passion, knowing what you're passionate about is key to leading well and effectively. One other question I would add is "What does a good job look like?" Or as countless business leaders and executives have asked: "What's our business? And how's business?"

Once you have clear direction on your vision from God and what He's calling you as an organization to be, you must fight like crazy to protect it and keep the main thing the main thing. We'll discuss this more in the "Subtraction" chapter. Andy Stanley says, "What can you do to keep your dream alive? Nehemiah did two things. He prayed, and he planned. Prayer keeps us looking. Prayer keeps the burden fresh. It keeps our eyes and hearts in an expectant mode." I hope you're beginning to see all these chapters work together. Yes, they can be read separately, but the entire book is trying to make one point and help you lead an innovative organization. In this one quote on vision, Andy Stanley, touched on prayer and keeping "our eyes and hearts in an expectant mode." He goes on to say, "New visions die easily. And understandably so. There is little to go on. Praying and planning will help you keep your vision alive. When your vision dies, part of you dies as well. Pray for the people who could help you launch your vision. And while you wait, plan! Develop a strategy. Dream on paper. Find the one or two things you can do and get busy." (*Visioneering* pp. 30, 31, 38) We'll discuss developing a strategy in the Organization chapter.

I hope you realize how crucial vision is to a healthy organization. This vision starts at the top but should be carried out throughout the entire organization. Other staff members have vision for their area of ministry, which should support and complement the overall vision of the church and senior pastor. When I was a worship pastor or tech pastor, I had a vision for the worship ministry or the technical arts ministry, but it was under the overall vision and mission of the church and didn't veer from what we as an organization were about. Within your own area of ministry, you should work hard to narrow your focus and operate out of your vision.

In the beginning of the book *7 Practices of Effective Ministry* (pp. 10–11), the authors say, "Focus is the key to achieving excellence and making impact. Each ministry environment should be designed to do no more than one or two things well." If you're over a ministry environment in the children's or youth area of your church, for example, you should lead with a vision and purpose in which you "do no more than one or two things well." Narrowing your focus (and sometimes subtracting, as we'll discuss later) will go a long way toward helping you make an impact. Craig Groeschel said, "Someone once said, 'If you chase two rabbits, both will escape. You can't underestimate the power of focus. Focus tends to let it breathe; lack of focus suffocates it.'" (*It* p.56–58)

I found listening to the free audio podcast on www.practicallyspeaking.org by the leadership of North Point Community Church to be extremely helpful in wrapping my head around this concept. On the podcast, Andy Stanley said, "Everything drifts toward complexity. Complexity makes organizations dumber. Complexity is so distracting that nothing gets done as well as it could get done were fewer things being done. For some reason in church life we add and we add and we add, and we chase the new fad, and we chase the new program, and we never subtract and things become so incredibly complex that we often times just fold up under the pressure." Reggie Joiner continued by saying, "A lot of churches get distracted from their vision and become ADD. It dilutes your potential to make an impact. It takes all of your energy, budget, staff, and resources and divides it in a hundred different ways instead of it being focused and excellent." Andy agreed and added, "Competition for resources, competition for rooms, competition within the organization. Ultimately, what gets squeezed out is not ministry to believers but evangelism. Complexity kills the spirit of evangelism in the church . . . All the resources are consumed trying to make insiders happy."

So, having a vision and sticking to it are crucial. After you have developed your vision statement you then should work with a team of key leaders to identify four or five key values that are based on the vision statement and then develop a set of belief statements that are based on the Bible. I have chosen to define values and beliefs differently. I like the way Ken Blanchard, author of *The One Minute Manager* and *Lead Like Jesus*, says it: "Values should define the way we act." In other words, your values will drive the behavior of the organization (i.e., we value that every follower of Christ should try to live like Jesus). Beliefs, on the other hand, reflect the theological and Biblical non-negotiables that you as a leader will never compromise. (i.e. We believe that Jesus Christ is the only way to have a personal relationship with God.) When God gives you a vision, it means He has a special and specific purpose for you and your organization. If you purpose and commit to lead by this vision, you can be a healthy, impactful, innovative organization.

One final thought: Having been on staff at Transformation Church, I can honestly say I've never been around a pastor that is as good a vision caster as Derwin Gray. If you have the opportunity to meet, interview him or attend one of his HD Leader Roundtables—do it! You won't regret it. The man flat out gets vision and oozes it.

"Give me a man who says this one thing I do, and not those fifty things I dabble in."
—Dwight L. Moody

"Most people have no idea of the giant capacity we can immediately command when we focus all of our resources on mastering a single area of our lives."
—Tony Robbins

"I cannot and will not recant anything, for to go against conscience is neither right nor safe. Here I stand, I can do no other, so help me God. Amen."
—Martin Luther

Mission

Do you have a personal mission statement?

Besides discovering and leading according to your vision, you must also lead based out of your mission. Where vision is a preferred future for your organization, mission is personal and influences how you lead, act and decide. For the purposes of this book, we looked at vision as it relates to the organization, and we'll now look at mission as it relates to the individual. Andy Stanley pointed out, "This generation has been ministered to by a number of individuals whose names are almost synonymous with their focus: Billy Graham and crusades. James Dobson and family. Bill Bright and evangelism. John Maxwell and leadership. George Barna and research. Gary Smalley and marriage." (*7 Practices of Effective Ministry* pp. 100, 101) Their mission defined them.

When I started my first full-time church (after college) I worked with a pastor named David Coleman, who had a personal mission statement. He recited it to me by memory and also had it framed in his office. He encouraged me to do the same, but I was young (twenty-one) and didn't think this was for me. Fast forward years later and I'm meeting with one of my mentors, Lee Ross, and he tells me of his personal mission statement and how important it is to have one.

Lee's personal mission statement is "To glorify God by being a positive, progressive, and Jesus-like example to my family, in my ministry, and to the people I meet." This time around, I took it seriously and after chewing on it for about a month and reading a couple of books that addressed it, I came up with my own personal mission statement: "To please God by being a Spirit-led leader as a loving husband, father, pastor, friend, and Christ-follower." Since then, I have shortened my personal mission statement or life philosophy to "Love God. Love people." I needed something short and sweet to remember.

Who's your role model when it comes to leadership? I hope it is Jesus. Of course, we all have people we look up to, admire, respect, quote, and read their books, but Jesus was and is the ultimate example of leadership. He is perfect. Jesus is also the biblical example of mission and having a personal mission. Jesus had two famous statements of His mission on earth. One was, "For the son of Man came to seek and to save what was lost" (Luke 19:10), and the other was, "For I have come down from heaven not to do my will but to do the will of him who sent me." (John 6:38) These two mission statements drove everything Christ did while He walked the earth. As I mentioned in the Decision chapter, He would not let anything deter Him from this, His mission.

What's a Mission Statement?

A personal mission statement is made up of two parts. First is common—to glorify God. We all are called to do this (Matt 22:36–39). The second part has to do with your shape and gift mix (like we talked about in the "Passion" chapter). Let's take a closer look at this concept of personal leadership. This concept of mission is crucial to the innovative leader. In *Lead Like Jesus*, the authors talk about this importance. They say, "Effective leadership starts on the inside. Before you can hope to lead anyone else, you have to know yourself. We call this personal leadership because it involves choice. Every leader must answer two critical questions: First, whose am I? and second, who am I?" (*Lead Like Jesus* pp. 20, 21)

My old mentor, Lee Ross, likes to say that, "Whose am I?" deals with Lordship and "Who am I?" is your purpose statement. In *Lead Like Jesus*, we see "the natural outcome of deciding to please God as well as turning over control of your life to Him is a change in your perspective. If you live a life that is not designed to please God or give Him control, your perspective will be inward and focused on self. If you live your life to please God and put Him in charge, your perspective will be outward and characterized by God-given confidence that will lead your life.

Early in His ministry, Jesus demonstrated His desire to please only the Father and turn control of His life over to Him." (*Lead Like Jesus* p. 21) Being characterized and known for God-given confidence is our aim as leaders. As John Maxwell says, "The most dangerous leader is an insecure leader." You can't be insecure as a leader—it's dangerous, and nobody wants to work with or follow an insecure leader.

This plays into innovation because innovation almost always involves change. Leading through change requires a great deal of God-given confidence and leadership skills. What is it about change causing us to be or feel insecure? I think it's because sometimes we try to bring about the change in our own flesh and natural strength and forget to tap into the supernatural reservoir we have in Christ and the leading of His Holy Spirit.

So, let's take this concept seriously and work on creating a personal mission statement. I've researched and studied this quite a bit and found there are a few simple elements to a good mission statement:

1. A mission statement shouldn't be long. Maybe a sentence or two.
2. It shouldn't be complex. Simple is best.
3. You should be able to recite it by memory on the spot. You know, like an elevator pitch.

Did you know many great leaders in history had mission statements that were no more than a sentence long? Abraham Lincoln's mission was to preserve the Union. FDR's mission was to end the Depression. Nelson Mandela's mission was to end apartheid. Mother Teresa's mission was to show mercy and compassion to the dying. Joan of Arc's mission was to free France. Moses' mission was to set his people free. Nehemiah's mission was to rebuild the walls of Jerusalem. Jesus said He'd come to "seek and save the lost." (Luke 19:10) I could go on and on, but I think you get the point.

If you follow these three simple guidelines, you should be able to come up with your very own personal mission statement. Your mission statement should challenge you to do what you may not be doing. It should challenge you to live your life like Jesus. This is why I shortened mine to "Love God. Love people."

Sound familiar? A twelve- year-old could remember it and I can remember it at gunpoint.

> *Pray also for me, that whenever I open my mouth, words may be given me so that I will fearlessly make known the mystery of the gospel, for which I am an ambassador in chains. Pray that I may declare it fearlessly, as I should.*
> *—Ephesians 6:19–20 (NIV)*

Paul, even in chains, knew Whose he was and who he was. He was a man on mission and would not even let being imprisoned stop him from what he was called to do. Paul was an innovative leader. Knowing whose you are and who you are can guard against insecurity and ineffective leadership. When you function from a sense of mission and purpose, you, like Christ and Paul, won't let anything deter or distract you from what you're called to do. Christ knew whose He was and who He was and if you do too, you'll be a fruitful and innovative leader.

"Observation—activity of both eyes and ears."
—Horace Mann

"A few observations and much reasoning lead to error; many observations and a little reasoning lead to truth."
—Alexis Carre

"To him that watches, everything is revealed."
—Italian Proverb

"You can observe a lot just by watching."
—Yogi Berra

Observation

Listening to culture

I was speaking to Church leaders in Miami one spring when someone in the audience raised her hand and suggested observation as a new -ion for how innovation comes about. I chewed on it for a while and then added it to my talk when I went on to future cities. I have found the act of observation and knowing what's around you is crucial to finding what God is up to and thus joining Him—which is where true innovation comes from. I like what Yogi Berra said, "You can observe a lot just by watching." I think watching is a form of listening. I also like the Horace Mann quote that says observation is an "activity of both eyes and ears." I think it hit the nail on the head. This book is largely a book on listening. In this chapter, we're going to look at listening to culture. Strange leaders listen to culture. One of my favorite Scripture passages demonstrates this—it's when Paul went to Athens.

> *So Paul, standing in the midst of the Areopagus, said: "Men of Athens, I perceive that in every way you are very religious.*

> *For as I passed along and observed the objects of your worship, I found also an altar with this inscription, 'To the unknown god.' What therefore you worship as unknown, this I proclaim to you.*
> *A few men became followers of Paul and believed. Among them was Dionysius, a member of the Areopagus, also a woman named Damaris, and a number of others.*
> *—Acts 17:22–23, 34 (NIV)*

An innovative leader who gets this concept of observation is a student of culture. Don't listen to those who say being a student of culture is wrong. It goes against our very calling to be missionaries and get to know the people we are trying to reach. Paul was a great example of someone who observed the people's "Unknown God" and used this as a starting point for a presentation of the gospel. Innovation goes hand in hand with observation. Mark Waltz said, "Wow is about innovation, and innovation is about addressing a constantly changing culture. We must be astute observers, conversationalists, and purveyors of change." (*First Impressions* p. 43) In this chapter, we'll discuss being astute observers. We'll talk about being conversationalists later and we've already discussed being a purveyor of change.

My friend Scott Hodge, pastor of The Orchard, once said he watches church planters to get ideas and inspiration. I, too, watch church planters, and I know we're not the only ones. Being a missionary and student of culture is crucial to fulfilling our calling to reach the lost and bring hope to the captives. I don't know about you, but I'm a learner and watcher (observer) of those I come in contact with. I observe reactions people have when I read a Bible in public or speak the name of Jesus. I'm constantly gauging people to see their receptiveness to the gospel.

As a church leader, I observe other churches. I watch how they lead, grow, organize, and structure. I try to attend other churches as much as possible. Thankfully, I've been blessed to travel quite a bit over the years and get to attend many churches. I've attended almost every church on the "Most Innovative Church" list and have learned something from each of them. At the time of writing this chapter, I was consulting full-time and not on a church staff, so I got to visit churches regularly as a church secret shopper consultant. I had eight months in Dallas of not being on staff at a church and got to visit some wonderful churches. Then I lived in the Atlanta area, and I got to visit great churches there in that region. At the time I wrote this chapter, I had visited six different churches throughout the Atlanta area in four weeks. Please note three churches were on the same day (two in the morning and one at night). I did try to be at my home church when I could.

Even before, when I was full-time on staff at a church, I would make it a habit to visit other churches on Saturday night and Sunday night. When I served in Charleston, SC, I would visit Seacoast Church on Saturday nights. When I served in Chapel Hill, NC, I would visit Providence in Raleigh on Saturday nights. When I served in Washington DC, I would visit McLean Bible Church on Sunday nights for their Frontline service and Wednesday nights for The Gathering. While in Dallas, I would go to churches like Fellowship Church (Ed Young) and The Village (Matt Chandler) on Saturday nights and even Irving Bible Church and Watermark Community Church on Sunday nights. No matter what your current situation is like, it would be wise for you to get out of your own church and observe what goes on at other churches. Don't even get me started on visiting churches while on vacation! This isn't just theory for me, these concepts are how I live my life.

I also serve as a secret shopper or mystery worshiper for churches across the country. Next month I'll be a secret shopper two out of the four weeks—once in Kansas City and once in Sacramento, CA. This allows me to observe all different types, sizes, styles, and shapes of churches. This also allows them to improve, grow and change based upon my observation. These churches bring me in to observe and share my experiences as a first-time guest at their church. Can you imagine the feedback, improvement, and growth you would receive by inviting a lost person in your community to visit and share their observations and experience with your leadership team? We can learn a ton from observation.

The Observers

I'd like to share a few stories about leaders who observed something and then responded and saw tremendous results all of which I would consider to be extremely innovative. They would say they were just responding to a need and listening to the Spirit. I agree. Let's look at two modern-day examples and first one from another generation. Obviously, there is a ton of examples, but I'm just going to share a few.

First, let's look at Hudson Taylor, who died in 1905. Hudson was a British Protestant Christian missionary to China and founder of the China Inland Mission (CIM). Taylor spent fifty-one years in China. According to Wikipedia, "The society that he began was responsible for bringing over 800 missionaries to the country who began 125 schools and directly resulted in 18,000 Christian conversions as well as the establishment of more than 300 stations of work with more than 500 local helpers in all eighteen provinces." Wikipedia goes on to say, "Taylor was known for his sensitivity to Chinese culture and zeal for evangelism. He adopted wearing native Chinese clothing even though this was rare among missionaries of that time." Taylor was able to preach in several varieties of Chinese. Historian Ruth

Tucker summarizes the theme of his life by writing, "No other missionary in the nineteen centuries since the apostle Paul has had a wider vision and has carried out a more systematized plan of evangelizing a broad geographical area than Hudson Taylor."

Next, let me introduce you to my friend, Brett Aljets. Brett used to be senior pastor of Whipple Creek in Vancouver, WA. Brett and his youth pastor were walking down the street in their community one day and saw some kids skateboarding. Brett knew his youth pastor was a good skateboarder and said, "Go tell those kids about Jesus."

So, his youth pastor, Christian, went over to the kids and began to skate with them and show them some tricks. The kids instantly liked him, and he had their attention. He said, "You know you're welcome to skate in the church parking lot. Why don't you come by this Thursday night and bring some friends?" They came and they brought more friends. The next Thursday night they brought more friends. On and on and the group continued to grow, so much so that they moved indoors (into their worship center). They put down plywood in their worship center and built ramps and jumps and allowed their place of worship to be turned into a skate park during the week.

This Thursday night gathering of skaters became known as Skate Church, and now years later, this church (which is not a mega-church) has seen well over three hundred kids come to know Christ. It all started with a pastor and youth pastor observing some kids skating.

Finally, let me introduce you to my friend, Toby Slough, a pastor in Argyle, TX. I had the pleasure of sitting next to Toby on a plane ride one time when we were both headed to the same conference. He began to share with me what God was doing at his church, Cross Timbers.

In the spring of 2009, when the economy had hit rock bottom,

God began to speak to Toby about how they could be sensitive to the times and observant of what was going on in the world with the economy. One Sunday, they were taking up the offering and pastor Toby simply encouraged people who needed the money to take it from the offering plate.

Over early months of this particular spring, Cross Timbers gave away half a million dollars to both members and nonmembers who were struggling financially in today's economy. When asked about it, Pastor Toby Slough said, "Well, we've given single moms and widows $100 gifts. We've taken $200,000 and spread it out to organizations—four local, two missions—who are feeding and clothing people in these tough times. We've paid utility bills for members of our church who are unemployed or underemployed." But Pastor Slough's favorite give away came in May of 2009.

The church gave 1,400 families $50 each and told them to give it to someone else. Katie Lewis, who was baptized this particular month, was one of the recipients. The gesture changed her life. Katie Lewis said, "I've been alone so long. Just to be thought of and to be remembered, to be welcomed, it's amazing. It's all I've ever wanted."

This movement started early one year when Toby told his congregation to take money from the collection plate if they needed it, even though church donations were down. On this remarkable day, they had the largest offering ever. Then, just after, Pastor Slough gave a ride to a man looking for a job, who had just used his last bus pass. Pastor Slough says, "In that moment, I just knew this is what our church has to be about. In these economic times, we can't be so into church business that we forget what our business is, and that is to help people."

This is being observant! And this is being a strange leader. To a ton of people, giving people permission to put plywood down in your worship center and skate inside or allowing people to take money out of the offering plate would definitely fall under the category of "strange." This is the very essence of strange leadership and when you're sensitive to the moving of the Holy Spirit, you'll be observant and ready to respond.

"It is often out encounter with culture that first reveals to us our own culture."
—Tim Chester, Unreached

"When ideas are detached from the media used to transmit them, they are also cut off from the historical circumstances that shape them, and it becomes difficult to perceive the changing context within which they must be viewed."
—Elizabeth L. Eisenstein, The Printing Press as an Agent of Change

"The spirit of Christ is the spirit of missions. The nearer we get to Him, the more intensely missionary we become."
—Henry Martyn, missionary to India and Persia

"Let's face it. We don't teach the Bible. We teach people the Bible. As vital as it is to know content, it's not enough. We must know our audiences. Christian communicators who want to know their audience must be aware of the culture that shapes them, motivates them, and often lures them away from God."
—Haddon Robinson

Contextualization

The critical need for relevance

Contextualization and observation go hand in hand—this is why they're next to each other in this book. To simply observe and not contextualize would be a shame and can be dangerous. Contextualization is also about listening to culture. I was talking with a pastor friend of mine, and we were talking about an infamous pastor who is known for bashing other pastors of growing churches, homosexuals, and President Obama. He's got the observing thing down, but he doesn't seem to get how to interpret and contextualize what he sees, hears, or thinks. To contextualize means to place a word or idea, for example in a particular context.

According to Wikipedia, contextualization (the term) was first used in missiology. Missiology is the area of practical theology that investigates the mandate, message, and work of the Christian missionary. Contextualization is used in the study of Bible translations in relation to their relevant cultural settings. The word continues to be used theologically, mainly in the sense of contextualizing the biblical message as perceived in the missionary mandate originated by Jesus in the gospel accounts.

Throughout this book and if you ever spend any time with me, you'll hear me say "we need to think like missionaries." I used to work for a pastor who was a missionary to Taiwan for fourteen years. He taught me a ton about how missionaries think, live, move, and thrive. Missionaries speak the language of the culture they're trying to reach. Missionaries learn the people, their culture, and their beliefs. Missionaries train and study and pray. I've got to serve alongside some amazing missionaries and noticed they are extremely intentional in how they go about their ministry. As you can imagine, I like missionaries. I've also been reading a lot of missional books lately and hanging out with several missional friends and leaders and their idea of living as missionaries or one sent really resonates with me. I hope to continue to grow in this area and am trying to get back to gospel-centered, Jesus-centered, missional living. We should all be living on mission.

> *Though I am free and belong to no man, I make myself a slave to everyone, to win as many as possible. To the Jews, I became like a Jew, to win the Jews. To those under the law, I became like one under the law (though I myself am not under the law) so as to win those under the law. To those not having the law I became like one not having the law (though I am not free from God's law but am under Christ's law) so as to win those not having the law. To the weak, I became weak to win the weak. I have become all things to all men so that by all possible means I might save some. I do all this for the sake of the gospel, that I may share in its blessings. Do you not know that in a race all the runners run, but only one gets the prize? Run in such a way as to get the prize. Everyone who competes in the games goes into strict training. They do it to get a crown that will not last; but we do it to get a crown that will last forever. Therefore, I do not run like a man running aimlessly; I do not fight like a man beating the air. No, I beat my body and make it my slave so that after I have preached to others, I myself will not be disqualified for the prize.*
> *—1 Corinthians 9:19–27 (NIV)*

Go! Live as one sent on mission

This is such a rich passage of Scripture. I wanted you to read it through to the end. Paul said he had "become all things to all men." To me, this is the essence of the concept and principle I'm advocating. I asked Larry Osborne, senior pastor of North Coast Church, his thoughts on contextualization and the gospel and he said:

> *I try to run everything through the grid of 1 Cor 9:19–27. That pretty much means that I consider the scriptures, the truth of the gospel, and the standards of righteousness to be universal and unchangeable—but the forms by which they are communicated and accomplished are always open to change. I try to have the mindset of a missionary, constantly searching for ways to contextualize the unchanging truth of God.*
>
> *Frankly, over my thirty plus years as the pastor of North Coast, I feel like we've been three different churches in terms of how our ministry interacts with culture and how we present the gospel's call to Jesus and righteousness. But at all times, we've maintained a deep commitment to Scripture, to practical righteousness, and to living out the one another of Scripture in community. But other than that, most things are fair game—and many have changed over the years.*
>
> *I've had numerous "zero-based" planning retreats in which we've as much as possible asked the question, "What would we do if we were starting all over again from scratch?" What would stop—and what would we start? This has helped us immensely in terms of staying open and hungry to innovation.*
> *—Larry Osborne, senior pastor, North Coast Church*

Interesting. I wrote this chapter (with my above-mentioned thoughts on thinking like a missionary) weeks before Larry responded to my e-mail and said, "I try to have the mindset of a missionary. I think wise, and even more important, effective leaders have the approach and posture of a missionary." As Larry said, it's a mindset that drives how you do what you do. It's the old saying, "The message never changes, but the methods do."

> *"I believe that NorthStar has become part of the fabric of the community in Acworth/Kennesaw (Georgia). Therefore, our messages and ministries in the community have the flavor of the area we are in. If we picked up and moved off somewhere else, the "what" we are doing may not change but the "how" it is done or said might."*
> *—Mike Linch, Senior Pastor of NorthStar Church*

I love this! They have "the flavor" of the area they're in. Now keeping in mind the last chapter on observation and all we've talked about so far, do you have "the flavor" of the area you're in? Do you intentionally take on the mindset of a missionary and think and act like one? Let's look at the same passage in The Message:

> *Even though I am free of the demands and expectations of everyone, I have voluntarily become a servant to any and all in order to reach a wide range of people: religious, nonreligious, meticulous moralists, loose-living immoralists, the defeated, the demoralized—whoever. I didn't take on their way of life. I kept my bearings in Christ—but I entered their world and tried to experience things from their point of view. I've become just about every sort of servant there is in my attempts to lead those I meet into a God-saved life. I did all this because of the Message. I didn't just want to talk about it; I wanted to be in on it!*
> *—1 Corinthians 9:19–23 (MSG)*

The apostle Paul, a hero of the faith and a great example of a missionary leader and pastor said, "I entered their world and tried to experience things from their point of view." (in *The Message*, of course). I don't know about you, but sometimes, a passage I've read several times can wash over me with a fresh insight or meaning when I read it anew in

The Message. Paul's closing thoughts in this passage are key—he said, "I did all this because of *The Message*. I didn't just want to talk about it; I wanted to be in on it!" Friends, this is the essence of being innovative. Not just talking about the message, but being in on it. Being in on what God is up to— what He's doing and where He's working. It bears repeating: we earnestly seek to see what God is up to and where He's at work and then we join him. I'm really not offering anything new here. I'm straight ripping off Henry Blackaby's *Experiencing God.*

> *So Paul, standing before the council, addressed them as follows: "Men of Athens, I notice that you are very religious in every way, for as I was walking along I saw your many shrines. And one of your altars had this inscription on it: 'To an Unknown God.' This God, whom you worship without knowing, is the one I'm telling you about.*
> *—Acts 17:22–23 (NLT)*

I mentioned these chapters on observation and contextualization go well together. I'd like to bring back the passage of Scripture (Acts 17) from the last chapter and offer it in the context of this chapter as well. See, Paul went beyond just observing the people in Athens—he thought like a missionary, "tried to experience things from their point of view," and used their altar "To an Unknown God" as a starting point and a discussion starter. He took something from their culture and world and used it as an icebreaker to tell them the deep truths of the gospel. It was a genius move and no doubt inspired by the Holy Spirit.

Paul and Jesus embodied contextualization. To the woman at the well, Jesus talked about "living water." (John 4) Often in Jesus's teaching He would just go with something near him or something he saw—from the wind to little children, to a mustard seed, to a fig tree, to a mountain. Jesus found things, ordinary things, that people could relate to and used them as a starting point to teach a new truth. If you can intentionally seek to contextualize the gospel and think like a missionary, it may lead you to a new and strange way (innovation) of doing ministry.

"Large numbers of small ideas allow an organization to reach levels of performance that are otherwise unachievable. Without them, it is impossible to attain excellence."
—Alan Robinson and Dean Schroeder, in Ideas Are Free

"I have not failed. I've just found ten thousand ways that won't work."
—Thomas A. Edison

"Great things are not done by impulse but by a series of small things brought together."
—Vincent Van Gogh

"Just because something doesn't do what you planned it to do doesn't mean it's useless."
—Thomas A. Edison

"Sometimes when you innovate, you make mistakes. It is best to admit them quickly, and get on with improving your other innovations."
—Steve Jobs

"Success is getting up one more time than you fall down."
—Rev. Darrell W. Boswell

"The greatest glory in living lies not in never falling, but in rising every time we fall."
—Nelson Mandela

Progression

When you fall, get back up. Press on!

Okay, friends, let's take a breath. We're up to the twelfth way innovation can happen, and you might be starting to get a little overwhelmed. I hope not, but you never know. I know I talk a lot about being intentional and being innovative requires we must work at it, but there is hope! This chapter and concept is here to put your mind at ease and help you relax. You won't turn into an innovation machine overnight, so don't try to. This journey to innovation is a process and progression.

I like the first Thomas Edison quote because it challenges me and puts things in perspective. Edison didn't invent something on the first try. He made progress with each attempt and eventually stumbled onto something that worked. Edison also said, "Restlessness is discontent and discontent is the first necessity of progress. Show me a thoroughly satisfied man and I will show you a failure." Maybe you have a "holy discontent" that Bill Hybels wrote about and this restlessness and discontent is driving you to make a change. This is wonderful—it means God is at work at what Edison said is the "first necessity of progress."

If you've made a decision (which we've already talked about) to be healthy and grow and feel God leading you to change (through the many ways this book suggests) or adapt (which is a future chapter), then you must start small and take short (but intentional) steps toward leading this change or adaptation.

> *Brothers, I do not consider myself yet to have taken hold of it. But one thing I do: Forgetting what is behind and straining toward what is ahead, I press on toward the goal to win the prize for which God has called me heavenward in Christ Jesus.*
> *—Philippians 3:13–14 (NIV)*

For some of you, I simply want to encourage you to keep pressing forward. Maybe you've been trying new things but keep failing. My prayer and desire for you is for you to fail forward. Meaning learn from your mistakes, dissect what didn't work and why and make a choice to push ahead with new information, new ideas and new approaches to making the necessary changes. The very word progression means forward or onward movement. The concept here is simple: keep progressing forward toward a desired goal or end you feel led by God to do. The change or solution may not come right away. We must remember God is just as concerned with the process as He is the destination. He's working on us (from the inside) as we seek to listen to Him and lead.

I asked some pastors about this concept of progression and failing forward and here are their responses:

> *"I would say, in one sense, everything I know has been the result of someone (either me or someone I've watched) failing forward. Wisdom and innovation are often the end result of paying dumb taxes. It's hard to know what will work, until you've exhausted many of the ideas that won't work. We've had venues fail, new programs bomb, and great ideas go nowhere. Each time, we've learned 'what not to do next time.'"*
> *—Larry Osborne, senior pastor at North Coast Church*

"One of our fail forwards happened at the very beginning of NorthStar. We listed every imaginable ministry on an information card (like we could possibly day one fill twenty things that every other church was doing.) We learned quickly that was not who we were or who we are going to be. The lesson was we better get rid of all of the things that we can't do well and focus in on a couple of key things that we were going to be great at! We truly did fail forward. If we had not learned our lesson that we couldn't do everything—we may (today) be good at tons of things but be great at nothing."
—Mike Linch, senior pastor of NorthStar Church
(I'll come back to Mike's quote in the Subtraction chapter. - GA)

"One of our failures was a capital campaign where we missed our goal by over $500,000. We tried to facilitate the campaign the same way that we did our previous campaign three years ago. We failed to consider how to effectively communicate and cast vision to a much larger church. We learned so much about the power of casting vision and casting it to a larger audience, and at the same time, we learned to trust God in how the vision is accomplished. The vision didn't happen the exact way we had planned. God had to stretch our faith, make us uncomfortable and show us another way."
—Pete Wilson, former lead pastor of Cross Point Church

To boldly go where none have gone before

W. A. Nance said, "Failure can be divided into those who thought and never did and into those who did and never thought." Let's break this down. If you move forward without thinking and proper planning and leading of the Holy Spirit—there's failure. But if you also have an idea (a God idea) and you never act on it—there's failure, too. The reason I'm encouraging you to keep pressing forward is because it will take a great deal of courage, faith, and bold leadership to lead through change and innovation. Change is not easy—just ask my friend Scott Wilson who wrote the book *Steering Through Chaos*. Being an innovative leader is not about being cool or trendy or even just relevant. Being an innovative leader is about following God where He leads and having the wisdom, maturity, courage, and faith to progressively and intentionally lead your people in the direction they need to go. Again, this probably won't happen overnight, but eventually, with enough determination and endurance, you'll get there.

The elephant in the room may be this whole concept of failure and failing forward. You might be thinking, Isn't failure a bad thing? Not necessarily. I was once on a flight and decided to read the American Airlines magazine that was in the seat back in front of me. In this particular issue, there was a fascinating article about innovative companies who actually reward failure. These companies understand you can't innovate without risk, and therefore, they celebrate when employees fail at trying something new.

One company in the article actually held an annual banquet and gave out awards for the biggest failures of the year, and the winner (the guy who blew it the worst) actually got sent on a vacation to Hawaii. No joke! As Stanford University engineering professor Jim Adams once noted, "Good companies reward success, punish failure, and ignore inaction. Great companies reward success and failure and punish inaction." Robert I. Sutton in the *Stanford Social Innovation Review*, spring 2003, wrote about what may seem to some to be "weird management ideas." The list of ideas included rewarding failure and he said, "When it comes to nonprofit innovation, these ideas can be essential."

As a leader and I'm especially talking to senior pastors, executive pastors, CEO's, COO's, and CFO's, you've got to intentionally work at creating a culture, one that is so hungry for innovation that failure is an option. Most companies and churches I know actually punish or fire the employee who fails—this is crazy to me. Now, being incompetent and not doing your job is one thing, but if an employee of mine is taking a risk and fails in an attempt at innovation, I'm going to pick them up, brush them off, and encourage them to keep progressing forward.

Remember Larry Osborne's quote: "Wisdom and innovation are often the end result of paying dumb taxes." Craig Groeschel spent a great deal of time and shared a huge amount of wisdom and experience about this whole failing and failing forward concept in chapter 8 of his great book, *It*. I'd encourage you to get it and read if you haven't already. As Craig stated, Peter was a great biblical example of failing and God using it. Peter failed a number of times, but he didn't let it stop him and was used by God in a mighty way.

In Robert Sutton's article I referenced earlier, he went on to say, "Unfortunately, every bit of solid theory and evidence demonstrates that it is impossible to generate a few good ideas without generating a lot of bad ones. If you want to eliminate mistakes, avoid dead ends, and succeed most of the time; you will drive out innovation. If a nonprofit wants to encourage people to keep generating new ideas, to test them in unbiased ways, and to avoid reverting to proven ideas and well-honed skills, rewarding success isn't enough; it has to reward failure as well, especially dead ends that teach new lessons and that enable people to have some fun along the way."

Later, Sutton said, "I am not saying that your nonprofit should reward people who are stupid, lazy, or incompetent. You should reward smart failures, not dumb failures. And if you want a creative organization, inaction is the worst kind of failure." I agree. The opposite of progression is inaction, and this is the worst kind of failure. You must press forward and take small steps when God leads and giant leaps when God leads. However He leads; it's our duty to obey and follow.

Rome wasn't built in a day. Houses are built brick by brick and wood stud by wood stud. You get the picture. The key is to take small, intentional steps toward the innovative change you want to see happen. Progression can lead to innovation.

"In preparing for battle I have always found that plans are useless, but planning is indispensable."
—Dwight D. Eisenhower

"The people who are doing the work are the moving force behind the Macintosh. My job is to create a space for them, to clear out the rest of the organization, and keep it at bay."
—Steve Jobs

"I came to the conclusion long ago that limits to innovation have less to do with technology or creativity than organizational agility. Inspired individuals can only do so much."
—Ray Stata

"Sometimes churches get so caught up in building the ministries, the property and even the advertising that we fail to think about the infrastructure that ensures customer satisfaction."
—Scott Vaughn

Organization

Your systems are perfectly designed to give you the results you're getting

My top two spiritual gifts are leadership and administration, so the subject of organization is something I love and gravitate toward. If you have the spiritual gift of administration, you love structure, systems, processes, and org charts. If you don't, those things probably drive you crazy. Regardless of your primary gifting, it helps to approach leadership with a thirty-thousand-foot view and try to see the big picture of what's going on in your organization. The way the body of Christ works is if this is difficult for you, surround yourself with other leaders who this is natural for.

In my travels, speaking, consulting, and conversations with leaders of all types, I've discovered a major reason they are not getting the results they desire is due to a system designed to give them the exact result they're getting. If your system is designed to fail, you will fail every time. If your organization's culture is one of creativity, innovation, trust, and you have a healthy system in place, there is no limit to what you as a team can accomplish (through the Holy Spirit). Do you think the Bible cares about organization? I do.

The next day, Moses took his place to judge the people. People were standing before him all day long, from morning to night. When Moses's father-in-law saw all that he was doing for the people, he said, "What's going on here? Why are you doing all this, and all by yourself, letting everybody line up before you from morning to night?" Moses said to his father-in-law, "Because the people come to me with questions about God. When something comes up, they come to me. I judge between a man and his neighbor and teach them God's laws and instructions." Moses's father-in-law said, "This is no way to go about it. You'll burn out, and the people right along with you. This is way too much for you—you can't do this alone. Now listen to me. Let me tell you how to do this so that God will be in this with you. Be there for the people before God, but let the matters of concern be presented to God. Your job is to teach them the rules and instructions, to show them how to live, what to do. And then you need to keep a sharp eye out for competent men—men who fear God, men of integrity, men who are incorruptible—and appoint them as leaders over groups organized by the thousand, by the hundred, by fifty, and by ten. They'll be responsible for the everyday work of judging among the people. They'll bring the hard cases to you, but in the routine cases, they'll be the judges. They will share your load and that will make it easier for you. If you handle the work this way, you'll have the strength to carry out whatever God commands you, and the people in their settings will flourish also." Moses listened to the counsel of his father-in-law and did everything he said. Moses picked competent men from all Israel and set them as leaders over the people who were organized by the thousand, by the hundred, by fifty, and by ten. They took over the everyday work of judging among the people. They brought the hard cases to Moses, but in the routine cases, they were the judges.
—Exodus 18:13–26 (MSG)

I thank God for including the story of Moses and his father-in-law, Jethro. In this story, we see Moses was a man with flaws and had made a poor decision on how to best go about judging the people. Maybe he didn't have the gift of leadership or administration. He did, however, have the wisdom to listen to someone who did, and the Bible tells us this gave Moses new strength to carry out whatever God commanded him. The people also flourished in their settings. It was a win-win.

The book *The Externally Focused Quest* by Eric Swanson and Rick Rusaw has some great thoughts on this as well. I could easily quote chapters of it for you, but I'll just encourage you to read it.

> *No good tree bears bad fruit, nor does a bad tree bear good fruit.*
> *—Luke 6:43 (NIV)*

It's crucial to recognize your system could be choking the life, health, creativity and innovation out of your organization. My encouragement to you is to have someone with the gift of administration evaluate your systems. This could be someone in your church (maybe a business leader who will volunteer), a gifted staff member, or an outside consultant who can come in and look at the big picture.

Can I get a milkshake?

Steven S. Little tells the story of how he came up with the name for his book. Steven, a frequent traveler and businessman had one joy at the end of long days: he longed to get back to his hotel room and order a vanilla milkshake from room service. Here's the story of his "milkshake moment."

> *When I finally got to my room an hour later, the first thing I did was call room service where I was greeted by Stuart. "Good evening, Mr. Little, this is Stuart in room service. How may I*

help you?" Stuart's voice brimmed with enthusiasm.
"Stuart, I'd like a vanilla milkshake, please," I said. A seemingly simple request, right? Well, not quite.
"I'm sorry, Mr. Little, but we don't have milkshakes," Stuart replied regretfully. I was crushed. Quickly, I regrouped.
"All right, Stuart, let me ask you this: Do you have any vanilla ice cream?"
"Yes, of course!" he responded with renewed enthusiasm.
"Okay, Stuart, I'd like a full bowl of vanilla ice cream."
"Yes, sir, right away, sir! Is there anything else I can do to serve you?" Stuart asked.
"Yeah . . . do you have any milk?"
"Yes, we have milk!" he replied confidently.
"All right, Stuart, here's what I would like you to do. Please send up a tray with a full bowl of vanilla ice cream, half a glass of milk, and a long spoon. Could you do that for me, please?"
"Certainly, right away, sir," Stuart responded triumphantly.
I hung up the phone and a few minutes later, there was a knock. Sure enough, at my door there was a tray with a full bowl of vanilla ice cream, half a glass of milk, and a long spoon—everything needed to make a vanilla milkshake. But of course, they didn't have vanilla milkshakes.
Now let me ask you an important question. Is Stuart stupid? Or is the system stupid?
—The Milkshake Moment pp. 6–7

I wonder, are there people in our churches and organizations who are dying for a milkshake, but everywhere they turn in our system they get told we don't offer milkshakes? Are there people with serving and hospitality and leadership gifts who are willing to sacrifice their time and make a difference in your organization, but can't seem to get through the assimilation process? Do you offer a 301 or Discovery-type class where people can find their SHAPE, their spiritual gifts, and get matched up with appropriate areas of service or do people in your church feel unneeded?

I remember once hearing Bill Hybels share how much it upset him because his dad was so gifted, such a strong leader and had so much to offer, and the pastor of the little church he attended never once tried to engage him and ask him to serve, lead, or help. One Scripture I've found myself quoting to church leaders often is when Jesus told his disciples to be "wise as serpents." (Matt 10:16) In *The Message*, verse 16 reads "be as cunning as a snake." I am often referring to this verse when I'm engaged in helping an organization with strategic planning and overall strategy.

I don't think there's anything wrong with strategy when it comes to church leadership. Of course, we need to always be sensitive and open to the Spirit's leading and sudden change, but God can be with us in the strategy and planning of any organization. So, as you set up your systems, structure, and processes I would suggest two thoughts: keep it simple and keep it fluid or flexible.

Neil Cole, director of Church Multiplication Associates said, "Simplicity is the key to the fulfillment of the Great Commission in this generation. If the process is complex, it will break down early in the transference to the next generation of disciples. The more complex the process, the greater the giftedness needed to keep it going. The simpler the process, the more available it is to the broader Christian population." (*Cultivating a Life for God* p.10) Albert Einstein said, "Out of complexity, find simplicity." I agree. You might have seventy-five staff members on your team, but this doesn't mean you can't approach your structure and processes in such a way in which they are simple to share, quote, and move people through. Did you know research strongly backs this principle?

The book *Simple Church* is full of thoroughly researched and proven principles. I want to strongly encourage you to read it if you haven't already. In *Simple Church*, the authors, Thom Rainer and Eric Geiger, tell us that "in general, simple churches are growing and vibrant. Churches with a simple process for reaching and maturing people are expanding the kingdom. Conversely, complex churches are struggling and anemic. Churches without a process or with a complicated process for making disciples are floundering. As a whole, cluttered and complex churches are not alive. Our research shows that these churches are not growing." (*Simple Church* p. 14)

Are you crystal clear?

I've seen this with my own eyes. One past spring and summer, I got to spend a lot of time at Church of the Highlands in Birmingham, AL, through my work with Association of Related Churches (ARC). Church of the Highlands was voted the fastest growing church in America in 2008. One doesn't have to hang around there too long to find out why. Their process is simple, easy to find, and accessible. They have a four-week process to move their people into discipleship and service. It happens every month without fail. The first Sunday night they have their 101 class where they hear from Pastor Chris Hodges the vision and mission of the church as well as his heart. The second Sunday night, they have an essentials class where they talk about doctrine and what they believe. The third Sunday night, they have a discovery class where they take spiritual gifts assessment and learn what their gifts are and where they would most find fulfillment in getting involved. The fourth Sunday night, they choose a ministry to be a part of and receive training to allow them to jump in and begin serving. This "Dream Team" approach is genius in its simplicity. It's obvious (every Sunday night there's a class), and it's nonstop. Chris Hodges has taught the 101 class every single first Sunday night of the church's fifteen years—whether it was Super Bowl Sunday or not. If you want to get involved at Church of the Highlands, they leave no doubt on what your next step is. This holds up to *Simple Church's* research that shows "simple churches are growing and vibrant."

I just took a break from writing for a second to check Twitter.

I've been receiving lots of great insight and suggestions from my friends on Twitter. This work truly is a collaboration. A few minutes ago, @SimpleChurch posted, "If you want people to understand why you are so passionate about your ministry process, you must be able to communicate it with ease." Good timing. I wholeheartedly agree. As we talked about a personal mission statement in the "Mission" chapter, our church's ministry process must be equally as simple and repeatable.

Most discipleship programs are very linear. Unfortunately, almost all of our spiritual growth is not. You must design a process and ministry that fits your people and your culture. When designing your systems and processes it's also important they be fluid and flexible. Hear me. I want you to have a definite and defined structure and process, but be flexible. Craig Groeschel, who leads a very large church, encourages his staff to be speed boats who can turn on a dime. Unfortunately, most churches (even medium size churches) move and react like oil tankers. Did you know if an oil tanker decides it wants to make a U-turn, it takes a mile and a half to do so? You can see why Groeschel would want his team to move like speed boats.

A few years ago, I was at a conference and got to spend some time with Rick Warren, including taking him to the airport. He mentioned Glen, his executive pastor of twenty-five years, was retiring, and he was now looking for a new executive pastor. Since I'm wired like an executive pastor, I thought I'd pick his brain. I asked him what he was looking for in his next executive pastor. Warren's reply was, "Nimble. He's got to be nimble." He went on to say, "Processes and systems are great and needed, but with an organization our size, we really need someone that is nimble and flexible—ready to change in an instant." I took those words to heart and let them sink in.

If Rick Warren and Craig Groeschel—two leaders of two of the largest and most innovative churches in America are looking for nimbleness and movement like speed boats, I think this is some pretty good insight. Scott Wilson said, "Vision is rock solid. Strategy is flexible." I agree. Like everything I've shared though, this won't happen by accident. You have to intentionally and strategically set yourself up to function like this.

This goes back to the chapter on Decision. If you are going to see innovation happen as a result of your organization, you'll have to make the decision to change we talked about in the second chapter. A decision to change and to be innovative means a decision for health and thus growth. If you are ready to make the necessary changes to make your organization healthy and function efficiently, then you must strive for a big-picture point of view and surround yourself with people who get it. I know growing churches who change their organizational chart yearly.

You must constantly be evaluating and reevaluating why and what you do and who does what. When one studies a growing and innovative church, one finds many staff members have changed positions over the years. They might have started out in one role, but have either grown or morphed into another role, been reassigned, or had a role or area of ministry hat outgrew their capacity for leadership and were thus changed to have less responsibility. Suffice to say, your team now should not look the same three to five years from now.

There was a time when Moses judging all the people might have worked, but he quickly outgrew it. I think one possible reason most churches in the US are under two hundred people and most of those are under one hundred people, is you have a pastor still trying to do everything (like Moses was), and he can only handle so many people. For a church to break a crucial growth barrier of two hundred to three hundred people, Rick Warren tells us, "The church must decide if it really wants to grow," "The role of the pastor must change," and "The members must be mobilized for ministry."

If you're not getting the results you want, check your system. You may be getting the exact results you're set up to get. If you're not seeing people mature and become more like Christ, check your process. Is it simple and easy to know what one's next step is? If you're not growing and seem to be hitting your head up against a growth barrier, check your structure. You must staff ahead of growth and design an organizational model that is built for five hundred to one thousand more people than you currently have. Again, all this will require a great deal of intentionality, but if you are set up organizationally in a healthy way, you will open the door wide for God to move and new innovations to happen in your ministry.

"The mind ought to sometimes be diverted that it may return the better to thinking."
—Phaedrus

"Don't try to come up with the proper answers; target coming up with good questions."
—Stanford professor Bill Lazier

"Every act of creation is first of all an act of destruction."
—Pablo Picasso

"The empires of the future are the empires of the mind."
—Winston Churchill

"I'm very easily distracted unless I have music on. Listening to music while I brainstorm makes me think of scenes that would fit the mood of the music I'm playing."
—Maggie Stiefvater

"Some men preach for an hour and it seems like twenty minutes, and some preach for twenty minutes and it seems like an hour. I wonder what the difference is."
—Harry Ironside

"All new ideas come with flaws, but we should encourage people to try to understand the intent behind the idea. If we take a new idea as a beginning point and then focus on the possibilities it presents, we can better see how to adjust those elements that need improvement."
—Andrew Papageorge, in Go Innovate!

Ideation

Break out the dry erase board!

Ideation is the process of forming ideas or images. I've found when most church leaders I talk to think of innovation or being innovative, this is what they are thinking of—their brainstorming or creative planning meeting. I hesitated to even include this chapter because my true heart is innovation is about being led by the Spirit, not sitting around thinking up ideas, but I realized God can be in the planning and brainstorming meetings. So I left this chapter in. My only caution to you is to realize this is just one of many ways innovation can come about. Please don't let this be the only way you practice. You'll miss out on so much! With this being said, let's talk about ideation and how it can lead to new ways of doing things and new ideas for your organization.

> *The Master said: "These people make a big show of saying the right thing, but their hearts aren't in it. Because they act like they're worshiping me but don't mean it, I'm going to step in and shock them awake, astonish them, stand them on their ears. The wise ones who had it all figured out will be exposed as fools. The*

smart people who thought they knew everything will turn out to know nothing." Doom to you! You pretend to have the inside track. You shut God out and work behind the scenes, Plotting the future as if you knew everything . . . .
—Isaiah 29:13–15 (MSG)

As I've taught on innovation, I've said one thing over and over: "Prayer isn't just how you start the meeting—it's the meeting." I think being prepared spiritually is about positioning ourselves or assuming a posture that frees us to respond to God's activity around us. Remember the *Experiencing God* concept. Throughout this book, I will talk about the posture in which we should approach something. For the act of ideation, when you gather to plan, dream, brainstorm, and create, you should approach with a posture that will free you to respond to God's activity around you and follow where He's leading.

Honestly, I love to plan. I love to attend brainstorming and creative planning meetings. I don't just do this at my church; I attend other church's creative meetings. When I lived in Dallas, I attended several other churches' planning meetings and had an open invitation to attend the worship planning meeting at Fellowship Church in Grapevine (Ed Young Jr.'s church) every Wednesday thanks to my friend, Pace Hartfield, who was their creative director. I love the dynamics of creative planning as a team and tossing ideas around—it's truly a fun and beautiful process. As I have had the opportunity to attend other churches' meetings, I've learned churches do these types of meetings differently. Yes, they have their similarities, but no two are the same.

A couple of years ago, I spoke at the National Church Music Conference in Indianapolis, and one of the classes I taught on was the creative planning process. I love to share ways I've experienced it and hear about other ways other leaders pull the best ideas from their team. Again, as long as you bring God, via the Holy Spirit, into the creative/brainstorming process, then I'm all for it—this is what separates us from the business world. We don't rely purely on our flesh. I believe God has gifted us with our imagination (which we'll talk about later) and can guide our time together by His Holy Spirit.

Get into the flow

You must partner with the Holy Spirit and invite Him into your meetings. Not only this, you must be intentional about how you lead such meetings. Some ways you can be intentional in the ideation process are by encouraging the dreamers, unleashing the power of synergy, creating atmospheres that foster ideas and innovation, and choosing a leader who manages the time and process well.

Encouraging the dreamers means there's no such thing as a dumb idea. My boss at Bent Tree was Scott Dyer, who used to serve for many years on the staff at Willow Creek Community Church. One of the ideas he brought from his experience there (this is why it's good to know of other churches' ways of doing this) was this concept of freedom to explore, create, dream, and stretch the limits of our God-given creativity and imagination. To intentionally create this freedom in our meetings, he would give us each balls (like Nerf balls or tennis balls) to hold in our hands. If someone ever shared an idea and someone else spoke up and said, "No" or "You're crazy!" or "We could never afford this"—if they shot the idea down in any form or fashion—we could zing them with the ball. Because we believed each team member (our meetings were a combination of paid staff and volunteers) had value and creativity, they were allowed to throw any idea out. (If you didn't allow it—you got pegged with a ball).

The next way you intentionally lead well through this process is to build off one another. This is collaboration (which we'll dive into thoroughly in the next chapter). As far as this brainstorming process goes, some of the best ideas I've ever seen come about came by one person saying something, another person adding to it, another person adapting it, another person saying, "And what if we did that plus this . . . ." and the end result was better than any of us could have dreamed on our own—this is synergy.

Andy Stanley, on page 9 of the preface of his book *7 Practices of Effective Ministry*, was sharing about their meeting they have with their staff leadership team at North Point Community Church every Monday morning. He talked about the dynamics of the meeting and how there can be tension, but said, "But we continue to meet. We continue to harness our differences for the sake of synergy. Consequently, we continue to learn and grow together." Have you ever really delved into the reality and power of synergy? The Oxford English Dictionary defines synergy as an "interaction or cooperation of two or more agents to produce a combined effect greater than the sum of their separate effects." Look up synergy in a thesaurus and you will see synonyms such as: alliance, collaboration, communion, concert, cooperation, harmony, help, helpfulness, participation, partnership, service, teaming, teamwork, and unity—all Biblical words we hold high. When a team taps into the reality of synergy and employs their gifts, the results are impressive and pleasing. Creativity grows exponentially on such a team.

We see this echoed in Scripture as Nehemiah rebuilt the wall of Jerusalem. In Neh 2:17–18, Nehemiah said, "Come, let us rebuild the wall of Jerusalem, and we will no longer be in disgrace . . . ." They replied, "Let us start rebuilding." Can you imagine him trying to build it all by himself? I know Nehemiah is often looked to as an example of leadership. Yes, he was "God's man". Yes, he had "a vision" and "a calling," but the reason he is so respected as a leader and has become a model we study and teach about is because he rallied the people and empowered them to do together what none of them could do alone.

While we're looking at biblical examples, one should consider the various other teams mentioned in Scripture, such as the disciples, elders, deacons, Pharisees—just kidding. Even creation was done through a Triune God, Who said, "Let us make man in our image, after our likeness." Synergy is potent, and you as a leader should be intentional about unleashing it in your team.

Setting the mood

The other piece you must be proactive in is creating atmospheres that foster ideas and innovation. Have you ever set in a plain, old, boring room and been asked to come up with an idea? It's brutal. Wise leaders try to make their team feel comfortable, creative, and like a party atmosphere. I love the way the worship office area at Irving Bible Church is set up with couches, a hammock, and cool stuff hanging from the ceiling—it's a creative space and thus encourages creativity.

Ed Young at Fellowship Church has basketball goals at either end of his conference room. As they meet and discuss ideas, they shoot hoops and let the ideas and inspiration flow. They know when to sit down and work, but if they get stuck or stumped, the basketballs come back out, and they play it out. I love this! Carlos Whittaker used to take his creative team at Buckhead Church in Atlanta down to the subway to be inspired by the urban vibe all around them. They would look at the people, the art, and graffiti around them, as well as the subway cars themselves.

My friend, Stephen Brewster, at Cross Point Church in Nashville, decorates the room his team is going to meet in based on the theme or series. He once decked their room out in winter and Christmas décor for a Christmas planning meeting in June. In the Revelation chapter, I mentioned I moved outdoors to write so I would be inspired and surrounded by nature. I was intentional in creating the atmosphere in which I was going to work.

Maybe you won't have basketball goals around your conference room table or hammocks hanging from the ceiling, but you can make an effort to decorate the room a little and put out fun things (like balls to throw at people) and candy and snacks for people to munch on. We also had candy and snacks in our meetings. Either store-bought or homemade, we brought the goodies. It probably doesn't hurt to add caffeine into the mix either. Some people on our team brought Coke, Pepsi and especially Mountain Dew; some brought coffee or Starbucks, but all had some shot of caffeine flowing through them.

When possible, try to do your planning offsite and in special locations. I've met in homes, on the beach, in cabins, and in a cool creative loft at the top of an advertising office that a volunteer in our church worked for (to name a few). This cool creative loft had a hammock and beanbags (you can't go wrong with a beanbag chair), and it was fully stocked with coffee and homemade goodies. One other important factor: always have a dry erase board handy. A good creative team will wear out a dry erase board. My friend, Terry Storch (digerati pastor at LifeChurch.tv) has dry erase paint on the walls of his office and writes all over every wall in his working space. I love it and hope to do the same in my new conference room. I think you get the picture. Make an effort to create an environment that breeds and welcomes creativity and innovation.

The last piece of the puzzle is to pick a leader to manage the process and time together. Now this doesn't have to be "the boss," it doesn't have to be the senior pastor or CEO, and it doesn't have to be the same person every time. You may rotate people in this role, or you may have one person who just stands out on your team and is gifted in guiding and leading this brainstorming process. Whoever it is, pick this person and let them write things down on the dry erase board as they come up. Let he or she direct the flow of the meeting, and give them the freedom to say things like, "Let's move on" or "Let's camp out here a bit and see what else comes to mind," etc. Empower and trust the leader to shape the outcome of the meeting, by directing traffic and making tough calls when needed.

I should go back and finish my story.

There was a time when we put our balls away and started to zoom in on what we were going to do and which ideas we were going to run with. You can't dream forever. Ideation without execution is a waste of time. If you're running the meeting, you need to keep an eye on the clock and realize when it's time to start homing in on what you actually hope to accomplish—especially if this is a weekly planning meeting for your weekend experience that is bearing down on you in a few days.

One of my former interns and guys I mentor has heard from me countless times he should read the book *Boundaries* by Henry Cloud and John Townsend. As a young, twenty-something leader, this book shaped, stretched, and challenged me, and as a result made me a more efficient and healthy leader. I reread the book in my late thirties to relearn its principles again. I understand it's okay to say no and set boundaries for myself. Whoever is leading your ideation process must know when to say no, too.

Your video editor may throw out a superb idea for a video or your drama director may—well drama directors are going to throw out ideas for anything to get them on the stage. Laugh, friends! Anyway, a gifted team member will throw out a good idea, but you need to assess the schedule for the week, the amount of other irons in the fire, and know if it's possible to pull it off or not. Here's a chart my friend Shawn Wood used (when he was the experiences pastor at Seacoast Church) He shared this with me years ago. This is what they use in their creative process at Seacoast.

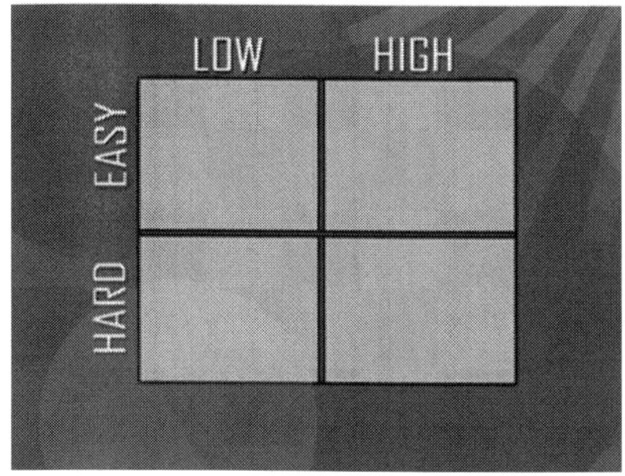

Some ideas are easy to do and have a high payoff—those are gold. Jump on them! Some ideas are hard to do but have a high payoff, and you need to make the call on whether or not your team is capable of healthily handling them this particular week or season in your organization's life. What you want to avoid is something that is hard to do and has a low payoff—there's a mistake and a waste of time. Run your ideas through this grid and make the right decision. Sometimes, you as a leader need to look a staff member in the eye (for the sake of their health and family) and say, "No. I appreciate you offering to do this, but I'm going to pass."

I know video editors who will receive a video project from their boss or senior pastor on Friday and spend their entire weekend up at the office working on it 'til the early morning hours and totally miss their family time. God help us. As a leader, you have got to see the bigger picture and value the health and relationship this staff member or volunteer team member has with their spouse and kids and not put them in a position where they have to choose between pleasing you or their family. You might get away with it a few times, but eventually the team member and their spouse will agree this is an unhealthy work environment and quit, burnout, or start submitting resumes other places.

The hard truth is the creative arts (music, drama, dance, staging/props, video and lighting) take a lot of time and work. These leaders and servants are gifted artists and take pride in what they do. Projects or events requiring the creative arts must be talked about way in advance and given plenty of prep time. This, senior pastor, means you know what you're speaking on before Saturday night.

Nancy Beach says, "There is a wall in some churches . . . this wall divides the artists preparing one part of the service from the teacher who will deliver the message. What contributes most to this wall is the overwhelmingly rapid pace of ministry combined with a lack of vision for what services could be if the wall were torn down." (*An Hour on Sunday* p. 241)

This wall exists for many reasons; from lack of vision, to lack of communication and planning, to pride on the pastor's part, to seminary training, to false assumptions. Whatever it takes, break down this wall, unleash synergy and start working as a team—a healthy team.

For more detailed and practical information on starting and leading a creative planning team and helping out your creative team, Google my articles "*No More Lone Ranger Worship Planning*" and "*Up All Night to Get Lucky.*" I hope they will be of help to you as you lead through this process of ideation. When led right and with the partnership of the Holy Spirit, wonderful things can occur, including new, strange ideas and innovation.

"I think the secret of directing is collaborating."
—Kathryn Bigelow, 2010 Academy Award winner for Best Director

"Great discoveries and improvements invariably involve the cooperation of many minds. I may be given credit for having blazed the trail, but when I look at the subsequent developments I feel the credit is due to others rather than myself."
—Alexander Graham Bell

"Coming together is a beginning. Keeping together is progress. Working together is success."
—Henry Ford

"I think it is in collaboration that the nature of art is revealed."
—Steve Lacy

"Collaboration is one of the best kept secrets of creativity."
—John Briggs

"Organizations are living systems, not machines, because they are made up of people. As innovators in a living system, we must learn to think more like gardeners than mechanics. When we view the organization as a living system, our perspective becomes one of how to provide the right environment or context for the organization to fulfill its purpose."
—Andrew Papageorge, in Go Innovate

"People who work together will win, whether it be against complex football defenses, or the problems of modern society."
—Vince Lombardi

Collaboration

None of us is as smart as all of us

In the last chapter, we talked about the power of synergy and planning as a team. Simply put, innovation is not a solo sport. The vast majority of the time, you don't come down from the mountain with the new plan or idea, but you arrive at an idea or new direction of ministry as a team. Ken Blanchard said it best when he said, "None of us is as smart as all of us." If you skipped the last chapter, go back and read what I said about synergy and leading a team. It's what I have to say about collaboration, teamwork, and synergy. Let's take a look at what the Bible has to say about the subject.

In Gen 6, Noah and his three sons built an ark to save their family. In Exodus 4, God teamed up Moses and his brother, Aaron, for a powerful collaboration in ministry. In Exo 17, Aaron and Hur worked together to hold up Moses' hands. In Acts 2, we see the Church selling their possessions and goods and giving to anyone as he had need. Also in Acts, we see collaboration, cooperation and teamwork from Paul and

Barnabas.

The Bible is full of people working together for a common purpose, goal, and mission. My absolute favorite example of collaboration though, has got to be Nehemiah. Talk about a leader rallying people to accomplish something. Wow! Scripture and God go out of their way to point out just how many worked on the wall. If you will, please indulge me by reading the entire passage from Neh 3. It really drives the point home. Notice how many times the word says "next to them" or "next to him." Over and over again. Tons of times.

Now, if you made it through this reading (and thank you if you really did read the entire passage) you realize how many times the phrase "next to him" or "next to them" was used. Nehemiah showed the true essence of leadership in influencing others and getting them to buy into his vision. There's no way he could have rebuilt the wall by himself—it was simply too much for one person. But when you count up the number of names this chapter lists, you start to understand the power of collaboration.

It's all about team

In preparation for this chapter, I read two great books—one from the church world and one from the business world. The books were *Doing Church as a Team: The Miracle of Teamwork and How It Transforms Churches* by Wayne Cordeiro and *Organizing Genius: The Secrets of Creative Collaboration* by Warren Bennis and Patricia Ward Biederman. I could include quote after quote from these two amazing books, but the best and proper thing for me to do is to encourage you to read them yourself if you really want to dive deeper into the subject and power of collaboration.

As I've traveled the world speaking, I've found myself

over and over opening my conferences or workshops with the following verse:

> *Each of you should use whatever gift you have received to serve others, as faithful stewards of God's grace in its various forms.*
> *—1 Peter 4:10*

When you operate as a team and encourage team leadership, you allow people to use their unique, God-given gifts. Pastor and author Wayne Cordeiro shares his philosophy and insight of the church needing to be a battleship, not a cruise ship. You see on a battleship, everyone knows exactly what his or her role is. From his experience on board the Reuben James, each person of the eight-hundred-member crew had a job, a function, a responsibility, and a purpose for being there. In contrast, some months later, Wayne and his wife went on a three-day cruise.

Wayne commented he noticed hundreds of lazy, sun-ripened human beings, lounging around the pool with just forty uniformed workers running around trying to keep them happy. In a moment of reflection, he heard the Lord say to him, "My church must be a battleship, not a cruise liner. If you are to pierce the darkness and rescue souls lost on the scratch, you cannot be a ship of spectators. Everyone must know why they are on board." He goes on to say, "When you do church as a team, the pastor does not do all the work while trying his best to get as many as possible to help him. It's everyone doing the work of the ministry, while the pastor is there to equip them." (*Doing Church as a Team* pp. 44–45)

So, it's important to remember collaboration as a staff and leadership team. It's also important to remember collaboration as a congregation or organization. Another type of collaboration

I love to see happening around the world is churches partnering with other churches. There are several examples of this, but ones I've gotten to witness up close are examples like Shaun King, when he was pastor of Courageous Church in Atlanta, partnering with people around the world to raise money for an inner-city Atlanta school, raise money for flood victims of Atlanta and raise support and buy tents for the people of Haiti after the earthquake.

When I spoke to church leaders in Atlanta a couple of years ago, I learned of Chip Sweeney at Perimeter in Atlanta and the organization called Unite!—a group of churches from Atlanta collaborating to end the city's human trafficking pandemic. I was blown away to hear of how these churches collaborate and support one another. I also got to see Healing Place Church and others with PRC Compassion (a group of churches in the South—part of ARC) who came together for disaster relief.

Like Wayne Cordeiro, I believe God designed us to work best in teams, not in solo acts. In the Bible, He uses phrases such as "We are Christ's Body and individually members of it" to remind us of our design (1 Cor 12:27). This flies in the face of many prevalent top-down leadership styles that are so widely accepted throughout the business (and church) world. As I've mentioned before, most churches in the US are under two hundred people. I think this issue and this lack of an intentional, strategic, and biblical choice to be collaborative could be contributing factors to this statistic.

My encouragement to you and strange leaders everywhere is to include others in your planning, decision-making, and strategy for the future of your organization. It might seem like you're sending a signal that communicates you're weak or "not in control," but as strange or new as this may be to you and your team, you'll be fruitful, more productive, more innovative, and more ready to deal with the constant issues that come up in shepherding and leadership.

"Motivation will almost always beat mere talent."
—Norman R. Augustine

"If he have faith, the believer cannot be restrained. He betrays himself. He breaks out. He confesses and teaches this gospel to the people at the risk of life itself."
—Martin Luther

"When I lose the sense of motivation and the sense to prove something as a basketball player, it's time for me to move away from the game."
—Michael Jordan

"People often say that motivation doesn't last. Well, neither does bathing—that's why we recommend it daily."
—Zig Ziglar

"Desire is the key to motivation, but it's determination and commitment to an unrelenting pursuit of your goal–a commitment to excellence–that will enable you to attain the success you seek."
—Mario Andretti

Motivation

Why did you buy this book?

Here we are, a little over a third of the way through these forty ways innovation can happen. I thought we should take a moment and get real and honest. What motivates you to be innovative? Why are you reading this? Maybe not all of you picked this book up with pure motives. Maybe you secretly hope to make it onto the "Most Innovative Church" list or you want to be a model other churches and organizations point to. It's not necessarily wrong to want to lead well and be a solid model for others to learn from. My hope is for us to approach innovation through a biblical lens (as I stated in the introduction), and we let Christ, His mission, and His calling on our lives drive us and fuel us.

Motivation is a powerful tool in the tool belt of an innovative leader. If you successfully motivate employees and volunteers, you can accomplish mighty things through an army of people sold out to your cause. The difference between leaders and team members who are motivated and those who aren't is night and day. As I wrote earlier, Wikipedia defines innovation as the process of introducing something new and for the sake of positive change. I mean seriously, if there is any group in the world who should be motivated to make improvements reflecting God's creative nature, it should be the Church, right?

In chapter seven of *It* (pp. 91–92), Groeschel talks about motivation. He gives an example of if he came up to you and asked, "Could you come up with a hundred thousand dollars in cash by the end of this week?" He goes on to say most of us would not be able to do this and would think, there's no way I could come up with that kind of cash. I can barely pay my bills. I think this is true for most of us, right?

He goes on to describe another imaginary exercise. He asks you to pick someone very dear to you—maybe your spouse, your parents, your kids, or a trusted friend. Suppose Craig told you "your special loved one is very sick. I'm referring to the you've-got-less-than-a-month-to-live sick." He goes on to say, "The doctors are certain that your loved one has no chance of living beyond the month unless you get them a very rare shot by the end of this week. And because of the scarcity of this shot, it is very expensive . . . .' How much is the shot?' you ask, determined to find the money. Soberly, I reply, 'The shot is one hundred thousand dollars.' What would you do? The short answer is you would do anything—whatever it takes to come up with the money (the money that a second ago you thought would be impossible to come up with)." As Craig writes, "You just became motivated. What changed? In the first scenario I gave you, no incentive. But the life-and-death stakes in the second scenario made you unstoppable. The spark of passion ignited the fuel for innovation." Get it?

We may not have a dying child who needs medicine, but we do have a dying world in need of a Savior. Craig Groeschel says, "At our church, we encourage people to do anything short of sin to reach those who don't know Christ." Again, I agree. In order to be properly motivated, we must understand the way God views those He died for and how much He wants to see them reconciled to Him. As we all know, He is not willing for any to perish (2 Pet 3:9). Hear me leader: this is crucial. If innovation is about listening, following, and joining God where He's at work, we've got to understand who He cares about and what He's up to in the world around us. Luke 15 gives some insight to Christ's heart for the lost. I've preached on Luke 15 here in the United States and in Haiti. It's a passage very dear to my heart. Let's take a brief look at His view on those far from God.

The Lost Parables

Personally, I love the beginning of this passage in Scripture, the Bible tells us Jesus had "a lot of men and women of doubtful reputation" hanging around Him, "listening intently." This is fascinating to me and we'll touch on it later. Continuing on.

Luke 15 starts out with The Story of the Lost Sheep. A man had one hundred sheep; one went missing. He left the ninety- nine to go look for it, and when he found the lost sheep, he put it on his shoulder and rejoiced. He celebrated.

Then you have The Story of the Lost Coin. A woman has ten coins. One goes missing. She tears her house apart looking for it. When she finds the missing coins she rejoices.

She celebrated.

Then you have The Story of the Lost Son. Listen to it in *The Message*:

> *Then he said, "There was once a man who had two sons. The younger said to his father, 'Father, I want right now what's coming to me.'*
>
> *"So the father divided the property between them. It wasn't long before the younger son packed his bags and left for a distant country. There, undisciplined and dissipated, he wasted everything he had. 'I'm going back to my father. I'll say to him, Father, I've sinned against God, I've sinned before you; I don't deserve to be called your son. Take me on as a hired hand.' He got right up and went home to his father.*
>
> *"When he was still a long way off, his father saw him. His heart pounding, he ran out, embraced him, and kissed him . . . 'I don't deserve to be called your son ever again.' "But the father wasn't listening. He was calling to the servants, 'Quick. Bring a clean set of clothes and dress him. Put the family ring on his finger and sandals on his feet. Then get a grain-fed heifer and roast it. We're going to feast! We're going to have a wonderful time! My son is here—given up for dead and now alive! Given up for lost and now found!' And they began to have a wonderful time.*
>
> *—Luke 15:11–24 (MSG)*

Did you notice the rejoicing, partying, and pleasure God takes in seeing the lost become found? This has got to be our heart, our goal, our desire, and what motivates us to make the necessary changes needed in our organizations. The gospel truly is good news, and when we operate and lead out of this hope and joy, we are open to doing anything (and I mean anything) God calls us to do. This proper motivation can steer you down a path to new and strange innovations in ministry.

"People of mediocre ability sometimes achieve outstanding success because they don't know when to quit. Most men succeed because they are determined to."
—George Allen

"To turn really interesting ideas and fledgling technologies into a company that can continue to innovate for years, it requires a lot of disciplines."
—Steve Jobs

"It is better to have one person working with you than three people working for you."
—Dwight D. Eisenhower

"There are only two options regarding commitment. You're either in or out. There's no such thing as a life in between."
—Pat Riley

"Dedication involves making the space to let young ideas take hold; every tree was once a seed and every company was once an idea."
—Zephyr Bloch-Jorgensen

"The person who makes a success of living is the one who sees his goal steadily and aims for it unswervingly. That is dedication."
—Cecil B. De Mille

"What this power is, I cannot say. All I know is that it exists . . . and it becomes available only when you are in that state of mind in which you know exactly what you want . . . and are fully determined not to quit until you get it."
—Alexander Graham Bell

Dedication

Blood, sweat and tears

In the last chapter, we talked about our motivation as leaders. In this chapter, we'll look at the crucial concept of dedication. Leading an innovative organization requires you are dedicated, committed, and sold out—this goes for your team as well. It's both—you must be dedicated, and you must surround yourself with people full of dedication to the vision of the organization. Your organization itself must also take on a spirit of dedication and commitment to be around for its community and purpose in the world for as long as God calls it to be.

As a leader, you must die to self—this means you care more about what God thinks than any hardships that may come your way as a result of your decisions and following where He leads. You must lead with a determination, drive, and commitment that will hold up under pressure. James said, "Consider it pure joy, my brothers, whenever you face trials of many kinds, because you know that the testing of your faith develops perseverance. Perseverance must finish its work so that you may be mature and complete, not lacking anything." (James 1:2–4 NIV) Throughout this book, I talk about the mindset the innovative leader must have. This is an example of this type of mindset—one who considers it joy when you face trials. The apostle Paul also was a great example of a dedicated man.

> *I eagerly expect and hope that I will in no way be ashamed but will have sufficient courage so that now as always Christ will be exalted in my body, whether by life or by death. For to me, to live is Christ and to die is gain. If I am to go on living in the body, this will mean fruitful labor for me. —Philippians 1:20–22 (NIV)*

Talk about dedication! Let's pick up at verse 27 in *The Message*:

> *Meanwhile, live in such a way that you are a credit to the message of Christ. Let nothing in your conduct hang on whether I come or not. Your conduct must be the same whether I show up to see things for myself or hear of it from a distance. Stand united, singular in vision, contending for people's trust in the Message, the good news, not flinching or dodging in the slightest before the opposition. Your courage and unity will show them what they're up against: defeat for them, victory for you—and both because of God. There's far more to this life than trusting in Christ. There's also suffering for him. And the suffering is as much a gift as the trusting.*
> *—Philippians 1:27–30 (MSG)*

You must plant roots

Now if you've been around for more than five years, you've tasted the sting of leadership. You've had a few battles, trials, and may have a few war wounds. Most of you reading this, statistically, haven't been in the same position for a long time. Imagine the drive, determination, and dedication it must require when you see people who have been serving in the same position for ten, twenty, or even thirty years. Rick Warren comes to mind, who recently celebrated thirty years of ministry at Saddleback Church. Bill Hybels comes to mind, who recently celebrated forty years at Willow Creek. I have many great heroes of the faith I keep an eye on. I've found those with a lasting, fruitful ministry have been at their church or organization for a long time. They made a commitment to stick to their vision and mission and have planted roots. This is something I deeply respect. In many situations, these leaders have outlasted their critics. Thomas Edison said, "Many of life's failures are people who did not realize how close they were to success when they gave up." I was watching The Idea Camp's sessions online from the Exponential Conference in Orlando, and I just heard my friend, Mark Batterson say, "We overestimate what we can do in two years, and we underestimate what we can do in ten. Don't think big. Think long . . . . Let your roots grow deep." Yes! This is my personal heart's desire. I've been laid off a few times due to a church's financial situation and unforeseen circumstances, and we've moved quite a bit, but my desire is to serve somewhere for decades.

In *Tribes* (p. 132), Seth Godin said, "Part of leadership is the ability to stick with the dream for a long time . . . long enough that the critics realize that you're going to get there one way or another . . . so they follow." In the church world, we all know not all critics will eventually follow. Some sheep leave and go with another shepherd. Such is life, and you have to be willing to accept this. Seth goes on to say, "The very nature of leadership is that you're not doing what's been done before. If you were, you'd be following, not leading . . . Leadership is scarce because few people are willing to go through the discomfort required to lead." (*Tribes* p.146, 55)

Leadership requires complete dedication and willingness to get uncomfortable—willingness to stick with it through the highs and lows of ministry. My encouragement and challenge to you is to lead with a dedication and commitment that says you will endure the hard times if this is what God asks of you. Hear my heart: If God's telling you to leave, then leave, but I think we often leave when the fire gets hot and not necessarily because it's what God desires.

Who are you locking arms with?

The second type of dedication I wanted to talk about is the dedication of those around you—your team. Let's look at this wild story in Mark 2:

> *A few days later, when Jesus again entered Capernaum, the people heard that he had come home. They gathered in such large numbers that there was no room left, not even outside the door, and he preached the word to them. Some men came, bringing to him a paralyzed man, carried by four of them. Since they could not get him to Jesus because of the crowd, they made an opening in the roof above Jesus by digging through it and then lowered the mat the man was lying on. When Jesus saw their faith, he said to the paralyzed man, "Son, your sins are forgiven."—Mark 2:1–5 (NIV)*

Talk about dedication! These four men were so committed to getting their paralytic friend to Jesus that they went to extraordinary measures—digging a hole in a roof. If I'm picking my team (volunteer or paid), I want these four guys. If I'm the crippled man, I'm grateful to God for the dedication of my four friends. Many great leaders have written about doing ministry with friends. I remember Bill Hybels in *Courageous Leadership* talking about doing life together as a team. Craig Groeschel in *It* talks about his team doing life together and having "refrigerator rights" (you'll have to read his book to find out more about this). The point is when it comes to whom you surround yourself with in leadership positions, you do get to choose. Jim Collins, in an interview with *Leadership Journal* entitled *The Good to Great Pastor* was asked, "Since discipline is so key, where do you most often see breakdowns in discipline?" His answer was, "Not being rigorous about who's put in leadership roles. In churches and other social sector organizations, the work is too important to let key seats on the bus be occupied by the wrong people." I'm sure you've heard of the concept of making sure the right people are on the bus and making sure the right people are in the right seat of the bus. If you're in a leadership role that allows you to hire or recruit (whether this be a senior pastor, executive pastor, elder, deacon, CEO, COO, whatever), you must build your team with passionate, dedicated people who are committed to your organization's cause and vision.

If I'm hiring the staff or recruiting the volunteers, I'm looking for the character of a person who reminds me of the four men who carried their crippled friend. Of course, competence, capacity, and chemistry are crucial and included in the process, but this concept of commitment and dedication is also key. I need to know they have my back and are going to stick with me in the tough times like David and his mighty men. If you're a team member, strive to be this type of team member. If you're a team leader, be intentional about whom you let occupy seats on the bus—this is part of protecting the vision.

Lastly, build and lead your organization to have the same dedication you and your team have. Jim Collins in the previously mentioned interview stated three things an organization must have to qualify as great. The third thing was endurance. "Making an impact over a long enough time, so that it's not dependent on the personality of one leader. If a church is effective during one pastorate, it may be a church with a stellar pastor, but it is not yet a great church."

You must be intentional and strategic to set up and lead your organization so it's dedicated, committed, and effective without you. You may be as dedicated as one can be (and think you can skip this chapter), but what happens if you die or leave the organization? Will it endure? Is it "built to last?" These are specific and deep questions that must be considered annually.

How does dedication play into innovation? Let's look at Thomas Edison's words again: "Many of life's failures are people who did not realize how close they were to success when they gave up." You may be days, weeks, months or years away from a significant and impactful breakthrough in ministry that will make an eternal, kingdom difference. You might be reading this, ready to walk away, and God's hoping you'll stick with it and follow Him into new waters.

My point is: skipping around is not the mark of an innovative and strange leader. Innovative and strange leaders endure the tough times, and it's through these tough times (as we'll talk about later) innovation is born.

"The highest form of worship is the worship of unselfish Christian service. The greatest form of praise is the sound of consecrated feet seeking out the lost and helpless."
—Billy Graham

"'Not called!' did you say? 'Not heard the call,' I think you should say. Put your ear down to the Bible, and hear Him bid you go and pull sinners out of the fire of sin. Put your ear down to the burdened, agonized heart of humanity, and listen to its pitiful wail for help. Go stand by the gates of hell, and hear the damned entreat you to go to their father's house and bid their brothers and sisters and servants and masters not to come there. Then look Christ in the face—whose mercy you have professed to obey—and tell Him whether you will join heart and soul and body and circumstances in the march to publish His mercy to the world.
—William Booth, founder of the Salvation Army

"I asked participants who claimed to be "strong followers of Jesus" whether Jesus spent time with the poor. Nearly 80 percent said yes. Later in the survey, I sneaked in another question, I asked this same group of strong followers whether they spent time with the poor, and less than 2 percent said they did. I learned a powerful lesson: We can admire and worship Jesus without doing what he did. We can applaud what he preached and stood for without caring about the same things. We can adore his cross without taking up ours. I had come to see that the great tragedy of the church is not that rich Christians do not care about the poor but that rich Christians do not know the poor."
— Shane Claiborne

"A true revolution of values will soon cause us to question the fairness and justice of many of our past and present policies. On the one hand, we are called to play the Good Samaritan on life's roadside, but that will be only an initial act. One day we must come to see that the whole Jericho Road must be transformed so that men and women will not be constantly beaten and robbed as they make their journey on life's highway. True compassion is more than flinging a coin to a beggar. It comes to see that an edifice that produces beggars needs restructuring."
—Dr. Martin Luther King, Jr.

"How far you go in life depends on your being tender with the young, compassionate with the aged, sympathetic with the striving, and tolerant of the weak and strong. Because some day in life you will have been all of these."
—George Washington Carver

"I would rather feel compassion than know the meaning of it."
—Thomas Aquinas

Compassion

What breaks your heart?

What is compassion, and why is it seen by some to be strange? Compassion is defined as a feeling of deep sympathy and sorrow for another who is stricken by misfortune, accompanied by a strong desire to alleviate the suffering. It is sensitivity mixed with action. Listening to the need and responding. The strange and innovative leader is one who listens. In this chapter we'll look at listening to the needs around us and around the world.

> *If someone forces you to go one mile, go with him two miles. Give to the one who asks you, and do not turn away from the one who wants to borrow from you.*
> *—Matthew 5:41–42 (NIV)*

I don't know about you, but this passage of Scripture seems just plain strange. "If someone forces you to go one mile, go with him two?" Are you serious? "Do not turn away from the one who wants to borrow from you." You've got to admit Jesus had some strange teachings (meaning new). Jesus was a strange leader, and what we need to understand and grasp as leaders is Jesus was full of compassion. His heart bled for people while He walked the earth. His heart still bleeds for a hurting world.

I used to say I had a heart for social justice. I still do, but it's turned out to be a controversial subject, and some people think anyone who mentions social justice is placing a cause above the gospel. Not so. To me (I can't speak for everyone with a passion for social justice), the gospel is paramount. Christ is preeminent. Nothing takes precedence over Christ and his gospel message. However, part of being a Christ-follower is living like Christ lived and having a heart, eye, and sensitivity to the things He does. So now I say I have a heart of compassion. People are less likely to criticize and stereotype me because they know of Christ's heart of compassion.

Many in my generation and younger, especially college students, are really into compassion and social justice. Yes, there can be unhealthy extremes and people who place the cause above the gospel, but I'm not going to go to the other extreme and live a life void of compassion and love for humanity. There are many issues that are near to my heart and many other great leaders as well. I'm passionate about AIDS and ministry to those with AIDS as is Rick Warren and people like Bono. I'm also passionate about clean water, which is a very serious issue. Did you know 88 percent of disease in the world is attributed to dirty water?

I'm passionate and have a burden for ending slavery because I think Christ wants to abolish slavery as well. Pardon me (I always take the opportunity to ask this wherever I speak): Did you know more slaves exist today than at any time in human history? You should know this, and it should break your heart. We pray as a family every night for the 27 million slaves around the world. I share stories with my kids of rescue missions from organizations like International Justice Mission (IJM). I wrote more about this issue in the book *Wasabi Gospel* by Shawn Wood and encourage you to check it out. A movie I recommend all Christians see is *Call + Response*. Find it and watch it.

I haven't always been sensitive to and aware of this issue. In 2008, I was speaking to Church leaders gathered in Atlanta. I asked them what they, as a city and as the Church (big "C") in their city, were passionate about and working together (collaboration) to achieve. I was expecting to hear evangelism, working to close strip clubs, or maybe even ministry to the homeless. They, without hesitation, said, "Child sex trafficking." I immediately responded back, "You mean overseas, right?" They went on to tell me Atlanta (where my wife is from and where we used to live) was the number one city in the United States for child sex trafficking. Las Vegas was number two.

My whole flight back to Dallas all I could think about was this issue that had been brought to my attention. You see, before this day, I didn't know there were more slaves alive today than any other time in human history. I thought slavery ended with Lincoln and an issue like child sex trafficking was something that maybe happened in Thailand or somewhere very far away—not in my own backyard. I returned home and did a lot of research and found my own city of Dallas was also heavily involved in human trafficking—most major cities are. I write this for one reason and one alone: You have now moved from ignorance to awareness.

What you do with this information is on you. I pray these words will disturb and disrupt you and your world. I pray you will find ways to be a part of the solution of ending slavery in our lifetime, which many think is possible. Louie Giglio and the Passion Conference launched the End It Movement, which I fully support and encourage you to look into. If this strikes a chord with you, go to my blog and search for the post entitled *I'm an Abolitionist*. Read this for action steps and organizations that are making a difference. Will you join me?

I'm also passionate about the poor and ministry to homeless people. There are numerous ways I try to involve myself in homeless ministry. (I won't get into them here—this isn't about me.) I will, however, share that I'm inspired and encouraged by many other pastors and leaders I watch around the country who have a burden for the poor as well and lead by example. I enjoy reading stories via Twitter, Facebook, and blogs about what many revolutionaries are doing to fight poverty and serve the homeless in their various cities. Why should this matter? Let's look at the words of Christ Himself:

> *The Spirit of the Lord is on me, because he has anointed me to preach good news to the poor. He has sent me to proclaim freedom for the prisoners and recovery of sight for the blind, to release the oppressed... —Luke 4:18 (NIV)*

Jesus said He had come to preach the gospel to the poor, to heal, and to set the captives free. As we've already stated in previous chapters, His mission must become our mission. His heart, His love, His burden, and His compassion must become ours. Not because it's cool, trendy, the college kids are into it, or Bono or Oprah said we should care but because Christ was a man of compassion and is a God who cares for the broken, the weary, the poor, and the imprisoned. I'm still wrestling with all of this and seeking to see the world through Christ's eyes. Look at these strong words from James:

> *Real religion, the kind that passes muster before God the Father, is this: Reach out to the homeless and loveless in their plight, and guard against corruption from the godless world.*
> *—James 1:27 (MSG)*

> *Pure and undefiled religion in the sight of our God and Father is this: to visit orphans and widows in their distress, and to keep oneself unstained by the world.*
> *—James 1:27 (NASB)*

How do we live this out?

In just the last year, God has opened my eyes to this crucial ministry we are called to. I've had great conversations with my mom about ministry to widows, as she was a young widow when my dad died from a heart attack. This past week, a dear man in my church died, and I plan to visit his wife and check on her.

For the past four years, I have traveled to Kenya and Haiti three times and have a growing heart for orphans. I've been having conversations with my wife about one day adopting a child (even though we are blessed with three wonderful kids). I don't have it figured out, but I'm reading God's word, and I'm trying to let it change me, challenge me, disturb me, and direct me. This must be the constant battle that goes on for the strange leader. You read something in God's word, and you chew on it, wrestle with it, and choose whether or not to obey and act on God's Word and the Spirit's leading. Remember: Jesus is our perfect leadership model, and Jesus was a man of compassion. Let's look at a couple of passages of Scripture that give us a tiny glimpse into Christ's heart of compassion.

> *Jesus called his disciples to Him and said, "I have compassion for these people; they have already been with me three days and have nothing to eat. I do not want to send them away hungry, or they may collapse on the way."*
> *—Matthew 15:32 (NIV)*

> *Two blind men were sitting by the roadside, and when they heard that Jesus was going by, they shouted, "Lord, Son of David, have mercy on us!" The crowd rebuked them and told them to be quiet, but they shouted all the louder, "Lord, Son of David, have mercy on us!" Jesus stopped and called them. "What do you want me to do for you?" He asked. "Lord," they answered, "we want our sight." Jesus had compassion on them and touched their eyes.*

> *Immediately they received their sight and followed Him.*
> *—Matthew 20:30–34 (NIV)*

And let's not forget the importance Jesus placed on loving our neighbor:

> *"Teacher, which is the greatest commandment in the Law?" Jesus replied: Love the Lord your God with all your heart and with all your soul and with all your mind. This is the first and greatest commandment. And the second is like it: Love your neighbor as yourself. All the law and the prophets hang on these two commandments."*
> *—Matthew 22:36–40 (NIV)*

Are there models of people and churches living this out? Yes! Praise God there are several who get this concept of compassion. By far and away, the church that I've seen embodies this concept and boldly lives this out the most is Matthew Barnett and The Dream Center (originally based in Los Angeles and now also in New York). The Dream Center Food Trucks go out to serve the community five days a week, going to thirty-one sites in some of the poorest areas of Los Angeles, including many of the inner-city projects and high crime areas, to both the young and the elderly. They reach 1,500 people in over 400 families each day they go out. Each month they're able to feed over 32,000 people in over 9,000 families.

Get this: The Dream Center in LA feeds and clothes hundreds of people every single day of the week (not to mention housing people on their campus and the ministry of their mobile medical unit throughout the city, plus dangerous ministries throughout some of the toughest neighborhoods in the city, including Skid Row), and they didn't make the "Most Innovative Church" list. Are you kidding me? Talk about a huge oversight or misinterpretation of what innovation is. The city, government, and police love The

Dream Center and have seen the crime rate drop over the years of their ministry, and someone doesn't think this is innovative? Say what? I say this to encourage you.

Please don't get caught up in these lists and discouraged if you're following God courageously and don't make the list. A lot of great churches get overlooked every year. The Dream Center is a perfect example of this. Visit www.DreamCenter.org for more information on their amazing ministry. I've personally been there and taken a tour of what all they're doing, and I've told many people a trip to the LA Dream Center is something I think every minister should do. The Dream Center encourages it and will house you and your staff for a week so you can get a close-up look at what God is doing through them.

The Dream Center in LA has inspired several other Dream Centers to spring up all over the country. Churches like Healing Place Church, Seacoast, and Church of the Highlands (just to name a few) all have their own Dream Centers and are ministering to their community in strange and innovative ways. Five years ago, we launched Mission Joplin out of our Joplin Campus at Forest Park where I serve as a campus pastor.

I get excited every time I hear of a church starting a Dream Center (or something like it) in their community. It's through these wonderful ministries that the body of Christ gets to be the hands and feet of Jesus to a hurting, sick, and broken world. It's also through these innovative ministries that cities and communities are tangibly touched and moved by the compassion of Christ-followers and witness churches going beyond their four walls.

Compassion moves us all

Compassion is contagious, and once a church starts looking beyond their four walls and making a difference in their neighborhood and community, the world takes notice. Look at what happened when Rick Warren and Saddleback Church did their 40 Days of Love and

40 Days of Service in Orange County—it was all over the news. People were shocked a church would do something other than prepare for Sunday (forgive me if that stings a little). My friends Charles Lee and Greg Russinger started JustOne.

JustOne is a nonprofit organization that was formed to stimulate greater global awareness about extreme poverty and to provoke compassionate ideas and intelligent giving in order to provide sustainable relief. They are a collective voice for the victims of social injustice—the one(s) living in geographical and situational poverty; the one(s) orphaned through death, disease, and desertion; the one(s) trafficked into slavery throughout the world. You can find out more about them at www.Just4one.org. JustOne has hubs and networks throughout the country. When I was in Dallas, we worked to start a new hub there. I'm proud Dallas is being impacted by this great organization.

I mentioned that leading with compassion is about listening to the need. Greg Surratt, founding pastor of Seacoast Church, is a great example of a leader who listened to the need of his community. Seacoast has campuses throughout South Carolina and North Carolina. One of Seacoast's campuses is in North Charleston, SC—where I went to college and lived for eight years. The North Charleston Dream Center was born out of Greg Surratt listening to the need of this city.

Greg read in USA Today that North Charleston was listed as number seven on the Top Ten Most Dangerous Cities in the US list. When Greg realized this and knew he had a campus there, he knew something must be done. He asked, "What are we going to do about it?" And thus, the birth of the North Charleston Dream Center. In January of 2009, when their North Charleston Dream Center Free Clinic opened up, their local paper gave it front page coverage, every TV station was there, and the mayors of North Charleston and Hanahan both spoke. Compassion moves people and catches the eye of even skeptics of Christianity. It's a concept twenty-first century leaders must grasp and practice to be effective in our postmodern, post-Christian world.

Rick Warren is a leader I greatly respect and I love his PEACE plan that God gave him a vision and heart for. I encourage you to check out www.thepeaceplan.com and see how you and your organization can get involved with this global movement. I know I'm leaving countless compassionate leaders out of this already long chapter. I'm simply sharing stories of people I know and have experienced firsthand. I know there are many other stories that need to be told.

The main point of this chapter is to remind you innovation is about following the Holy Spirit. Sometimes, the Holy Spirit will lead you to act and lead out of a heart of compassion. God may want to do a new thing in your community, but it may be born out of a compassion He places deep within you. It might be you being the answer to something that breaks your heart. Is there a risk of being called strange for serving the poor, ministering to the homeless, and feeding the needy? Absolutely. This is strange leadership, and I'm hoping you'll embrace it and live lives marked by compassion.

"There's a basic philosophy here that by empowering... workers you'll make their jobs far more interesting, and they'll be able to work at a higher level than they would have without all that information just a few clicks away."
—Bill Gates

"The beauty of empowering others is that your own power is not diminished in the process."
—Barbara Colorose

"The vision is really about empowering workers, giving them all the information about what's going on so they can do a lot more than they've done in the past."
—Bill Gates

"Delegating means letting others become the experts and hence the best."
—Timothy Firnstahl

"Give up control even if it means the employees have to make some mistakes."
—Frank Flores

"Surround yourself with the best people you can find, delegate authority, and don't interfere as long as the policy you've decided upon is being carried out."
—Ronald Reagan

"Don't be a bottleneck. If a matter is not a decision for the President or you, delegate it. Force responsibility down and out. Find problem areas, add structure, and delegate. The pressure is to do the reverse. Resist it."
—Donald Rumsfeld

Delegation

Get this, and you get the whole enchilada!
In this book, we're looking at forty ways to lead an innovative organization—not just how to be an innovative leader. It is just as important the entire organization and your team members realize their full potential as it is for you, the leader. I'm not just writing to the big dogs at the top of an organization, I'm writing to all involved in some sort of leadership. Whether you're the children's pastor, youth pastor, worship pastor, small group pastor, volunteer or paid, responsible for a few or for many—I'm writing to you.

> *And he gave the apostles, the prophets, the evangelists, the shepherds and teachers, to equip the saints for the work of ministry, for building up the body of Christ...*
> *—Ephesians 4:11–12 (ESV)*

I've spent my career in vocational ministry based on the Ephesians 4 philosophy of ministry. I believe my calling is to equip the saints for the work of ministry, and I've led, structured, changed, adapted, and made decisions based on this principle. Delegating to and empowering those under you is key to leading a healthy organization. Doing so allows you to be all you can be by concentrating and focusing on what only you can do, and it allows others to do what they're gifted and passionate about— making your whole team stronger.

One reason your organization is healthier when you delegate was expressed well in the Donald Rumsfeld quote: "Don't be a bottleneck. If a matter is not a decision for the President or you, delegate it. Force responsibility down and out." There are few things I hate worse than a bottleneck. I've spoken, written, and vented to friends about my feelings of the bottleneck I see in most church leadership—it drives me crazy.

I think my passion and holy discontent stems from something (a bottleneck) that stunts growth and makes an organization unhealthy. We have to fight for health and make strategic and intentional decisions that set us up to win. One of the intentional decisions you'll have to make as a leader is to give away what you can and empower those under your authority. Authors Ken Blanchard and Phil Hodges say, "Failure to empower is one of the key reasons that teams are ineffective." (*Lead Like Jesus* p. 27) I agree.

One thing I had to learn early on as a leader was to multiply myself and build ministries that were not centered on me. When I was on staff at Bent Tree I created and led a volunteer leadership team. I would constantly tell them in our meetings that the ministry I oversaw couldn't be "Greg-centric." I intentionally gave away the ministry and literally worked myself out of a job. Seriously, ask my former boss. You always hear people say their goal is to work themselves out of a job—I actually did! This volunteer leadership team I created now leads the ministry each week and makes sure Sunday happens. I had studied, read, learned, and believed long ago in lay leaders and empowering them for ministry. I built a team of volunteer leaders who truly took ownership in the ministry (this was by design), and it was a beautiful thing to behold.

In 2007, I wrote a blog entitled *When Volunteers take Ownership.*

In this article, I share my thoughts on giving away the ministry and choosing your battles. I share a story of not liking a background that was used behind the lyrics of a song. I asked another person if they liked it, and they said they did. I decided not to go to the person who had created the graphics for the week and override them. I let it go, even though it wasn't a background I, personally, would have chosen. If I didn't allow the volunteer to get creative and choose their own backgrounds, they would eventually give up or quit and say, "You do it." I had things only I could do—putting in the music or message backgrounds each week wasn't one of them. I delegated that to someone who was passionate about this and saw creating backgrounds as their ministry and act of service.

We are the Body

This concept of delegation and gift-based ministry has been engrained in me since my early twenties. I had the divine honor of hearing Ray Johnston, senior pastor of Bayside Church, speak at a conference in the year 2000. His topic was on the body of Christ, and I'll never be the same after hearing him share his well thought out concepts on how the body of Christ was designed and works together for good. A few years ago, I got the privilege of returning the favor when I went to his church to consult and do a secret shopper visit. I thanked him in person and told him how much his talk over a decade ago meant to me.

Basically, you must realize God has intentionally not given you every gift there is. He wants you to be dependent upon other parts of the body. You might be a foot, but you're going to need a hand and eye, etc. Every leader, including you and me, has weaknesses. There's only been one perfect person, and his name is Jesus Christ. Other than Him, we all have shortcomings and need the help of the body of Christ.

Again, this is by God's design. I hope you'll take comfort and relief in this fact. The success, fruit, and future of your organization do not rest squarely on your shoulders. Other people have a part to play, and the sooner you learn, accept, and implement this, the quicker your organization can become healthy and thus grow. As your staff and leaders learn the importance of their ministry and input, the organization's values will eventually become the operating values, and your church's culture will thrive. When your team takes ownership in the vision and mission of the organization (which happens through the delegation of your authority and leadership), your organization can excel.

> *And he went up on the mountain and called to him those whom he desired, and they came to him. And he appointed twelve (whom he also named apostles) so that they might be with him and he might send them out to preach and have authority to cast out demons.*
> *—Mark 3:13–15 (ESV)*

To summarize, do what only you can do. Lead in such a way you encourage gift-based ministry. Ask the hard questions of "What are you called to do?" and "What can you give away?" What can you delegate that someone else can do better? And the crazy thing is, because it's in their area of passion and gifting, they'll come up with new ideas (innovation) before you will. In the "Organization" chapter we looked at Moses's conversation with his father-in-law, Jethro, who encouraged him to delegate and thus multiply himself. Jesus multiplied Himself through His disciples, which He handpicked, taught, and empowered (gave authority to).

Recently, I got to spend some one-on-one time with Hugh Halter. He was talking about some of the books he'd written and a new one that was getting ready to come out. He spoke of living on mission and living like a missionary. But something that caught my attention was when he said, "The more you become an equipper, the cheaper you can do ministry." Wow. Think about it. For some of you, this is just pure gold. Most of us have limited funds, limited budget, and volunteer staff. Chew on this statement, and ask God to reveal to you why it's so crucial you delegate and empower others.

To wrap this chapter up, I'd like to go back to what I said at the beginning. What we're discussing in this book is how to lead an innovative organization. This concept of delegation is crucial for you to grasp and implement if you want to be as effective, healthy, and innovative as you possibly can be. The hard truth is the "innovation" that comes from your organization may very well come from your team and not you as the leader. You need to accept this and encourage it.

Some of the best ideas don't come from the top, but from people on the ground serving in their areas of passion and giftedness. A good leader knows how to lead other leaders and free them up to create, risk, lead, and execute. If you'll do what God has called you to do and allow others to do what God has called and equipped them to do, your organization will be healthy and thus prime for innovation to take place.

"The survival of the fittest is the ageless law of nature, but the fittest are rarely the strong. The fittest are those endowed with the qualifications for adaptation, the ability to accept the inevitable and conform to the unavoidable, to harmonize with existing or changing conditions."
—Anonymous

"The real security of Christianity is to be found in its benevolent morality, in its exquisite adaptation to the human heart, in the facility with which its scheme accommodates itself to the capacity of every human intellect, in the consolation which it bears to the house of mourning, in the light with which it brightens the great mystery of the grave."
—Thomas Babington Macaulay

"Stay committed to your decisions, but stay flexible in your approach."
—Tony Robbins

"The measure of intelligence is the ability to change."
—Albert Einstein

"Those who cannot change their minds cannot change anything.
—George Bernard Shaw

"It is not the strongest of the species that survives, nor the most intelligent, but rather the one most adaptable to change."
—Leon C. Megginson

Adaptation

How flexible are you?

I dare say probably no other of the principles contained in this book can set you up for innovation quite like the principle of adaptation. Now, I'm building on the spiritual chapters on prayer and seeking God—those are primary, but as far as what you can personally and organizationally do in your own human strength, this is king. Having a mindset of adaptation is vital and healthy to every innovative and growing organization.

Simply put, adaptation means adjustment. Every innovative company, organization, and church gets this concept and has set up their systems, structure, and processes to be able to operate with this mentality. In the chapter on organization, I said, "If Rick Warren and Craig Groeschel—two leaders of two of the largest and most innovative churches in America—are looking for nimbleness and movement like speed boats, I think there's some pretty good insight." Like everything I've shared though, this won't happen by accident.

You have to intentionally and strategically set yourself up to function like this. There's the word again: intentional. I imagine by now (halfway through this book) you're either loving or hating seeing the word in print. Forgive me—you'll see it many more times.

An innovative leader is an intentional leader.
—@GregAtkinson

I was watching the TV show *Chuck* once and the Buy More store manager (Big Mike) asked his employee (Casey) a funny but powerful question. He said, "Are you strong enough to bend like a reed and not break like a KitKat?" Wow. I'd like to ask every church, company, and organization I get the pleasure of consulting with this opening question. I'm afraid too many of us are about to break like a KitKat candy bar.

It's interesting; Big Mike said, "Are you strong enough . . . ?" You and your organization must work at being flexible, fluid, and nimble. Just like I have to work out, exercise, and stretch daily to be able to still touch my toes, you have to build up enough strength to be able to "bend like a reed." Throughout this book, you'll find me using phrases, words, and concepts like "mindset" and "posture". You as a leader must make up your mind and approach your leadership with the posture of a willingness to adapt when called for.

Vijay Govindarajan at the 2013 Willow Creek Association Global Leader Summit said, "If you want to lead in the future, you have to adapt to change." Innovation at its very core is change— it's the introduction of something new to make a positive change. Innovation will likely occur because the way things were being done weren't right, weren't relevant any longer, weren't healthy and something needed to be done, etc. If you lead with a closed mindset like, "We've always done it this way and so shall it forever be," then you will really wrestle with this concept.

How crucial is this concept of adaptation?

When it comes right down to it, the organizations I view as healthy and innovative have made an intentional choice to be so. They operate with a mindset and posture that is willing to change when needed. This is true for organizations and churches both large and small. I've seen large churches (like Saddleback and LifeChurch.tv, who I mentioned earlier) have a way of operating which allows them to adapt and thus be innovative. I've seen too many large churches to count who have the oil tanker mentality and getting anything new done is like passing an act of Congress. I've seen small churches and church plants operate out of a mindset of adaptation and be willing to bend and flex when needed, and I've seen small churches (who should be set up to turn like a speed boat) be so set in their ways that they have no possibility of being innovative and making positive change.

This one simple, little concept is literally holding back their growth. There is a reason most churches in North America are in plateau or decline, and this is largely due to them forgetting their first love (Rev 2:4) and not making intentional decisions that we're discussing throughout this book—like the first decision to be healthy and decide to grow—mixed with this concept of being able to adapt when needed. I'm not advocating you change everything all the time—this would be chaos. I'm talking specifically about times, moments, and seasons in your church or organization's life when you face a crisis of belief and a tough decision, and you can either adapt or stay the same (die).

I know what some of you may be thinking: Where's your biblical basis for this? Are you kidding me? You don't think God has adapted and changed His ways over time? Do we still keep all the laws those in the Old Testament kept? Do we live like the Pharisees? Did God not come up with a new plan—a new covenant? Check out how this verse is worded in *The Message*:

> *By coming up with a new plan, a new covenant between God and his people, God put the old plan on the shelf. And there it stays, gathering dust.*
> *—Hebrews 8:13 (MSG)*

Wow! Say what? "God put the old plan on the shelf. And there it stays, gathering dust." What a beautiful picture of adaptation and change by the Creator of the universe. In the summer of 2013, I wrote a piece about lessons I learned from Netflix. One of the lessons was "adapt or die." Blockbuster didn't adapt to the changing world and systems around them and they went bankrupt. Don't be like Blockbuster!

Richard Innes of ACTS International in his devotional on February 4, 2010, was writing about adaptation and change and said, "This same principle applies to many areas of life. No, we don't want to make changes where change is not to our advantage, but there are times when we do need to make changes. When it comes to communicating the gospel, while the message itself never changes, our way and means of communicating it have to change in order to communicate effectively to the particular group we are addressing. One size doesn't fit all! Also, whether we approve or disapprove, many things around us change, and if we don't adapt, we get left behind."

How can you know when you need to adapt? I'm glad you asked. A few different ways: One is when the Holy Spirit takes away your peace about something or prompts you to change. Another way is when enough people complain, seem frustrated, stop growing, or in some way seem like they're not healthy. When this happens, it might be time to look at a new way of doing things. Another way is to ask the right questions (which we'll discuss in the "Information" chapter) and have an evaluation process set up for your team, leaders, volunteers, and entire organization.

The old saying, "If ain't broke, don't fix it" is not always true. Sometimes, something may have been working for a long time but needs to die or be cut (which we'll discuss in the next chapter on "Subtraction"). Sometimes something is very broke, but for whatever reason, you just don't see it or notice anymore and thus remain limping along. This is one reason why I love serving as a secret shopper. I get to come in with fresh eyes and say, "Hey—this isn't working. It's broke and needs to change." Time after time, pastors will tell me, "You know we've been doing this so long we didn't even stop to ask why."

I'm writing to urge you, friends, to ask "Why?" I'm encouraging you to have a mindset and structure which is prepared and equipped to handle any adaptation which comes your way. I'm all for vision and mission, but at the same time, sometimes, there needs to be tweaks, changes, or an abandonment of an old way of doing something. Our God is the Living God. He's alive and on the move. He's constantly disturbing us, interrupting us and thank God—pursuing us.

If you want to keep up with Him (and this is a challenge)—to duck when He ducks, turn when He turns, and jump when He jumps, you'll have to be ready to adapt. If you get this, friends, adopt this, and live by this, there's no end to the innovations in ministry that could flow out. And yes, when you make changes and adapt your ministry or organization, you may be seen as strange at first, but this is par for the course.

"Less is more."
—Ludwig Mies van der Rohe

"The problem is never how to get new, innovative thoughts into your mind, but how to get the old ones out. Every mind is a room packed with archaic furniture. Make an empty space in any corner of your mind, and creativity will instantly fill it."
—Dee Hock

"Take a relief. You draw it, you carve it out. Later you build it up from a flat surface. There is no other way to do a sculpture—you either add or you subtract."
Urs Fischer

"You will find that it is necessary to let things go; simply for the reason that they are heavy. So let them go, let go of them. I tie no weights to my ankles."
—C. JoyBell C.

"It was strange, really. A couple months ago, I had thought I couldn't live without him. Apparently I could."
—Gabrielle Zevin, Memoirs of a Teenage Amnesiac

"Life moves on and so should we."
—Spencer Johnson, Who Moved My Cheese?

Subtraction

Less is more. Bank on it!

Three words. I've based my ministry philosophy and how I lead for the past twenty years on three simple words: less is more. I'll never forget years ago at a Catalyst conference hearing Andy Stanley teach on *The Blessedness of Subtraction*. He said, "No ministry has a forever shelf life." That message was used by God to greatly shape me and open my eyes to the possibility that sometimes we need to bring the axe down on a ministry.

Back in 2007, I wrote an article entitled *Less is More* for both the MinistryCOM website and *Vision* Magazine. To end the article, I said, "Paul, when speaking to the Corinthians, said he'd rather say five words that people could understand than a bunch that made no sense. That's my heart in this philosophy. I'd rather see your church do a few things well than a lot of things average or poorly." This pretty much sums up this chapter, which honestly, shouldn't have to be too long to get the point across.

Andy Stanley in his opening to chapter 13 in *Deep and Wide* gave the following example or scenario. Think on this:

> *Chances are, if you stand up next weekend and present a new vision for your church, you probably won't feel much resistance. New ideas always pique people's interest. For those who've been praying for something new to happen, your new vision may feel like an answer to prayer. If you lead an evangelical church and your vision includes reaching unreached people, you might even get an amen or two. If you're real good, you might even get a smattering of applause. As long as you keep it biblical and intangible, you'll be fine. But once Nelly McCloud finds out that your new vision requires her to give up her Sunday school classroom . . . well, that's when the fun begins, doesn't it?*
> *—Deep and Wide p. 277*

Nobody likes to have their ministry subtracted or taken away. Believe me, I've been there, and I know. Rick Warren in his article *How to Break Through the 200-300 Barrier* said, "The Bible says real clearly 'Except a grain of wheat fall into the ground and die, it abides alone. But if it dies it then bears fruit.' In order for a church to grow there are some things that have to die. That's why it takes unselfish people for a church to grow." Hold on to your seats. This might get uncomfortable and be a little painful, but if you get this and practice it, you will thrive.

> *Brothers, I do not consider that I have made it my own. But one thing I do: forgetting what lies behind and straining forward to what lies ahead, I press on toward the goal for the prize of the upward call of God in Christ Jesus.*
> *—Philippians 3:13–14 (ESV)*

Let me frame this chapter and principle like this: For some of you to do something new and innovative that God is leading you to do, you're going to have to say "no" to some other things— maybe many things. You must constantly narrow your focus (like we discussed in the Vision chapter). Maybe, just maybe, the "innovative" thing God wants to do in your organization is not to add anything, but to champion and focus in on what you're strong at and called to do by subtracting anything which takes away from this. Make sense?

If you look up innovation in the thesaurus, one of the words is "addition." One of my biggest fears in writing a book purely on innovation (the act of doing or introducing new things) is people would assume I'm suggesting we keep adding onto our already full plates and become busy and complex churches. Nothing could be further from my heart. Hear this loud and clear!

I think God calls us to do a few things really, really well and focus in on those things. These forty chapters on innovation are principles to help you hone in on what God is up to in your midst and join Him where He's at work and calling you to act. Yes, this could mean cutting a number of things and adding something new (occasionally) or this could mean simply doing more of what you're really gifted and called to do (less is more).

Are you a simple church?

The reason I don't want this chapter to be long is because it's already been covered so well by much better authors. If this concept or idea intrigues, scares, challenges, excites, or teases you, I want to strongly suggest you pick up three great books on this subject. The must-read book on the subject is *Simple Church* by Thom Rainer and Eric Geiger. Seriously, I could post pages and pages of quotes from the book, but it's much easier to just encourage you to read it for yourself. It's a groundbreaking and hugely powerful book and concept.

The second book I'd like to suggest you read is *7 Practices of Effective Ministry* by Andy Stanley, Reggie Joiner, and Lane Jones. For this concept, skip to practice #3: Narrow the Focus. You can also listen to a free podcast online at www.practicallyspeaking. org. The most recent book I've read on this subject is *Deliberate Simplicity* by Dave Browning. These books go into great detail on this whole "less is more" concept and as I said, are written by much better authors than myself. I sincerely mean this.

> *"Any intelligent fool can make things bigger and more complex. It takes a touch of genius–and a lot of courage to move in the opposite direction."—E. F. Schumacher*

I do want to get your mind in this place of simplicity by reading off the list of companies which *Simple Church* lists in the beginning of their book. These companies, the book suggests, show "the simple revolution has begun." These are companies who get it when it comes to simplicity and less is more. They are leaders in their field, and it is due in large part to their grasp of this concept—the companies are Apple, Google, Southwest Airlines, Papa John's, and they also mention graphic designers, interior designers, marketing gurus, and then the book proves growing and vibrant churches know this as well.

Some of you may read this list of companies and immediately know why they're listed; for others, you might have to chew on this for a while. Picture the two search engines Google and Yahoo. Look at how clean and simple Google is. Look at how busy and cluttered Yahoo is. Google has about twenty to forty words on their homepage. Yahoo has hundreds. Guess which one is more successful, more used, and makes the most money? You got it: Google. Less is more!

I'd like to add In-N-Out Burger to the list of companies who get it as well. Have you been to In-N-Out? Oh, it's glorious! Anytime I travel to the west coast, it's always on my radar to stop in there, and I usually tweet about it and send pictures. What's so special about them? They picked a few things, and they knock them out of the park. When you walk in to an In-N-Out burger, the sign reads, "Ordering is as easy as 1, 2, 3." Why you ask? Because they only offer three things on their menu. There are only three options and because of their pure focus and decision, they made on what they do best; they're a favorite of many.

As the book *Simple Church* shows us through their extensive research, growing churches get this, too. Craig Groeschel said, "In my observation, ministries that have it tend to be focused on a limited set of targets. They do a few things as if all eternity hinged on their results, and they do these things with godly excellence. They clearly see the vision and drive toward it with laser-guided precision. Those who have it know what they are called to do and what they are not called to do. Their vision is characterized by specificity, selectivity, exclusivity . . . ." Amen! Craig went on to say, "To have it, you'll have to choose not to do everything." (*It* pp. 54, 60) Did you see it? "Choose"—there's the intentional concept again. Craig Groeschel believes "to be great at a few things and experience it, you'll have to say "no" to many things."

The last I checked, LifeChurch.tv (who, by the way, was listed as the most innovative church in America by *Outreach* magazine) only does five things: weekend experiences, missions, small groups, kids, and students—that's it. Church of the Highlands (who, by the way, was once listed as the "fastest growing church in America" by *Outreach* magazine) is extremely focused. I've had the opportunity to hear their pastor, Chris Hodges, speak several times on his focus and vision. They are very picky about what they do, and they won't let anything deter them from keeping the main thing the main thing.

Please don't roll your eyes or pass them off as mega-churches you can't relate to. Hear my heart. When God is blessing something, it can be helpful to take a look under the hood and find out what they're doing right. Make no mistake—they have the hand of God on them and what's happening is a God-thing, but they are participants with the Holy Spirit and are making hard and wise choices as leaders. Their success hasn't been easy and doesn't come without a cost. They made a decision (which we talked about in the beginning) to be healthy, focused and to grow, and they have stuck by this decision no matter how painful it may be.

Pruning something is not easy.
In fact, it's downright painful.

> *The Vine and the Branches*
> *"I am the true vine, and my Father is the gardener. He cuts off every branch in me that bears no fruit, while every branch that does bear fruit He prunes so that it will be even more fruitful."*
> *—John 15:1–2 (NIV)*

There's a fascinating concept growing leaders like Craig Groeschel, Andy Stanley, and Reggie Joiner (just to name a few) teach. They talk about this whole "pruning" principle Jesus taught in John 15. It's one thing to cut off a branch "that bears no fruit"—killing something which is already dead is pretty obvious and easy. I shouldn't say easy—I'm sure somebody in your organization will still want to fight for it and revive it.

Several years ago, I was speaking at the NRB Convention, and one of my classes was on television broadcasts. There were a variety of people in the room, and most had inherited a TV ministry they didn't have a passion for anymore and wasn't doing well. I had a

God-moment where the Holy Spirit spoke straight to my heart and prompted me to say, "For some of you, you need to hear this: Stop trying to revive something God's trying to kill." You would not believe the mood in the room after I said that. There was a mixture of gasps, tears, relief, and stunned looks. After the class was over, I had some people come up to me and say I had spoken straight to them, and they knew it was time to pull the plug on their church's television ministry. I thanked God who led me to say it and gave Him the glory.

When something is not bearing fruit and needs to be propped up, for me, it's an obvious call to kill it. Chris Hodges says they don't prop up any ministry in his church. If it needs a pulpit announcement to beg people to come to it, it will quickly be cut. The tougher part of leadership is pruning back branches which are bearing fruit, as John 15 suggests. There may be some things in your organization which are working, but are not the best things for you to be doing. This is where it gets tricky, personal, and emotional and thus will need to be surrounded with a great deal of prayer, wisdom, and discernment from the Holy Spirit.

A great example of this was years ago when North Point felt led by God to cut 7:22. If you've never been to 7:22 or even heard of it, let me tell you: it was awesome. On a couple different occasions I would travel hours to attend one of their meetings, which took place every Tuesday night. I especially loved attending back in the day when Louie Giglio was the speaker. This was a cutting-edge ministry which was reaching thousands (thousands) of single adults and twenty-somethings every week.

After years of what appeared to be great success, North Point reevaluated and decided to kill 7:22. Were they in decline and seeing a drop in attendance? No. The leadership, including Andy Stanley whom I earlier quoted as saying, "No ministry has a forever shelf life," felt the ministry had run its course, and it was time to end it. They had a good reason for it and had launched a new campus (Buckhead Church), which was mainly reaching the same demographic. Still it was a hard decision. Did they upset, disappoint, and disturb some people? Absolutely. Many people struggled with the decision, but for them, they felt it was the right one. To the outside observer, 7:22 seemed to be innovative (and for a season it was), but when God led them to cut, kill, or subtract the ministry, this for North Point was being innovative (Spirit-led).

Please know, they (North Point) were thinking this way day one. This principle is for churches of all sizes. It means you do very few things, and you do them well. Know when to say "maybe later" and when to say "no". Church plants often choke because they try to do too much early on. For some of you, you may just need to say "maybe later" to some well-intentioned members who have a passion for a particular ministry or program. I had a church planter recently ask me to coach him. He sent me a list of all the ministries he wanted to do from the beginning. It was far from a simple church. I told him I would not be able to help him, and we probably weren't a good fit. I doubt his church plant will make it off the ground. He wants to offer something every day of the week and they will be spread too thin.

I asked Kem Meyer, communications director at Granger Community Church about the pruning process they once went through. Kem said, "People are busy and life is hard. They have too much information bombarding them from everywhere and not enough time to make sense of it all—much less the motivation to act on it. We've found the value we provide grows in direct proportion to how easily people can find and say yes to their next step. And, the opposite is also true: the value we provide decreases in direct proportion to how hard we make it for people to find and do what they're trying to do. The minimalistic approach to our ministry organization (broad categories for volunteer, groups, and events versus individual listings per each ministry) is about breaking a big leap into smaller, incremental steps."

Kem went on to say they got rid of "all individual ministries . . . men's, women's, new beginnings, spiritual gifts, singles, couples, homecare, meals for moms, etc. Essentially, we consolidated eighty options down to four. Anything that happens at the church is going to show up under events, groups, volunteer, or get help. When everything is communicated as being important, you actually end up communicating nothing is. That's why we elevated the macro categories and demoted individual options under those categories." Did you catch that?

> *"When everything is communicated as being important, you actually end up communicating nothing is."—Kem Meyer*

Maybe you need a to-don't list

In *Simple Church*, the authors define focus as "the commitment to abandon everything that falls outside of the simple ministry process." Craig Groeschel asks a hard question in his book *It* which needs to be wrestled with thoroughly. He asks, "What are you doing that isn't directly contributing with high impact to your vision? The answer to that question needs to be eliminated." Again, I reply, "Amen!" Now I know this is easier said than done and tremendous fear may come over you when you read something like this. Don't worry: we'll discuss courage in the Execution chapter.

I so appreciate the mindset, focus, and Kingdom heart to share wisdom from the leadership of North Point Community Church. Andy Stanley, Reggie Joiner, and Lane Jones said, "If you really want to make a lasting impact, then you need to eliminate what you do well for the sake of what you can potentially do best." Remember what pastor Mike Linch of NorthStar Church shared in the Progression chapter? They learned to get rid of all the things that they couldn't do well and focus in on a couple of key things they were going to be great at. He went on to say if they had not learned the lesson that they couldn't do everything they may "be good at tons of things, but be great at nothing."

What do Craig Groeschel and LifeChurch.tv and Andy Stanley and North Point have in common? They both teach the concept of having a "to-don't list." I won't go into detail on this. I think you get the picture, plus you can read their books and get more insight into creating your own "to-don't list" for your organization. On May 12, 2010, Rick Warren said on Twitter, "Never add without subtracting. Pro teams do it when adding players. Great cafes with menus. Healthy churches with programs." I agree. What wisdom. Please read that tweet again and really wrestle with it, friends.

Even my one church I served, Forest Park, has cut numerous ministries over the years for the sake of growth and healthy change. Need examples? Sure! Over the last fifteen years, Forest Park has cut having a daycare, women's ministry, men's ministry, children's choir, handbells, Sunday night worship, Valentines banquet, annual summer picnic, bus ministry, New Year's Eve party, Tuesday night visitation and Wednesday night teacher training.

I've served as pastor for twenty-plus years, and I will be the first to admit: this is hard. It's easier said than done. I don't take this lightly. Have I subtracted a ministry? Yes. It was very difficult and feelings got hurt. Will I do it again? Yes. We're already planning to cut one of our annual outreach events because we weren't seeing fruit from it. Our people love it, but it's not effective. Please hear me: This is not easy. Leadership takes guts. I want to encourage you, friends, to see innovation in a holistic way—to have an innovative mindset. I want to go back to something I alluded to earlier. For some of you, innovation (in your context and circumstance) might not be to add anything. You may need to adopt an innovative mindset, and innovation for you is to simply narrow your focus, subtract some things, and do what you're strong at even better. I hope you'll take this to heart.

Again, I know this isn't easy. Remember Rick Warren's words: "It takes unselfish people for a church to grow."

"Courage is contagious. When a brave man takes a stand, the spines of others are often stiffened."
—Billy Graham

"The man who makes no mistakes does not usually make anything."
—Bishop W. C. Magee

"Only those who risk going too far can possibly find out how far they can go."
—T. S. Eliot

"I have not failed. I've just found 10,000 ways that won't work."
—Thomas A. Edison

"Sometimes when you innovate, you make mistakes. It is best to admit them quickly, and get on with improving your other innovations."
—Steve Jobs

"Unless you try to do something beyond what you have already mastered, you will never grow."
—Ronald. E. Osborn

"Great deeds are usually wrought at great risks."
—Herodotus

"Necessity is the mother of taking chances."
—Mark Twain

"A ship is safe in harbor, but that's not what ships are for."
—William Shedd

"I would rather fail in an attempt at something new and uncharted than safely succeed in a repeat of something I have done."
—A. E. Hotchner

"Today's successes hold the poisons that will kill tomorrow's innovations."
—Larry Osborne at the Exponential Conference

Exploration

This is the great adventure!

"Two roads diverged in a wood, and I . . . I took the one less traveled by, and that has made all the difference." Ah, such amazing and insightful words from Robert Frost. This chapter and concept of exploration, experimentation, and taking risks is something I've been thinking on for a long time. As a matter of fact, this is the last chapter I'm writing (though it's not #40)—I waited to write about this until last. I've spent months thinking about this concept, researching, polling leaders, and finding out who the cartographers and topographers of our generation are.

Where would we be without the cartographers, explorers, inventors, and risk takers of the past? In grade school, we all read and learned about explorers like Lewis and Clark, Christopher Columbus, and Magellan. I can't imagine what our world would be like without inventors and experimenters like Benjamin Franklin and Thomas Edison, and modern-day innovators like Steve Jobs and Bill Gates. There are some bold, brave, and passionate leaders around the world who are charting new territory still today. Like

Star Trek, they are boldly going where no one's gone before.

Believe it or not, I still think there's much in our ministries and in this digital world left to explore and discover.

I have a little bit of natural explorer in me. I'm not saying I don't have my comfort zones and don't get challenged, stretched, and disturbed by God; I do, but I also have a little risk side of my life I enjoy. One of the ways this fun exploration happens for me is when I visit a new city (and I travel quite a bit). I love to explore new, local restaurants I've never been to before and have no guarantee it won't make me sick. With me, anything goes. I've tried sushi in several cities with friends and hear me: I don't like sushi. I'm not a sushi eater. I just try it for the fun of it and to see if it's grown on me yet. It hasn't.

Usually, when I arrive in a new city (and I just did this last week in Nashville), I ask where the local Mexican restaurant is. I don't want a chain like On the Border. I want to find a real, local Mexican restaurant with people who barely speak English. I'm constantly trying new ones, hoping to stumble across a great one (to discover something new and worth remembering). Have I gotten some bad Mexican food before and got sick? Absolutely. My wife thinks I'm crazy. I enjoy it. I also tried a new Indian restaurant one time and got sick as a dog—doubled over with stomach cramps. I was in Cincinnati last summer, and I tried Skyline Chili—it was excellent! Yes, I've taken bigger risks, but this is an example of something minor (like eating) to get your creative and explorative juices flowing.

> *"Therefore let all Israel be assured of this: God has made this Jesus, whom you crucified, both Lord and Christ." When the people heard this, they were cut to the heart and said to Peter and the other apostles, "Brothers, what shall we do?" Peter replied, "Repent and be baptized, every one of you, in the name*

of Jesus Christ for the forgiveness of your sins. And you will receive the gift of the Holy Spirit."
—Acts 2:36–38 (NIV

When I think of a Biblical explorer and risk-taker, I think of good ol' Peter. Yes, Peter was brash, short-tempered, and a little rough around the edges, but he was a man of faith—before and after the resurrection. After the resurrection, Peter became even more bold and confident in his risen Savior. Empowered by the Holy Spirit, he preached boldly to the early church (Acts 2) and also walked in power and faith, healing many. You must understand Pentecost was a true "first"—it had never happened before. They were going into new territory, and instead of freaking out, Peter stood up calmly and began to share the Scriptures with those present. I don't know how I would have reacted if I had seen something like Pentecost, but I have a great deal of respect for how Peter handled this new thing in the Church and seized the opportunity to share Christ.

Peter was also a man of faith and stood out from the other disciples before Christ's Resurrection. Let's look:

The Calling of the First Disciples
One day as Jesus was standing by the Lake of Gennesaret, with the people crowding around him and listening to the word of God, he saw at the water's edge two boats, left there by the fishermen, who were washing their nets. He got into one of the boats, the one belonging to Simon, and asked him to put out a little from shore. Then he sat down and taught the people from the boat. When he had finished speaking, he said to Simon, "Put out into deep water, and let down the nets for a catch."

Note: Sometimes, God will call you out into the deep water.

Also notice Peter's response of obedience and faith:

> *Simon answered, "Master, we've worked hard all night and haven't caught anything. But because you say so, I will let down the nets." When they had done so, they caught such a large number of fish that their nets began to break. So they signaled their partners in the other boat to come and help them, and they came and filled both boats so full that they began to sink. When Simon Peter saw this, he fell at Jesus's knees and said, "Go away from me, Lord; I am a sinful man!" For he and all his companions were astonished at the catch of fish they had taken, and so were James and John, the sons of Zebedee, Simon's partners. Then Jesus said to Simon, "Don't be afraid; from now on you will catch men." So they pulled their boats up on shore, left everything and followed him.*
> *—Luke 5:1–11 (NIV)*

You want to see more exploration and taking risk? Check out this awesome moment in Peter's life:

> *During the fourth watch of the night Jesus went out to them, walking on the lake. When the disciples saw Him walking on the lake, they were terrified. "It's a ghost," they said, and cried out in fear. But Jesus immediately said to them: "Take courage! It is I. Don't be afraid." "Lord, if it's you," Peter replied, "tell me to come to you on the water." "Come," He said. Then Peter got down out of the boat, walked on the water and came toward Jesus.*
> *—Matthew 14:25–29 (NIV)*

Talk about taking a risk! We see bold living, risk taking, and people walking by faith all throughout the Old Testament. Think of Moses sending out men to explore (including Joshua and Caleb) in Numbers 13. Think of Ezekiel and the Valley of Dry Bones

(Ezekiel 37). Think of David being bold enough to fight Goliath—not knowing how it would turn out, but led by a conviction His God was the one true God, and no one should "defy the armies of the living God" (1 Samuel 17). Think of Benaiah who "went down into a pit on a snowy day and killed a lion" (2 Samuel 23:20). Do you think innovation, exploration, and risk are something for the young bucks? Not something retired people are supposed to do? Let's look at Abram:

> *The Lord had said to Abram, "Leave your country, your people and your father's household and go to the land I will show you . . . . So Abram left, as the Lord had told him; and Lot went with him. Abram was seventy-five years old when he set out from Haran.*
> *—Genesis 12:1, 4 (NIV)*

Go. Where? "To the land I will show you." Just start walking, and I'll be with you. In other words: Explore. Walk by faith. Take a risk. Leave your comfort zone. And how old was Abram? Seventy-five! This concept is for every generation reading this book. Do not think I'm only writing to twenty-something-and- thirty-something-year-old church planters who love taking risk. No. I'm writing to you no matter what season of ministry you're in, and no matter what season of life.

Get out of the boat!

For some of you, to go to the next level in your leadership and see a breakthrough in your ministry, you're going to have to leave your comfort zone, explore, experiment, and try something you've never done before. On March 30, 2010, Mark Batterson (@MarkBatterson on Twitter) said, "We want signs to precede our steps of faith, but signs typically follow our steps of faith." Like Peter, God may be calling you to get out of the boat and attempt to walk on water or go out in the deep waters and try doing something God's way, even though you may have tried your own way for years.

The strange and innovative leader has a pioneering and entrepreneurial spirit. For some of you, this may come naturally. For some of you, you'll have to work at this and take huge leaps of faith along your spiritual and ministry journey. For some of you, your gift mix may be an apostolic (which is a pioneer, entrepreneur and innovator) on the APEST Gift Test developed by Alan Hirsch. I encourage all leaders to check out www.theforgottenways.org/apest/ for more information on this. It does cost $10, but it's worth it. My friend, Brett Aljets, talked me into taking it because he knew I was an apostolic leader (according to the test), and he wanted to affirm and confirm this in me. I think this test will open your eyes to how God has uniquely shaped you and prepared you for ministry.

I asked a few pastors I respect their thoughts on taking risks. I'm sure many more of you could share your own stories, but here are a few thoughts from various leaders:

> *I heard Craig Groeschel once say, "To reach people we've never reached before, we're going to have to do things we've never done before." Church planting isn't for everyone– and it's certainly not for those who are afraid to explore . . . . Exploring has to be done on all levels: The daily exploration of the how we do what we do (the daily tasks. Can we do better?), the weekly exploration of where we do what we do (Are we working the right fields this week... Does God have new territory for us to take?) and the seasonal exploration of why we do what we do (I know the purposes of the church never change, but our focus we have for this season does. Should we invest more in leadership development or outreach?). Being willing to experiment means you've got a God-given identity which stays strong when you*

fail. Failure shouldn't ever be looked at as a mistake as much as a learning experience. What have we learned which will help us grow?
—Brett Crimmel, lead pastor of Forefront Church in Denver

I think one of our greatest risks we've taken so far was when we moved our original campus (and only campus at the time) from a suburban, middle-class neighborhood to an economically and culturally diverse neighborhood in the city of Nashville. That shift not only affected the comfort and convenience of our current attendees but it also challenged our staff to do ministry in a completely different way. Loving and serving our community took on an entirely new face.
—Pete Wilson, lead pastor of Cross Point in Nashville

We took a risk from day one . . . the risk was that we could grow our church through no other evangelism training other than teaching our people to "love the Lord and to serve our community." We had no other plan for growth other than serving people. Looking back over thirteen years, there is no doubt that we made the right choice . . . but in the beginning it was a huge risk!
—Mike Linch, lead pastor of NorthStar Church in Atlanta

Best recent example I have is partnering up with the Advent Conspiracy. May not seem like a risk and probably wouldn't be for most churches, but for us, it was because we rely on year-end giving for building fund, general fund, etc. We gave away the Christmas Eve offering, which is typically when year-end gifts come in. Ended up giving away around 250K, and yes our general fund and building fund took a hit. But how do you measure the $$$ value of the Spirit's work in individual hearts,

which the Advent Conspiracy catalyzed?
—Pete Briscoe, senior pastor of Bent Tree Bible in Dallas

It all depends upon our definition of risk. Our ministry has taken tons of risks if you mean doing things that were out of the norm, not commonly done by other churches, or even considered crazy by others. But if you mean have we taken wild leaps without being pretty convinced of a high likelihood of success (or without a solid exit plan in place just in case our great idea didn't work), I'd have to say we haven't actually taken many risks. To me, innovation is not so much doing something risky that hasn't yet been done as much as it is doing something success fully that hasn't yet been done. In other words, by mentally modeling the outcomes of our actions, I was actually quite sure that a shared pulpit, multiple senior pastors, sermon-based small groups, video venues, closing down the church for weekends of service, and many other things we've done over the years would work even if most people at the time thought we were crazy.
—Larry Osborne, lead pastor of North Coast Church in San Diego

"Even if most people at the time thought we were crazy." Hmmm. Sounds like strange leadership. Wow. I love hearing stories of faith and risk from modern day pioneers and leaders, but the last quote from Larry Osborne is worth reading a few times. The depth of wisdom he shared is profound and a good word for this whole concept of strange leadership. He said they've done several things which "were out of the norm, not commonly done by other churches, or even considered crazy by others." Some might say they were strange. His wise words go on to put this whole chapter and concept into perspective. We're talking about calculated risks most of the time. I believe, like Abram and Peter, God will sometimes call you to do something or try something new that has no guarantee of success, but I agree with Larry—we should shoot for things which have "a high likelihood of success."

I've been around Larry enough to hear him speak on his style of leadership and thoughts on innovation. One thing that intrigued me about him and his church is I once heard him say when they are trying something new, they call it an "experiment." They let the people know up front this is something different they are trying, and they could fail. Notice how he mentioned having a "solid exit plan in place just in case." We talked about failure and the whole concept of failing forward in the "Progression" chapter, so I'll let you read there for more on failing and how God uses it, but I must point out if you try something new, explore, and experiment in your setting, there is the chance it might fail. Just accept this and create a culture which permits it.

Failure is an option.

"I give myself two epic fails a year."
—Bob Goff, Storyline Conference 2013

My friend, Bobby Gruenewald, innovation pastor at LifeChurch.tv says, "At LifeChurch.tv, we tell our staff, 'Failure is not an option. Failure is a requirement.' When you fail, it means you get to try again. You get another chance to create.

Harvard University Professor David Perkins said, "Mental risk-takers are more likely to produce creative results by working at the edge of their competence, where the possibility of failure lurks. Innovation doesn't happen with one lucky shot. It's the result of failure and refinement." What a good word.

My friend, Todd Rhodes of Leadership Network wrote about this on his blog. He wrote: "Question: Is your church willing to accept risk and failure when there are lessons to be learned? What is the last big risk that you took in your leadership that actually paid off in some type of innovation?

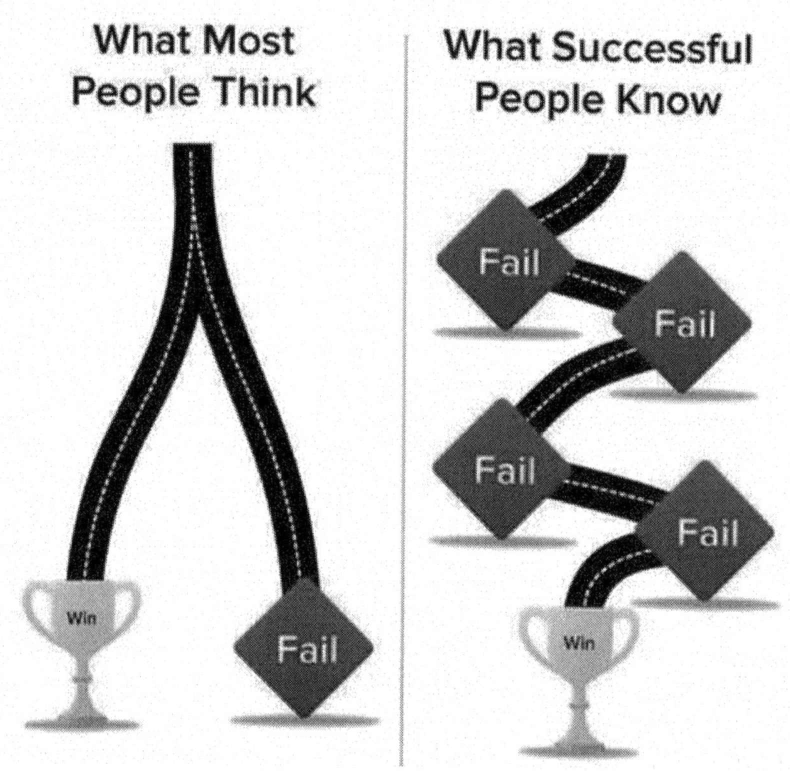

The godly may trip seven times, but they will get up again.
—Proverbs 24:16 (NLT)

According to leading authors on the subject, the keyword in those who innovate is risk. Did you know some of the companies we look at as being the best at innovation, such as Google, Apple, Pixar, and 3M, promote innovation through a culture where it's okay to take risks? A culture where failure is acceptable.

I believe whenever risks can be taken in a safe environment, innovation is much more likely to be successful. Another interesting caveat: while innovation can happen in both small and large organizations or churches, the larger your organization, the more dedicated resources you'll need to fuel the innovation process, and the more you'll need to risk failure. This is very hard (especially the failure part) as your church grows. Ben Arment once said, "The enemy of innovation is success." We'll delve into this in the last chapter.

I must again caution you: There is a difference between a calculated risk, following God and exploring and poorly executed plans. I've seen churches recently start an internet campus or started streaming their services live, and it was a disaster. There's no excuse for this. I'm not talking about doing sloppy or poorly prepared initiatives. If (and there's a big if) you feel called by God to stream your services live on the web, streaming TV, or start an internet campus, you must beta test behind-the-scenes for months before ever going public. You should have someone sitting at home, taking notes and giving feedback on what they saw (in their private viewing of the beta test) and then make adjustments based off the beta test audience's feedback—but this is for another book.

By faith

Throughout our Bible (Old and New Testament) and human history are stories upon stories of exploration, experimentation, walking by faith, and taking risks. My encouragement to you, my friends, is to join this great heritage of faith we've seen lived out over centuries.

Read Heb 11 and 12 in *The Message*. I'll just pull a highlight quote: "It's impossible to please God apart from faith."

Couple your seeking God in prayer (Inquisition) with faith and the belief "he exists, and he cares enough to respond to those who seek him." I'm also challenged and encouraged when I read the roll-call of faith in Heb 11. It's too long for me to include it here, but I encourage you to open your Bible and read it. Notice how many times the passage says, "By faith . . . " Let's look at one of the "by faiths"—the story of my favorite innovator, Noah.

> *By faith, Noah built a ship in the middle of dry land. He was warned about something he couldn't see, and acted on what he was told. The result? His family was saved. His act of faith drew a sharp line between the evil of the unbelieving world and the rightness of the believing world. As a result, Noah became intimate with God.*
> *—Hebrews 11:7 (MSG)*

There is an important lesson in this passage. Noah "was warned about something he couldn't see and acted on what he was told." Hebrews, in chapter 12, goes on to encourage us to look at the example of Jesus—the perfect role model for leadership and life.

> *Do you see what this means—all these pioneers who blazed the way, all these veterans cheering us on? It means we'd better get on with it. Strip down, start running—and never quit! No extra spiritual fat, no parasitic sins. Keep your eyes on Jesus, who both began and finished this race we're in. Study how He did it. Because He never lost sight of where He was headed—that exhilarating finish in and with God—He could put up with anything along the way: cross, shame, whatever. And now He's there, in the place of honor, right alongside God. When you find yourselves flagging in your faith, go over that story again, item by item, that long litany of hostility He plowed through. That will shoot adrenaline into your souls!*
> *—Hebrews 12:1–3 (MSG)*

Reading this passage in *The Message* is such an encouragement to us all. When you're struggling or wrestling with something God is calling you to do, the Bible encourages us remember the story of

Christ and reflect on it again and again. I like how the beginning of chapter 12 acknowledges "all these pioneers who blazed the way." Which pioneers? The ones in the roll-call of faith (Heb 11).

The Bible links faith and pioneering together. When we talk about exploration and taking risks, we're talking about a spiritual matter—a matter which requires a great deal of faith. When you lead from a place of faith, you are most like the pioneers before us (Heb 11) and ultimately like Christ, "who both began and finished this race we're in."

Throughout this chapter, I've referred to two acts: exploration and experimentation. These two concepts are similar and operate with the same respect to the risk factor. However, they are a little different too.

In exploration, you're willing to get lost. In experimentation, you're willing to fail. —@GregAtkinson

In exploration, you have no idea what you'll find, but yet, you explore. In experimentation you have an idea, you just don't know if it will work or not. See the difference?

What are you learning when you experiment?

Innovation has also been defined as "a creation, new device, or process resulting from experimentation." This principle of experimentation is something which is missing from most of our churches. I'm not talking about a wild, crazy attempt at something without any reason or Spirit's leading behind it. I'm talking about having a notion. The thought of "with God nothing is impossible" and you're willing to attempt something which has never been done in His name and for His glory (if you have a peace about it). It's what Steven Furtick talks about when he says to act, pray and believe with "audacious faith." Speaking of having a notion about something (and this can truly be a God-thing), Thomas Edison said, "When I have fully decided that a result is worth getting I go ahead of it and make trial after trial until it comes"—this, my friends, is experimentation.

Gary Hamel and Gary Getz, in *Funding Growth in an Age of Austerity* say, "When it comes to innovation, consistency counts. Over time, small ideas compound, learning from experimentation accumulates, and competencies grow stronger. Teams develop a collective memory and avoid making the same mistakes twice. With this in mind, a company should commit itself to a relatively small number of medium-term innovation goals." (*Harvard Business Review*, July–August 2004, p. 83)

Does your organization learn from experimentation and commit itself to innovation goals? If we believe God is doing a new thing (Isa 43:19), and we look around our organization and see dated, stale, dying, or dead elements and programs, we've got to take a hard look at what we're doing and make intentional and strategic strides toward seeking where God is doing a new thing in our community.

On the Practically Speaking podcast (www.practicallyspeaking.org), Reggie Joiner tells the story of Emily Hill. She was at a church in Texas and wanted to do a Kidstuf program for families, and they had an adult Sunday school model. They flew in influential people from North Point to teach them. Their church killed (or subtracted) their adult Sunday school and created a different kind of concept for children. In the first year, about 30–40 percent of the people left. In the second year, the number of people had returned, and they started growing at a rate they'd never grown before. They were willing to take a risk, willing to cut back and start to do a few things better, and as a result, they began to grow. Reggie says, "You can't immediately judge your success by what you see the first six months, even the first year sometimes." I saw this at my own campus where I pastor. The first year I was there we really didn't experience much growth. The second and third year, we exploded with growth. Give it time, friends.

This is a good word for some of you who resonate with this

chapter and this concept. Maybe you're full of faith and are wired to be an innovator and pioneer—ready to go where no one's gone before. Be aware things may not come to fruition overnight. It might take months for you to see the benefits of the change you implemented. I do, however, suggest you set regular checkpoints (once a month, once a quarter, or annually) where you evaluate the new innovation you started and see if it's working. If it's not, you need to have your exit plan ready to go and be willing to stop doing it. Again, let me remind you of these wise words: "No ministry has a forever shelf life" (Andy Stanley).

Scott Wilson points out something worth noting. I think it's pertinent to have a realistic expectation and perspective of this concept. As Scott says in his book, "If we think everybody on our staff and in leadership in the church is going to stand up and cheer" when we implement and lead through change, we're deceiving ourselves. He shares a few people may "thrive on change," but the "vast majority of people" are "risk averse." He encourages leaders to not "underestimate the threat of change to your people." His wise counsel is when you lead from an awareness of this reality, "you'll be more patient with their resistance and more thorough in your communication." (*Steering through Chaos* p.66–67)

Please know exploration, experimentation, and taking risks— no matter what type of organization you lead—will take an extremely well thought out communication plan. With this being said, let's look at and celebrate some modern-day cartographers.

The modern-day explorers

When I think of modern day explorers in the ministry world, several friends come to mind. Charles Hill saw a need to resource churches in small towns and created The Sticks Conference, believing there was a need to equip leaders throughout the country in small towns. I have been a part and still am of The Sticks Conference, now under the leadership of my friend, Artie Davis. Charles Lee, a pastor who had the idea (he didn't know if it would work) to start a different kind of conference—a conference that was free, regional, and where the speakers facilitated discussion and accepted no honorarium. He created The Idea Camp, which I had the honor of speaking at the first one in Southern California. Both The Sticks Conference and The Idea Camp have exploded with growth and gone regional, meeting throughout the country and streaming online. The Idea Camp also recently spurred off a new conference just for nonprofits. Both Charleses are friends of mine and busy guys, and I have a great deal of respect for these modern-day explorers and risk-takers.

In the world of online ministry (which is uncharted territory), I think of my friends in Internet campus ministry. People like Brian Vasil at Potential Church and my old buddies Tony Steward and Brandon Donaldson who used to run the Internet Campus at LifeChurch.tv. These guys blazed a trail in doing church online and in a type of ministry which has only been around since 2005. They are known as veterans in a new but growing ministry of the Church, including present day trailblazers like Nils Smith and Jay Kranda.

My friend Paul Watson, who I used to meet weekly with for prayer and Bible study, is a digital missionary. You can follow his activities, thoughts, and lessons at www.pauldwatson.com. Like many missionaries around the world who raise support and serve full-time to spread the gospel, Paul raises support like a missionary, but his mission field is the Internet, and he engages people in communities online. Like his dad, David Watson—a well-respected missionary, he's blazing a new trail in the way people are evangelized and discipled in the twenty-first century. My friend Barry Whitlow started a unique new outreach church in the Nashville area specifically designed to reach new people in the community who do not attend any church on Sunday. This unique church is called Studio Church. What makes Studio unique is they only use multimedia and the creative arts in their services. They feel using in their services the same communication style as the people they are trying to reach use every day will help them introduce their target to God's amazing grace and love found in Jesus. Their outreach and growth strategy includes creating a unique monthly Community Outreach Church Service which will be high-quality, relevant to the unchurched, and designed to serve as a bridge to the community for people who do not attend any church on Sunday. I'm keeping my eye on them!

Maybe you skipped over the chapter on Mission and rolled your eyes when I asked you to create a personal mission statement. You might need to go back, explore who you are and what God's called you to do so you can dive in with all your being.

Jesus is absolutely worth it, and the strange and innovative leader gets this. You may be called strange (imagine Francis Chan walking away from a senior pastor's salary at a mega-church to go into the unknown), but if you're following the Spirit's leading, you're right where you should be.

"The ear of the leader must ring with the voices of the people.
—Woodrow Wilson

"The most basic of all human needs is the need to understand and be understood. The best way to understand people is to listen to them."
—Ralph Nichols

"One of the most sincere forms of respect is actually listening to what another has to say."
—Bryant H. McGill

"I like to listen. I have learned a great deal from listening carefully. Most people never listen."
—Ernest Hemingway

"You can make positive deposits in your own economy every day by reading and listening to powerful, positive, life-changing content and by associating with encouraging and hope-building people."
—Zig Ziglar

"Wisdom is the reward you get for a lifetime of listening when you'd have preferred to talk."
—Doug Larson

Conversation

Listen to the people

So far, we've talked about listening to the Spirit, listening to the culture, and listening to the need. In this chapter, we're going to talk about listening to the pain and specifically how God speaks through people. In Henry Blackaby's *Experiencing God*, he says God speaks through Scripture, prayer, the Holy Spirit, people, and circumstances.

This chapter is very special to me as God has used several people over the years to speak into my life. I'm so grateful for my studying of *Experiencing God* and my eyes being opened at a young age of how God uses people to help us discern His will for our lives. Since I had been taught this, I've always been sensitive to the Spirit and what God is up to when people speak into my life or I have a conversation with a lost person. This also goes back to the book Spurgeon wrote on the Holy Spirit.

Earlier in the book, I talked about the posture in which we approach God. In this chapter, I'd like to talk about the posture in which we approach people we encounter daily. Do you honestly believe you can learn something from anybody? Young, old, smart, dumb, male, female, trained, or uneducated—we can all learn from people. We learn both good and bad, positive and negative, and the right and wrong way to do something but learn, we do.

In Luke 24, we read of two men walking on the road to Emmaus who encounter Jesus. In verses 25–27, it reads, "He said to them, 'How foolish you are, and how slow to believe all that the prophets have spoken! Did not the Messiah have to suffer these things and then enter his glory?'" And beginning with Moses and all the prophets, he explained to them what was said in all the Scriptures concerning Himself.

And of course, we remember the last verse in the story. Verse 32 reads, "They asked each other, 'Were not our hearts burning within us while he talked with us on the road and opened the Scriptures to us?'"

This conversation on the road to Emmaus is one of my favorite conversations in Scripture. My favorite part is the men recalling how their hearts burned within them as they heard Christ speak. Can you imagine it? I can. God broke my heart over pride in my life in the Fall of 2013 and my heart burned. I'm serious. It burned within me. We'll talk more about God speaking through Scripture in the Illumination chapter. As per our conversation on innovation, your next idea or breakthrough in ministry could be just a conversation away.

Maybe God wants you to speak to a coworker, neighbor, family member, barber, or friend at the gym who doesn't know Christ. Maybe God knows something they say or the way they feel about the Church will shape your thinking and open your eyes to a new way of doing things. It's really pretty elementary. If you want to know how to reach lost people—ask them. If you want to be relevant in your ministry—get to know the people you're trying to reach. You must constantly think like a missionary. This is something I'm continuing to learn as I hang out with all my missional buddies and was a part of Forge Joplin. And this exact concept of interacting with everyday people in coffee shops and restaurants is featured in a book by my friend, Hugh Halter.

The other day on Twitter, I noticed Rick Womack said, "Out of 132 contacts that Jesus has with people recorded in the New Testament, 6 were in the temple, 4 were in the synagogue, and 122 were in the mainstream of life." Could it be 95–100 percent of most pastors' conversations are with people already in the church? Wow. I hope not.

What a huge opportunity we'd be missing out on if this were the case. I wonder . . . .

John Ruskin said, "I believe the first test of a truly great man is his humility. I do not mean by humility, doubt of his powers. But really, great men have a curious feeling that the greatness is not in them but through them. And they see something divine in every other man." Do you see something divine in every other person? Are you humble enough to believe you can learn from anyone? An innovative leader is teachable and proactively (intentionally) engages in conversations with all types of people, especially people who believe differently than he or she.

Remember this quote from Mark Waltz (of Granger): "Wow is about innovation, and innovation is about addressing a constantly changing culture. We must be astute observers, conversationalists, and purveyors of change." (*First Impressions*, p. 43)

Be an astute conversationalist. Astute means clever, cunning, ingenious, or shrewd. There's the word again: "cunning." Remember, Jesus told us to be "cunning as a snake." (Matt 10:16)

If Jesus is our model for leadership, and He instructed us to be shrewd or cunning as a snake, could it be He wanted to apply it to our conversations as well as Mark suggests? I dare say so. I think God would have us be clever, intentional, and strategic in how we engage others in conversation in order to place ourselves in a posture in which we can be enlightened, grow, and change our outlook on a particular situation. Innovation is a mysterious thing. You never know where it will come from. The key is to be intentional enough to place yourself in a situation or conversation which God can use to lead you to new ways of doing things.

Innovation from the bottom up

So, we've discussed a few different ways God can speak to us through conversation. Blackaby teaches God speaks through the Church and godly people. I agree. I also believe God speaks through lost people. They are keys to us, understanding their fears, desires, hopes, and dreams and thus reaching them.

Another way God speaks is through your team. Please hear me senior pastors and CEOs: God can and will speak through those under your authority. If you think every new idea and innovation must come from the top, you will severely limit your organization. One of the roles of those in executive leadership is to get to know the people who work for them. I've heard some CEOs of major Fortune 500 companies who say they spend 30 percent of their time walking the floor and speaking to employees—trying to get a pulse on their organization. Eric Schmidt, CEO of Google said, "The most clever ideas don't come from the leaders but rather from the leaders listening and encouraging and kind of creating a discussion. Wander around and try to find the new ideas." Eric gets it and in return, Google is seen as one of the most innovative companies in the world.

> *"Seek first to understand, then to be understood."*
> *—Stephen R. Covey, 7 Habits of Highly Effective People*

> *"There is no such thing as a worthless conversation, provided you know what to listen for. And questions are the breath of life for a conversation."*
> *—James Nathan Miller*

I wanted to place these quotes here in the chapter to chew on and really process through. I'll start with Covey's quote. As a leader, you must first seek to understand and then to be understood. This leads to success and effectiveness in your life, work, and ministry. It also speaks to the posture in which we are to approach people.

Maybe you are buying what I'm selling. Maybe this resonates with your spirit, and you know this concept is true. Maybe God has used people at various times in your life to speak to you and help you discern God's plan or will. Maybe you don't wrestle with the "why," but the "how." How can you be a better conversationalist? The James Nathan Miller quote is intriguing to me as well.

He suggests, "There is no such thing as a worthless conversation, provided you know what to listen for," and I agree—you can learn from anybody. He also says, "Questions are the breath of life for a conversation." There's a nugget. Ask questions.

I hope it goes without saying when I talk about conversation, I'm talking about a two-way deal. If you simply meet with somebody and do all the talking, you won't learn anything. A conversation means you give and take, share and listen. We'll talk more about the listening aspect in the chapter on Auscultation, but for now, let's focus on Miller's nugget of asking questions.

If you ever have the privilege of sitting down with someone wiser, smarter, older, more experienced, more godly, more (you fill in the blank), please take the opportunity to pick their brain. I meet with people all the time just to ask them questions. I ask and then I listen. I follow up with a question and then I listen. I'm very intentional to not be the only one talking and to place myself in a posture as a student.

If you ever have the distinct privilege and honor of talking with an unbeliever, please don't do all the talking. Use questions to breathe life into your conversation, but really seek to understand. Seek to listen to the pain in their life. Go deeper. If they say they are sick of "organized religion" or "so-called Christians," seek to understand where this area of pain or frustration is coming from. Many times, the answer to something which troubles an unbeliever is what turns out to you to be a new innovation in ministry. You might be seeking to change or adapt to an idea or way of doing things which was prompted by your conversation with the lost person. Trust me. God spoke through an animal. He can speak through anyone He chooses.

Lastly, I'll just close with a challenge. You must have your antennae up at all times. You never know when, where, or through whom God will choose to speak or what He is up to behind the scenes. This requires a great deal of sensitivity. As we discussed earlier, you need to have a keen sensitivity to the Holy Spirit in all matters of life, especially in your meetings, interactions, and conversations with people. So take a dose of humility, a teachable spirit, and a posture which says you can learn from anyone into each conversation you have, and see what God does.

"Is not the commission of our Lord still binding upon us? Can we not do more than now we are doing?"
—William Carey

"The spirit of Christ is the spirit of missions. The nearer we get to Him, the more intensely missionary we become."
—Henry Martyn, missionary to India and Persia

"The Great Commission is not an option to be considered; it is a command to be obeyed."
—Hudson Taylor

"We are debtors to every man to give him the gospel in the same measure in which we have received it."
—P. F. Bresee, founder of the Church of the Nazarene

"In the vast plain to the north I have sometimes seen, in the morning sun, the smoke of a thousand villages where no missionary has ever been."
—Robert Moffat, who inspired David Livingstone

"If a commission by an earthly king is considered an honor, how can a commission by a Heavenly King be considered a sacrifice?"
—David Livingstone

"Any church that is not seriously involved in helping fulfill the Great Commission has forfeited its biblical right to exist."
—Oswald J. Smith

Commission

Don't we all have the same mission?
It has been several chapters since we looked at our motivation and why we do what we do. As we continue on this innovation journey, I wanted to again lift your eyes upward and onward to the biblical commission which should drive us. This will be a short chapter but needs to be expressed.

> *Then Jesus came to them and said, "All authority in heaven and on earth has been given to me. Therefore go and make disciples of all nations, baptizing them in the name of the Father and of the Son and of the Holy Spirit, and teaching them to obey everything I have commanded you. And surely I am with you always, to the very end of the age."*
> *—Matthew 28:18–20 (NIV)*

Let's look at the same passage in *The Message*:

> *Jesus, undeterred, went right ahead and gave his charge: "God authorized and commanded me to commission you: Go out and*

> *train everyone you meet, far and near, in this way of life, marking them by baptism in the threefold name: Father, Son, and Holy Spirit. Then instruct them in the practice of all I have commanded you. I'll be with you as you do this, day after day after day, right up to the end of the age."*
> *—Matthew 28:18–20 (MSG)*

Jesus, as the perfect leader, left no doubt as to what we, His followers, should be about. A commission is an authoritative order, charge, or direction. Christ entrusted us with this awesome charge and then encouraged us He would be with us, "day after day after day"—every step of our journey.

Because we are people who have been sent, everything we lead, change, plan, move, adapt, and do should be based on this goal of making disciples. Everything should flow out this direction we've been given. And so, when it's necessary to change or to try something new (innovation) in order to accomplish this already stated God-given goal (the Great Commission), we need to do whatever it takes to reach the goal.

To the ends of the earth

> *"But you will receive power when the Holy Spirit comes on you; and you will be my witnesses in Jerusalem, and in all Judea and Samaria, and to the ends of the earth."*
> *—Acts 1:8 (NIV)*

My heart for missions and the Great Commission is shaped by this passage of Scripture. We must take the gospel to our Jerusalem, our Judea and Samaria, and to the ends of the earth. I like the simplicity and biblical way in which Church of the Highlands has established their missions ministry. They have three areas which their people can get involved in: local missions, national missions, and international missions. I think this is Scriptural and should be the missions strategy for all churches. How your particular church fleshes these three areas out is where you can differentiate and be creative.

For Church of the Highlands, they are involved in a number of local outreaches, including hosting and supporting their own Dream Center (like the ones we talked about in the Compassion chapter). Nationally, they are very involved with ARC, a church planting organization I've done some work with. I know for a fact they support (prayerfully, financially, and physically—by sending their people to serve) church plants around the country. Internationally, they send a number of student and adult teams on foreign missions trips to serve, lead, train, and evangelize. When I wrote this chapter they had mission trips planned to Santo Domingo, DR, Ghana, Rwanda, China, Brazil, Guatemala, South Korea, Czech Republic, Kenya, Nepal, and India. Amazing.

My last church had a similar strategy for missions.

They did local outreaches and ministries, including Mission Joplin, which I mentioned earlier (a ministry to clothe and feed poor or needy people). We participate in national mission trips, and we have several international mission trips. I've been on trips to Kenya and Haiti, but we also have trips to Brazil, Thailand, Cambodia, and various other countries depending on the year.

Now, your church may not have the attendance, resources (people and money), and opportunities Church of the Highlands has, but you can start somewhere. Hopefully, you're involved in your backyard—your Jerusalem—doing local outreach, service, and ministry. There are a number of avenues to be involved nationally. There are also a number of ways to be involved internationally, and I encourage you to do so. Take the model of local, national, and international and make it your own. Tailor to your people, your vision, and your passion.

Years ago, when I was in college, I made up my mind I was a WIT leader. Whatever It Takes. Period. I will do whatever it takes to reach people far from God. I have no sacred cows and nothing I won't cut, change, or try. Because I've given my life to the Great Commission, I will follow God wherever He leads and do whatever He asks. As we seek to lead out this commission, innovations and adventures are sure to follow. God be with you as you *go!*

"We must be global Christians with a global vision because our God is a global God."
—John Stott

"A congregation that is not deeply and earnestly involved in the worldwide proclamation of the gospel does not understand the nature of salvation."
—Ted Engstrom, World Vision

"Getting information off the Internet is like taking a drink from a fire hydrant."
—Mitchell Kapor

"These technologies can make life easier, can let us touch people we might not otherwise. You may have a child with a birth defect and be able to get in touch with other parents and support groups, get medical information, the latest experimental drugs. These things can profoundly influence life."
—Steve Jobs

"The single biggest problem with communication is the illusion that it has taken place."
—George Bernard Shaw

"A beautiful thing happens when we start paying attention to each other. It is by participating more in your relationship that you breathe life into it."
—Steve Maraboli, Unapologetically You: Reflections on Life and the Human Experience

Globalization

The Digital Church

Globalization has been described as an ongoing process by which regional economies, societies, and cultures have become integrated through a globe-spanning network of communication and trade. The term is sometimes used to refer to the spread of technology. For the purposes of this book, I'm going to use the term to talk about technology and the worldwide or universal Church.

The Stanford Encyclopedia of Philosophy says, "In popular discourse, globalization often functions as little more than a synonym for. . . the proliferation of new information technologies (the "Internet Revolution")." This is the first of two chapters (the other being Auscultation) where I even mention technology.

Too many people think technology is synonymous with innovation, and I strongly disagree. I've dedicated thirty-eight other chapters to showing how innovation can come about. However, the use of technology for good is something I believe God is redeeming in an innovative way, so in this chapter, we'll look at the globalization of our world and also my heart for the big "C" Church.

Did you know, according to the Internet World Stats website, about 3.3 billion people (or 46.4 percent of the world's population) access the Internet? Did you know according to a UN study, around 6 billion people have access to mobile phones? Yep: the most widely used form of technology and communication is held in your hand everyday—your mobile phone. The world is getting smaller and smaller through technology. I interact regularly with people from around the world via e-mail, Facebook, Instagram, and Twitter. I used to play a game called Words with Friends frequently with a missionary in China. She was usually awake the same time I am, and we played back and forth over our iPhones.

> *And as he taught them, He said, "Is it not written: 'My house will be called a house of prayer for all nations'?"*
> *—Mark 11:17 (NIV)*

I've found Twitter and Facebook to be a tremendous global prayer chain. I've had occasions (like when my oldest child, Grace, broke her wrist years ago, when I've been sick or stressed, when we found out my wife has kidney issues, and most recently, when my son, Tommy, got very ill) where something happened, and I sent out a simple Twitter or Facebook message requesting prayer I have received hundreds of responses from people around the world saying they are praying for me/us and offering words of encouragement. The world truly is getting smaller through technology.

I've also seen how technology can allow you to form relationships and is a networking machine. I'm a natural networker anyway and love meeting people, but the Internet is networking on steroids. For two years, I traveled doing my own speaking tour called the Church 2.0 Local Forum, where I would meet with church leaders in a given region of the country. I went to over twenty-two different major cities. I met with thousands of leaders face-to-face, but I felt as though I already knew lots of them because of how we had already been interacting over Twitter and Facebook. As a matter of fact, the only promotion and marketing for the tour was done via Twitter and Facebook. I would simply create an event page on Facebook, announce I was coming to a particular city, let word spread virally, and then arrive and see who showed up. It was a great experiment and experience in networking via the web. By the way, the result of those meetings and conversations around the country is this book you hold in your hand.

I've also held other events that were totally created via Twitter such as Train Friday—a social experiment when we had people from three states drive to Dallas, TX, to ride a train from downtown Dallas to Fort Worth and then spend the day hanging out in Fort Worth—this was a mixture of Christians and lost people responding to the buzz we created via Twitter.

We also held IHOP Tuesday on a day when IHOP was giving away free pancakes nationwide. We got the word out, we were going to meet at a particular IHOP in Dallas and people drove hours to get there, again including lost people. We had an interesting discussion with a Universalist who showed up, and I've tried to stay in touch with her.

I was once invited to speak on a tech panel for a monthly meeting of interactive marketing and search engine optimization (SEO) professionals in the Dallas area. One of the leaders of the group followed me on Twitter and invited me to come share my thoughts on the use of Twitter and how they could get the most out of Twitter for their businesses. This was a great opportunity for me to rub shoulders with a group of non-Christians and share what I do and how I see God redeeming technology. The group was fascinated, and I received several positive comments after the meeting. I used the tool of technology, and specifically Twitter, to open the door to a face-to-face meeting where I could show them I was a fun, normal guy and not all Christians are freaks (you know what I mean).

Meet-ups

I'm also very intentional and proactive about how I use Twitter (which I'll talk more about in the Auscultation chapter). When someone messages me who is local, I immediately follow up with a message back to them saying, "Hey. I see you live around here. Would you be up for grabbing a coffee or lunch together? I'd love to get to know you." I've had countless encounters and meetings with people I did not know but found through Twitter.

One memorable meeting was with the professor of Emerging Media at the University of Texas, Dallas. He actually teaches on the use of new media, such as Twitter and Facebook. For some strange reason, he followed me on Twitter, kept up with me, and was fascinated with my Church 2.0 Local Forums and my travels to teach people about how God was using technology. He messaged me one time when I was at a baseball game. I clicked on his profile and saw he was in Dallas. I sent him a message asking if he was interested in us doing lunch. He said yes, and we eventually met for lunch and had a great discussion. He was a vegan, and I'm, well—not—so our lunch was interesting to say the least. He suggested a special restaurant, and let's just say I stopped to eat again after our meeting. Again, this man was not a believer, but he was interested in me and what I was doing and my thoughts on technology and the Church. He couldn't believe churches would actually see technology as a good thing and seek to use it.

Another by-product of globalization is how news travels so quickly now. News stories are posted on Twitter before the news stations and newspapers have time to get the word out. When I was driving down the street in LA one year, I got a direct message (via Twitter) Michael Jackson had died. When Ted Kennedy had a stroke, I knew about it because of Twitter. Why is this important? Because my generation doesn't read the newspaper or watch the news. I never do. I get my news via technology.

When I ran into my friend, Cynthia Ware, at a conference, she mentioned Ted Kennedy having a stroke. I stopped her, and I said, "The only reason I even know what you're talking about is thanks to Twitter. Isn't it amazing?"

Another example of this phenomenon is when the airplane went down in the Hudson. Passengers on board were tweeting about it long before the news got hold of it. Another example of the use of social media is the situation in Iran in 2009. When journalists were kicked out of Iran, the people took to the web and started getting the story out virally. For a long while, many people's Twitter profile pictures were green in support of a free Iran. We carry a revolutionary tool around with us in our hands, and it's changing the face of news.

Even fairly recently, we've seen the devastation in Haiti and the relief efforts quickly spread around the world. The Red Cross raised support by having people text "Haiti" on their mobile phones. Several blogs and websites raised support and money to help out Haiti and later Chile. The world, through social media and the web quickly became smaller as we were brought face to face with the tragic realities of life after the earthquakes. This example of globalization points to the fact churches or organizations don't have to reinvent the wheel. Instead of trying to raise support themselves and make a little dent, most churches just encouraged their people to text and support the Red Cross. This proved to be most effective.

It takes time, work, and the right mindset:

> *We continually remember before our God and Father your work produced by faith, your labor prompted by love, and your endurance inspired by hope in our Lord Jesus Christ.*
> *—1 Thessalonians 1:3 (NIV)*

Several years ago, I wrote a blog entitled *Diving into Social Media* for Leadership Network's Digital Blog, and it got a lot of comments. It seemed to hit a nerve. In the blog, I talked about how some people give a weak attempt at social networking and social media strategies and then blame the technology when it doesn't "work." Here's an excerpt from the blog post:

> *I'm chewing on something, and honestly, it's still stirring in me, so you're reading thoughts in development—kind of like me thinking out loud. If "new wine must be put into new wineskins," I think new strategies and tools to reach, connect, engage, and mobilize people must be employed with new mindsets.*

The following is from my friend, Bill Seaver's MicroExplosion blog:

> *"A lot of companies are considering trying some new marketing approaches these days. They have become enamored or curious about the new social media tools, which are widely publicized and are trying to determine how it can work for them. This is a good spot to be in, but I've realized something is still missing. What's missing is the appropriate mindset needed to use the social media tools, techniques, and strategies well.* ***The old mindset won't work with the new tools.*** *They don't mix. Seth Godin wrote an entire book about this called* ***Meatball Sundae****.*
>
> *New marketing only works with the new mindset. Simply using the new tools with the old mindset won't bring about the marketing change you need and want."*

Many of you know I work with churches, organizations, and companies of all kinds. I'm brought in as an innovation consultant, and these days, almost all want to talk about using social media to build their brand and reach more people. What I've noticed is they get excited talking about these new tools and desire to use them but haven't had a change in mindset (like Bill said) and thus are striking out. I'm thinking of two cases in particular: One with a well-known Christian organization who desperately wants to reach the next generation and brought me in to consult on how to use social media to connect with them. The other is with a fitness/health company with whom I consult on using social media to help get their message out and expand their business.

Both want to tap into the buzz (or what Tony Steward calls "the awesomeness")—the latest tools and technology. Mind you: this isn't a bad thing. I do like to keep it in perspective and realize these are all just tools, but I like that they want to enter this world. The problem I see with these two organizations (and honestly, with a ton of churches, including my own) is they don't dive in. They try to dip their toes in the water and hope they catch a fish. A fisherman gets dirty, gets wet, and smells… I know when I fish, I don't wear my best clothes, and I don't expect to cast once and catch a bass on the first throw. You have to have patience. You have to be committed...

Some churches I work with don't "get" Facebook. Most really don't "get" Twitter. And don't get me started on SnapChat! There's only a handful of churches using Instagram and SnapChat in effective ways. My assessment is that most churches haven't been patient enough and don't live in those worlds.

One organization I work with had previously tried using Facebook in a broadcast-type model (we put out some info about our ministry and you come check it out). It didn't work and they blamed Facebook. I'm now working with them on how to engage people on Facebook and tools like those. You don't just put it out and say, "Come get."

You must strive for engagement. My friend Nils Smith recently blogged about this and encouraged church leaders to use social media to have conversations. He pointed to Dave Adamson, who recently said that "at North Point Church they strive to use more questions marks than periods." Read that again. Facebook is a social network, which means that conversation is central to the platform and the best way to create a conversation is to ask a question."

Another great tip from Nils Smith is to see social media as a place to celebrate and tell more stories. Smith say, "It sounds simple, but we focus more on our what God has ahead and too often don't take time to pause and look at all that God has done. Whether it's a ministry highlight or a personal testimony, capturing and sharing stories is critically valuable to your Facebook page content."

My prayer, heart's desire, and encouragement/challenge to you are to wrestle with Bill Seaver's quote: "Simply using the new tools with the old mindset won't bring about the marketing change you need and want."

I share this with you to challenge you to prayerfully think through the philosophy your organization has with technology, specifically, social media, and how you will strategically and intentionally use it as a tool and means of communication (two-way communication). I also share it to encourage you to endure and give your strategy time to work. It will take months and even years to grow a following on tools like Facebook, Instagram, and Twitter, but if you stick with it and consistently use those tools (with the right mindset); you'll eventually see fruit from them.

The world is in your hand

I once did a blog post entitled Must Have Mobile Strategy. With the realization that six billion people have mobile phones, it would behoove churches who are serious about fulfilling the Great Commission to design, strategize, and be intentional about tapping into the power of mobile technology.

I think one of the most basic and easy ways to communicate to people whose language you're trying to speak and reach them where they are (like a missionary) is to have a mobile version of your church or organization's website. Obviously, you must first have a main website—this is a given, but when I'm consulting with a church, the first thing I do is pull up their website on my phone. The standard now is for a website to be responsive. What's that? When a website is responsive, the layout responds (or, adapts) based on the size of the screen it's presented on. A responsive website automatically changes to fit the device you're reading it on (including your mobile phone).

There are several amazing stories of how churches are using the Internet for outreach and evangelism. Just read the January/ February issues of any Outreach magazine, which are their innovation issues, and you'll see story after story of churches that did extremely innovative things to create buzz, give people a place to connect, and start much-needed discussions. The stories tell of churches using the Internet in powerful and innovative ways to reach people far from God.

Some churches, following the leading of the Holy Spirit, have started a new innovation: an Internet campus. This is where people from around the globe gather online to worship. I will say I don't think an Internet campus is for every church, and I would caution a church to really pray through the why? and how? of how to go about starting one if they feel led by God to do it.

Another new form of outreach and communication for churches is creating an app for AppleTV or Roku (streaming services). I think this is awesome and my friends have a company to help you do it. In 2016, Apple's CEO, Tim Cook, made this bold statement: "The Future of TV is Apps." If you're serious about reaching beyond your four walls, look into this new opportunity.

We're in this together

Lastly, as we close this concept of globalization, I'd like to share my heart for the Church (capital "C")—which I believe is God's heart, too. You don't have to spend too much time with me to hear me start talking about my passion for the Church and the kingdom. I can't stand any spirit of competition between churches and believe we're all in this together.

A while back, it was announced on ChurchMarketingSucks.com that Gateway Church in Dallas is going to finance the Table Project and keep it free for other churches, and not just big mega-churches; it's the same kind of thing Life.Church has done with the YouVersion Bible app, the Church Online Platform, Church Metrics, and free resource downloads at Open. A lot of churches have shared their graphic resources, such as Church on the Move with *Seeds*, Southeast Christian Church with *Stuff I Can Use*, Elevation Church, and others.

Just recently Rock RMS went public and it's getting all the buzz. I'm working to transition our church over to it. Rock RMS is a free church database management software that does everything from community engagement, children check-in, reporting, online giving, calendar and event registration, and more. From their website: "Rock RMS is crafted to make you a ministry superhero with a balance of simplicity and power. Oh, and it's community supported (that means you can afford it)." The only cost you would have is hosting for your church, which is minimal.

Now don't be fooled because the software is free. Willow Creek Community Church uses it. I heard about it from a staff member at Max Lucado's church. This new, free church resource is legit! Check it out. I love seeing the church helping the church. We should be extravagant with one another and with the world.

It takes all types of churches to reach all types of people.
—@GregAtkinson

I'm not a hater on the mega-church or a hater on the house church. I believe God is using both in terrific ways to evangelize, build community, and grow in discipleship. My heart is for churches to share information, resources (including people and money), and relationships with other churches.

I believe Church leaders ought to be meeting with other Church leaders. Get to know the pastor down the street. Ask them if there's anything they need and how you can best pray for them. It will blow their mind and point them to God's heart for his body and his Bride. Every Saturday night, I text the local pastors in my city and tell them I'm praying for them. In the Collaboration chapter, I shared how some churches and organizations are working together for good. I think this is a piece of the globalization puzzle and a way in which together we can be innovative.

In April of 2013, I was the Keynote speaker at the ReConnect Conference in Ontario, Canada. In my Keynote talk, I said, "I don't just pastor my congregation. I pastor thousands through Facebook and Twitter (and now Instagram), and I get to consult with more than I can in person through my blog, phone and video conferencing. It's about leveraging these things— these tools for God's purposes."

If you start to picture the world as getting smaller and smaller through technology and see your role in reaching people of every nation, tribe, and tongue, you're on your way to new ideas, innovations, and breakthroughs in your ministry. When you seek to support, pray for, and befriend other churches and organizations, you love on the Bride of Christ and take another step closer to God's heart. And when this happens, you'll be ready to join God where He's at work—which could be at the church down the street.

"Innovation = revolution not evolution."
—Dawn Grover

"Most good things have been said far too many times and just need to be lived."
—Shane Claiborne

"Every generation needs a new revolution."
—Thomas Jefferson

"If by the mere force of numbers a majority should deprive a minority of any clearly written constitutional right, it might, in a moral point of view, justify revolution."
—Abraham Lincoln

"The more I get to know Jesus, the more trouble he seems to get me into."
—Shane Claiborne, The Irresistible Revolution: Living asan Ordinary Radical

"The greatest revolution of our generation is the discovery that human beings, by changing the inner attitudes of their minds, can change the outer aspects of their lives."
—William James

"Every revolution was first a thought in one man's mind."
—Ralph Waldo Emerson

Revolution

"Revolutions never go backwards."

That subheading above is a great, old proverb. The strange and innovative leader often acts like a revolutionary or leads a revolution—be it small or large. Revolution is about a mindset. One of the definitions of revolution is a sudden, complete, or marked change in something (i.e., the present revolution in church architecture.) As we survey the global Church, we see marked changes happening left and right. The thesaurus lists transformation as a synonym of revolution. Don't we all want to see our churches, organizations and communities transformed for the glory of God? I do—therefore I'm a revolutionary leader. Often, when people think of a revolution in Christian history, they immediately think about Martin Luther, the Reformation, and new theology. All of this was revolutionary, and Martin Luther was definitely a revolutionary leader, but this chapter is not about something as major as the Reformation—though it's worth noting and appreciating.

Dave Browning says, "The church has always undergone change, reformation, and revolution. But today, the major reforms taking place in the church are in the area of methodology rather than message, in practice more than theology. According to church growth expert Peter Wagner, "The radical change in the sixteenth century was largely theological. The current reformation is not so much a reformation of faith (the essential theological principles of the Reformation are intact) but a reformation of practice." (*Deliberate Simplicity* p. 19–20)

Browning goes on to shed light on a hard truth: "Yet for the church—which often institutionalizes its practices—reforms in methodology can prove every bit as epic as reforms in theology." Ah—but there's hope! Browning concludes his thought by saying, "Fortunately, the significant changes that used to take decades, if not centuries, for the church to embrace are now happening in months and years." (*Deliberate Simplicity* p. 20) I agree.

For some of you, your call is to lead through change or transition in your own context. Maybe God is leading you to be more relevant, purposeful, missional, or global. For some of you, maybe you can revolutionize through your weekly sermons. A.W. Tozer spoke of this new breed of preachers in his short article "*rophetic Preaching*—he dropped some pretty powerful words:

> *"If Christianity is to receive a rejuvenation, it must be by other means than any now being used. If the Church in the second half of this century is to recover from the injuries she suffered in the first half, there must appear a new type of preacher. The proper, ruler-of-the-synagogue type will never do. Neither will the priestly type of man, who carries out his duties, takes his pay and asks no questions nor the smooth-talking pastoral type, who knows how to make the Christian religion acceptable to everyone. All these have been tried and found wanting. Another kind of religious leader must arise among us. He must be of the old prophet type, a man who has seen visions of God and has heard a voice from the throne. When he comes (and I pray God there will be not one but many), he will stand in flat contradiction*

to everything our smirking, smooth civilization holds dear. He will contradict, denounce, and protest in the name of God and will earn the hatred and opposition of a large segment of Christendom. Such a man is likely to be leaned, rugged, blunt-spoken, and a little bit angry with the world. He will love Christ and the souls of men to the point of willingness to die for the glory of the one and the salvation of the other. But he will fear nothing that breathes with mortal breath. This is only to say that we need to have the gifts of the Spirit restored again to the Church. And it is my belief that the one gift we need most now is the gift of prophecy."

—A. W. Tozer

Preachers—read that again and let it soak in.

You only have to read the Bible through once to pick up on the theme of revolution. Isaiah, Jeremiah, Ezekiel, Amos, Joel, Hosea, Zechariah—these men were fully accepted of God but fully rejected by men. Peter and Paul were revolutionaries. Jesus was a revolutionary leader. In his Sermon on the Mount, He shook things up. Look at how many times He says, "You have heard it said. . . , but I tell you. . . ." Jesus had revolutionary teaching and concepts. Check out Matthew 5:21–22, 27–28, 31–35, 38–39, 43–44.

Jesus, as I've stated, is our role model for leadership, and throughout Scripture, we see his innovation through revolution. Jesus did not go with the status quo, and he definitely wasn't a people-pleaser. When you get a chance, just read through Mark chapter 2. Jesus was messing everybody up and didn't do what He was expected to do throughout the chapter.

Some revolutions are welcomed, respected, and seen as positive things (the point of innovation)—but even those have their critics. I think of revolutions like the printing press. Boy has that changed our world, but it had its critics. The Internet was a revolution, but it still has its haters. Movements like Promise Keepers back in the day were considered a revolutionary way to engage men in ministry, but I remember feminist groups protesting at their gatherings. Great revolutionaries like Martin Luther, Abraham Lincoln, Martin Luther King, Jr., and even Keith Green all had great messages and challenged the status quo—they shook things up and they were laughed at, mocked, threatened (Lincoln and MLK were eventually murdered), and definitely seen as strange.

Modern day revolutionaries are also received with mixed reviews. Leaders such as John MacArthur, Rob Bell, Shane Claiborne, Neil Cole, Frank Viola, George Barna (who wrote a book called *Revolution*), Francis Chan, Len Sweet, Louie Giglio, Michael Frost, Alan Hirsch, Hugh Halter, Mark Driscoll, Darrin Patrick, JD Greear, and my friends Shaun King, Dino Rizzo (who wrote *Servolution*—a revolution through serving) and Charles Lee—to name a few. Please know I don't agree with all of these current revolutionaries. Some of us don't see eye to eye, but they are leading their own revolution none the less.

People who lead a revolution are often seen as strange to the world around them (think John the Baptist—well, that dude was just strange, but you get the point). From Old Testament to New Testament, we see revolutionaries who at the time were ostracized, ridiculed, mocked, and seen as strange to their contemporaries.

Think of Martin Luther whose refusal to retract all of his writings at the demand of Pope Leo X in 1520 and the Holy Roman Emperor Charles V at the Diet of Worms in 1521 resulted in his excommunication by the pope and condemnation as an outlaw by the emperor.

Think of modern day revolutions like the Black Lives Matter movement and as I'm typing this, Colin Kaepernick started a revolution by not standing for the National Anthem, to protest the oppression of African-American people that still goes on to this day.

You may not agree with Kaepernick (and that's your American right, just as it is his to non-violently protest), but he is being joined by more and more athletes and at the time of this writing, his jersey was the #3 jersey sold in the NFL—and 1st among quarterbacks.

Guess what? Kaepernick is a backup quarterback! What that tells you is that the revolution that he set out to start has taken on legs and garnered support (whether you like it or not). Somebody is buying his jersey. We'll address some of this racial tension in the Bonus Chapter.

But like all revolutionaries in their time (good or bad), he's seen as strange by most. Right before I turned in this second edition, USA Today reported "Colin Kaepernick's gesture to kneel for the national anthem was repeated by high school players in a number of places before games Friday night." Wow. Now that is a revolution.

If you follow the example of Christ and lead a revolution (again, large or small).... If you feel like saying, "You've heard it said...but I tell you...." If you sense God leading you to shake things up and do things differently than the way they've always been done, then put your battle armor on and be brave. Be bold. Be courageous. Be revolutionary. Be strange!

"Imagination is more important that knowledge."
—Albert Einstein

"The soul without imagination is what an observatory would be without a telescope."
—Henry Ward Beecher

"A man to carry on successful business must've imagination. He must see things as innovation, a dream of the whole thing."
—Charles Schwab

"There is a boundary to men's passions when they act from feelings but none when they are under the influence of imagination."
—Edmund Burke

"To achieve the impossible, it is precisely the unthinkable that must be thought."
—Tom Robbins, Jitterbug Perfume

"The common question that gets asked in business is, 'why?' That's a good question, but an equally valid question is, 'why not?'"
—Jeffrey Bezos

"Play is the oxygen for imagination, which sparks creativity, which ignites innovation, which generates paradigm shifts."
—Len Sweet

Imagination

"There is nothing that cannot be achieved by firm imagination."

I love and resonate with that Japanese proverb above. Of all the subjects I've been asked to speak on, the imagination is far and away one of my favorites (behind innovation). I've had the privilege to speak at a number of pastors' conferences on the subject of being a creative communicator. I've often encouraged pastors to "paint a picture with your words. Don't underestimate the power of the imagination."

This reality really hit home for me several years ago. I was doing some consulting with Prestonwood Baptist Church in Plano, TX. I had done a seminar for their entire creative, worship, and tech leadership team. Their worship pastor at the time, Todd Bell, invited me back to speak to their entire teaching team (they had several teaching pastors plus interns), including Pastor Jack Graham, who at that time was the President of the Southern Baptist Convention.

I had prepared a class based on using visual aids, video clips, and illustrations to enhance your message and was ready to go when God interrupted me the night before. God, in His gentle whisper, reminded me Jack Graham is heard on radios all over the world and all of what I was prepared to teach on wouldn't apply to those simply listening over the radio and not able to see a video clip. God laid it on my heart I should include the part on imagination I had taught at previous conferences. I added it in last second and thanked God for redirecting my good intentions. Something I said to them and I say at every conference I speak at, is to not be afraid of having your video screens go to black and then say something like, "Close your eyes and listen as I read this story." or "Close your eyes and listen as I read this passage of Scripture."

> *I think most communicators underestimate the power of the imagination. Want to improve your effectiveness as a communicator? Paint a picture with your words.*
> *—@GregAtkinson*

The honest truth is too many communicators rely too much on tech; they're lazy in their preparation and it shows. If you were to preach on a Sunday and the power went out and you couldn't use any visuals, PowerPoint, or videos, and your sermon fell apart, you're basically admitting you had nothing to say. Videos and graphics are supplemental enhancements—they can't be the meat of what you communicate. Read those last two sentences again.

Please know I'm all for using media and have taught on it widely, but I always caution my audience to not let the "tail wag the dog." You should never say, "Hey, I found this cool video clip. Let's build a message around it." This way is backwards. Plan to preach what God has laid on your heart, rooted in Scripture, and if there happens to be a video clip which supports or illustrates one of your points, great! But it must be in a supporting role. I'll step down off my soap box and move on to the power of tapping into the imagination.

> *"Watch out for false prophets. They come to you in sheep's clothing, but inwardly, they are ferocious wolves. By their fruit, you will recognize them. Do people pick grapes from thorn bushes or figs from thistles? Likewise, every good tree bears good fruit, but a bad tree bears bad fruit. A good tree cannot bear bad fruit, and a bad tree cannot bear good fruit. Every tree that does not bear good fruit is cut down and thrown into the fire. Thus, by their fruit you will recognize them."*
> *—Matthew 7:15–20 (NIV)*

Not only is Jesus the perfect model for leadership, He is the perfect model for communication. Jesus was the greatest preacher who ever lived. You only have to read the gospels once to see how Jesus captured the imaginations of all who came to hear Him. Jesus understood if you can capture one's imagination, it will take them on a glorious adventure and have far greater impact than a picture or video we try to show them.

Often, I've used the example of Moses parting the Red Sea. I've asked classrooms full of people to close their eyes and picture the giant walls of water on each side of them, with fishes, whales, and sea creatures swimming about, but not breaking through the walls of water. Then, I would show them a drawing of Moses parting the Red Sea which some artist came up with and I'd ask: "Which was better? What you saw in your mind or this picture of a drawing?" It was always what they had pictured in their mind.

How does this play into innovation? If you want to lead an innovative organization and an innovative team, you've got to capture the imagination of those you work for, under, and with.

You might say: "I thought you said all true; biblical innovation comes from God." I believe this, yes, and this doesn't contradict that. God has given us our imagination as a gift. Why else would you have it? Jesus knew the power of imagination and He often tapped into His with parables and stories. When you unleash the imagination of yourself and your team, you open up a world of possibilities for innovation in your organization.

> *"Creativity is part of God's divine nature, and He has given it to us as a gift. Like so many of God's gifts, creativity is often neglected or wrongfully used. . . .Imagination is the first storytelling tool. To properly tell a story, you must see it in your mind."*
> *—John Walsh, author of (The Art of Storytelling p. 88)*

> *"We can apply this understanding to our own creative efforts at many levels. On the most superficial level, we learn from the prophets that the tools best suited for communicating to the imagination are image, parables and sometimes even bizarre activity! At a deeper level, we learn that if we are to effect permanent change in people's hearts, we must do more than simply teach them facts or reduce them to some emotional experience. Like the prophets, we must learn to reach out to the heart as well as the mind by speaking to the imagination. We must allow our audience the freedom to make realizations on their own, as with the parables of the prophets, particularly the prophet Jesus!"*
> *—Michael Card, (Scribbling in the Sand pp. 60–61)*

Imagination is for adults, too.

Do you realize as you lead your staff, your volunteer teams, and each and every meeting you're a part of, you have the opportunity (if you'll seize it) to speak directly to the imagination of each person in the room? The companies in the business world who are recognized as innovative are full of dreamers and leaders and employees who regularly tap into their imagination.

David Enyart said, "Frequently, creativity and imaginativeness are casualties of ministerial education. Ministers start to mistrust or ignore their own creative impulses; they come to view imagination as a child's play toy rather than an essential tool for vibrant communication." What a shame. I can only imagine (yes, I meant to say that) how many churches are led by imagination-less leaders. Please allow me to free you, my brothers and sisters: God has gifted you with an imagination for a reason. It was no accident, and it wasn't just for silly games or fantasies when you were a child. Your imagination is a sharp tool which, if you tap into it, God can use it to lead you to something new and innovative in your leadership.

I want to share another quote from Michael Card's amazing book *Scribbling in the Sand* –it's on my must-read list. This quote is from p. 55-56. Michael relays this concept much more effectively than I can. Here are his thoughts on the imagination:

> *"Our imaginations are involved in every area of our lives, in everything we do or say or are. It is no wonder that God is so intent upon recapturing them. Therefore, we must seek to understand the imagination biblically, that is, Christ-centeredly.*
>
> *The imagination is the bridge between the heart and the mind, integrating both, allowing us to think/understand with our hearts and feel/emote with our minds. It is a vehicle for truth. Through the use of images, metaphors, stories and paradoxes that demand our attention, it calls for our interaction. The*

> *imagination is a powerful means for communicating truths about God, and so God shows an awesome regard for the imagination in His word.*
>
> *Because we are called to creativity, a working, gut-level understanding of the imagination is vital. It can be our greatest strength or our greatest weakness. To harness the imagination, or better yet, to bring it under submission to Christ is something about which we don't talk or pray or do enough."*

Michael Card, whom I respect, believes having a "working, gut-level understanding of the imagination is vital." Not only this, he thinks it can be "our greatest strength or our greatest weakness." Wow! What if you or someone on your team has this glaring weakness which has never been pointed out? What if you're not tapping into the power of the imagination and your leadership, team, service, and ministry are suffering because of it?

Mark Batterson wrote an article titled *Postmodern Wells*.

In it, he said, "Don't get me wrong: the message is sacred. But methods are not. And the moment we anoint our methods as sacred, we stop creating the future and start repeating the past. We stop doing ministry out of imagination and start doing ministry out of memory." Are you doing ministry out of imagination or out of memory?

Some of these chapters are no-brainers and easy to agree with. Some of these chapters you'll need to wrestle with and chew on and let it sink in over time. For some of you, this might be one of those chapters. My encouragement to you is to study Scripture, particularly Christ in the gospels and see how He engaged the imagination in His ministry, communication, and leadership. Mull over the fact you even have an imagination and ask the deeper question: Why? Why didn't your imagination fade away during adolescence? How can it be a crucial tool in your tool belt today as a leader? And how can God use my imagination and the imaginations of those I lead and work/serve with to lead us into new and innovative ways of doing ministry?

"The vital connection between the Word and prayer is one of the simplest and earliest lessons of the Christian life."
—Andrew Murray, With Christ in the School of Prayer

"It is in the process of being worshipped that God communicates His presence to men."
—Reflections on the Psalms, C. S. Lewis

"I had then, and at other times, the greatest delight in the holy Scriptures, of any book whatsoever. Oftentimes in reading it, every word seemed to touch my heart. I felt a harmony between something in my heart and those sweet powerful words. I seemed often to see so much light, exhibited by every sentence, and such a refreshing ravishing food communicated that I could not get along in reading. Used oftentimes to dwell long on one sentence, to see the wonders contained in it, and yet almost every sentence seemed to be full of wonders."
—Jonathan Edwards, quoted in Jonathan Edwards and the Bible by Robert E. Brown (Bloomington: Indiana University Press, 2002), p. 3.

"This book contains the mind of God, the state of man, the way of salvation, the doom of sinners, and the happiness of believers. Its doctrines are holy, its precepts are binding, its histories are true, and its decisions are immutable. Read it to be wise, believe it to be safe, and practice it to be holy. It contains light to direct you, food to support you and comfort to cheer you. It is the traveller's map, the pilgrim's staff, the pilot's compass, the soldier's sword, and the Christian's charter. Here paradise is restored, heaven is opened and the gates of hell are disclosed. Christ is its grand object, our good is its design, and the glory of God its end. It should fill the memory, rule the heart, and guide the feet. Read it slowly, frequently, and prayerfully. It is a mine of wealth, a paradise of glory, and a river of pleasure. It is given you in life, will be opened in the judgment, and will be remembered forever. It involves the highest responsibility, will reward the greatest labor, and will condemn all who trifle with its sacred contents."
—Anonymous

Illumination

Staring right into the face of God

How would you like to stand toe-to-toe with God and stare Him dead in the face? Guess what? You can! Because the Bible is God's Living Word and John 1 tells us Jesus is the Word. Every time you read your Bible, you are staring face-to-face with God. I've mentioned before in *Experiencing God*, Blackaby teaches us we can discern God's will through Scripture, prayer, the Holy Spirit, people and circumstances. This chapter is about how God speaks to us through His word.

> *Open my eyes that I may see wonderful things in Your law.*
> *—Psalm 119:18 (NIV)*

I've talked a lot about the mindset and the posture in which we should approach certain things. What is the type of posture you come with to read God's word? Do you scan it quickly or do you savor it? Do you have days when you read it out of duty and kind of check it off your list? I'm sure we all do. My intent in this chapter is to encourage you to be intentional about praying God would "open your eyes" each time you stop to encounter Him through His word.

In the Inquisition chapter, we discussed how we go seek God in prayer, and He speaks to us in His still, small voice—the whisper. In the Revelation chapter, we discussed how God comes to us and surprises us sometimes. Revelation is rare and precious. Illumination can happen daily. God primarily chooses to reveal Himself now through His word, so this is the grid which we must put everything through.

You might think you heard God's whisper or thought your dream meant something, but if it contradicts Scripture, it's misleading. The Bible trumps everything else. God's word is paramount. The Intersection (which we'll discuss in a later chapter) is when prayer, Scripture, the Holy Spirit, people and circumstances all line up and point in the same direction—this is a true God moment which can change the course of your life. So how does illumination play into innovation? Glad you asked.

> *All Scripture is inspired by God and is useful to teach us what is true and to make us realize what is wrong in our lives. It corrects us when we are wrong and teaches us to do what is right. God uses it to prepare and equip His people to do every good work.*
> *—2 Timothy 3:16–17 (NLT)*

I like the *New Living Translation* of the above verse. It reads, Scripture "teaches us to do what is right" and "God uses it to prepare and equip His people to do every good work." God uses His word to prepare and equip you to do good works. What may be something new, innovative, or a breakthrough in ministry to you in your situation may be something you find buried in the treasure of Scripture.

When you pray the Bible would be illumined right before your eyes; you're praying the living word, truly would come alive in your heart and life. "His divine power has given us everything we need for life and godliness through our knowledge of Him who called us by his own glory and goodness" (2 Pet 1:3 NIV).

> *For the word of God is alive and active.*
> *—Hebrews 4:12 (NIV)*

Do you want to hear from God? Be led by Him? Know what the right thing to do is? Get in His word. Consume it. Devour it. In order to lead you must be led. Let God through His Holy Spirit lead you in all things. God's word is "living and active"—it really has the answer, wisdom, direction, and guidance you need and are desperately searching for.

> *Do not conform any longer to the pattern of this world, but be transformed by the renewing of your mind. Then you will be able to test and approve what God's will is–his good, pleasing and perfect will.*
> *—Romans 12:2 (NIV)*

I'm using lots of Scripture in this chapter because it's appropriate and has to do with this whole concept. Romans 12 tells us we need our mind renewed. As we daily renew our mind, God is able to whisper to us and teach us. The spiritual life is about positioning ourselves or assuming a posture which frees us to respond to God's activity around us. When we are transformed by God's word, we are ready to respond to His leading.

> *Dear friend, listen well to my words; tune your ears to my*

> *voice. Keep my message in plain view at all times. Concentrate! Learn it by heart! Those who discover these words live, really live; body and soul, they're bursting with health.*
> *—Proverbs 4:20–22 (MSG)*

Again, you may know this passage of Scripture well, but we receive a fresh breath of air and perspective looking at it in *The Message*. God tells us to keep His message "in plain view at all times. Concentrate! Learn it by heart!" And the good news! "Those who discover these words live, really live." Now we must understand this in the full view of the totality of Scripture. James 1:22 calls us to live the word, not just read it. We must "do what it says", which is what some of the other chapters are about (Commission, Compassion, Execution, etc.).

So, if we sincerely pray before we read God's word, even a simple, little prayer like Psalm 119:18 and approach Scripture with a hungry and sensitive heart—combined with a posture of reverence and teachability, God can then open our eyes and speak to our hearts. When this happens, and you obey, there's a good chance you'll find, as a result, yourself doing something innovative.

Again, God is the One doing a new thing (Isa 43:19), and because He is omniscient and transcends time, He has put hidden gems in His word which will speak to us today so relative and practical you would think He wrote it yesterday. Do you really believe a book written thousands of years ago can tell you how to live, learn, and lead today? I do. The good news is God desires to share His heart with you. He's not hiding from you or playing games.

Jeremiah 29:11–14 tells us, "You will seek me and find me when you seek me with all your heart. I will be found by you," declares the Lord." So my encouragement for you to is to seek

God with all your heart (with pure motives—just to know Him, His heart and His will) and see what happens—it just may lead to something new.

"The vital connection between the Word and prayer is one of the simplest and earliest lessons of the Christian life."
—Andrew Murray, With Christ in the School of Prayer

"It is in the process of being worshipped that God communicates His presence to men."
—Reflections on the Psalms, C. S. Lewis

"I had then, and at other times, the greatest delight in the holy Scriptures, of any book whatsoever. Oftentimes in reading it, every word seemed to touch my heart. I felt a harmony between something in my heart and those sweet powerful words. I seemed often to see so much light, exhibited by every sentence, and such a refreshing ravishing food communicated that I could not get along in reading. Used oftentimes to dwell long on one sentence, to see the wonders contained in it, and yet almost every sentence seemed to be full of wonders."
—Jonathan Edwards, quoted in Jonathan Edwards and the Bible by Robert E. Brown (Bloomington: Indiana University Press, 2002), p. 3.

"This book contains the mind of God, the state of man, the way of salvation, the doom of sinners, and the happiness of believers. Its doctrines are holy, its precepts are binding, its histories are true, and its decisions are immutable. Read it to be wise, believe it to be safe, and practice it to be holy. It contains light to direct you, food to support you and comfort to cheer you. It is the traveller's map, the pilgrim's staff, the pilot's compass, the soldier's sword, and the Christian's charter. Here paradise is restored, heaven is opened and the gates of hell are disclosed. Christ is its grand object, our good is its design, and the glory of God its end. It should fill the memory, rule the heart, and guide the feet. Read it slowly, frequently, and prayerfully. It is a mine of wealth, a paradise of glory, and a river of pleasure. It is given you in life, will be opened in the judgment, and will be remembered forever. It involves the highest responsibility, will reward the greatest labor, and will condemn all who trifle with its sacred contents."
—Anonymous

Meditation

More than meets the eye

Jonathan Edwards gave us a little insight into his spiritual life. He said, oftentimes, he would "dwell long on one sentence (of the Bible), to see the wonders contained in it." In the last chapter, we looked at how God can speak to us through His holy word. How partnering with the Holy Spirit, He can illuminate the verses to us and make the words come alive in our hearts and lives.

As I said, for some, this happens daily; for others, this happens on occasion. It really does come down to the amount of time you spend in the marvelous book. Sometimes, however, God will withhold all of a particular passage of Scripture from us for various reasons.

Maybe we're not ready to comprehend all the nugget contains. Maybe we approached our quiet time this particular day casually and irreverently, and He doesn't want to be taken for granted. Maybe we scanned the page, quickly rushing through our scheduled time in the word, and He doesn't want to be rushed. For whatever reason, God sometimes will wait to open our eyes and hearts to all He has for us.

> *Study this Book of Instruction continually. Meditate on it day and night so you will be sure to obey everything written in it. Only then will you prosper and succeed in all you do.*
> *—Joshua 1:8 (NLT)*

The Bible instructs, encourages, exhorts and challenges us to study it continually. In addition, it goes on to tell us to "meditate on it day and night." I'm coming out of a season where I've personally been meditating on Psalm 103 for over three years. I think I'm ready to move on and feel God had laid the Sermon on the Mount, Romans, and Hebrews on my heart as the next places for me to dive deeper.

I like to use the phrase "chew on" something for a while. My wife can't stand when I say I'm "chewing on something" and thinks it's unprofessional and not something an author should say in a book. I'm a good ol' Carolina boy, and for me, I like to use the phrase "chew on something", so forgive me if it drives you crazy, too.

The last three plus years of chewing on Psalm 103 have been unbelievable. Of course, I try to read my Bible regularly and vary where I read, but I keep coming back to Psalm 103 over and over again. It brings me peace and gives me clarity, comfort, and direction. When I've been stressed and started having anxiety attacks, I've laid in the bed with my eyes closed and had my wife read Psalm 103 to me, sometimes repeating it. I love what John Chrysostom said about the Scriptures— "the more familiar they become, the more they reveal their hidden treasures and yield their indescribable riches." I don't know about you, but I can vouch for this.

I went through a season in my life where I camped out in Ps 51 for a long time. Those words were words of life, hope, and cleansing I so desperately needed. I felt a bond with the psalmist as if I had written those words myself.

Another season in my life I spent over a year in the book of James. Another season I spent in the book of Romans. I don't have to tell you (but I don't mind reminding you), God's word is a priceless treasure. We know all Scripture is God-breathed (2 Tim 3:16) and thus cannot be treated like just any book. Don't get me wrong. I'm a reader. You wouldn't believe how many books I read each year. But I realize these are simply that—books. The Bible is "living and active" (Heb 4:12). It has stood the test of time and is a "lamp unto our feet" (Ps 119:105).

I'm sure you hold the word of God in the same esteem I do and have just as much reverence for it. My point is if we truly believe the Bible is God's word to us and is different from all other books, then we must devour it and meditate on it day and night.

W. Tozer encouraged us to "constantly practice the habit of inwardly gazing upon God." Brother Lawrence wrote an entire book dedicated to practicing the presence of God. Jesus Himself told Satan in the wilderness, "Man does not live on bread alone but on every word that comes from the mouth of God" (Matt 4:4). Ideally, we should have the same relationship with our spiritual food as we do with our physical food. How long can you go without food? How long can you go without water? How long can we truly last without quality and consistent time in the word? I'm preaching to myself here, friends.

For a moment forget about being innovative and let's just focus on enduring and lasting in ministry. While I'm writing this, I asked a number of friends to do guest posts on my blog so I could concentrate on this book for a season and not have to worry about my blog. One of the guest posts was by a pastor and friend (Michael Robison) who wrote about how only one out of ten pastors retire from their position. Why? Burnout, stress, mental, and physical deterioration and moral failures. He ended the blog post with the encouragement, "Don't let yourself become one of those statistics!"

Friends, if the Bible encourages everyone to meditate day and night, how much more true is it for pastors and those on the front lines of ministry? Please hear me. I want you to be healthy and grow as an organization. I want you to be innovative and creative and full of life. But none of it matters if you aren't healthy and growing personally. If you don't get anything else I'm saying, hear my heart: Bathe in Scripture. Soak it up. Chew on it. Treasure it. Marvel in it. When you're done with this book, it can sit on a shelf and collect dust, but may it never be with our Bible.

Let's dig deeper

I know what some of you are thinking: I'm in the Bible daily or every week. Allow me some grace to dig a little deeper. You know what I've found over the years? Pastors and ministers of the gospel, for the most part, really struggle with having a consistent quiet time. Follow me now.

Many pastors can't read their Bible without preparing for a sermon or looking for an illustration (it's work to them). Many youth pastors can't simply spend time getting to know God; they, too are searching for material and illustrations. Many worship leaders who are also songwriters turn to Scripture to find the perfect lyric for a new song.

Are any of these things wrong? Of course not. Preachers should base their messages out of Scripture (youth pastors, too). Songwriters in the Church should sing songs inspired from the word of God. Just don't let this be the only time you turn to the Bible—this is where things can get unhealthy, and I've talked with enough pastors to know what a struggle this is.

What I'm suggesting will require a great deal of discipline. You need time on your calendar for sermon preparation, and you also need devotional time, and the reading of Scripture simply to know God more and fall more in love with Jesus—so schedule it and put it on your calendar, too. This, my friends, is just the basics—a healthy starting point. What this chapter and the principles contained within are about is carrying the word of God around with you in your heart and mind. Chewing on it. Meditating on it day and night.

You may meditate on a verse, passage, or chapter of Scripture for weeks, months or years before you see something new and get new ideas and inspirations. That's okay. Remember, God's not in a rush. He cares about the process more than the destination. We may want to be innovative, but He desires we be holy. We may want to lead strong and he just wants us to be healthy in every way.

> *My son, do not forget my teaching but keep my commands in your heart for they will prolong your life many years and bring you prosperity. Let love and faithfulness never leave you; bind them around your neck, write them on the tablet of your heart. Then you will win favor and a good name in the sight of God and man. Trust in the Lord with all your heart and lean not on your own understanding; in all your ways acknowledge him, and he will make your paths straight. Do not be wise in your own eyes; fear the Lord and shun evil. This will bring health to your body and nourishment to your bones.*
> *—Proverbs 3:1–8 (NIV)*

Being an innovative leader first requires you are a leader—not just this, but a healthy leader. A strong, wise, and healthy leader knows to ask for help and "lean not" on his or her own understanding. James 1:5 encourages us to ask for wisdom when we feel we need it. When you consume the word, allow it to shape your thoughts, desires, dreams, and motives; you open up the possibility for God to not only do something new (innovative) through you; you open up the possibility for God to do something significant and eternal through you.

Don't you want your life to make a kingdom difference? Don't you want to storm the gates of hell? I do. I'd encourage you to read and reread this chapter, but more importantly, read and reread God's word. Ask the Holy Spirit to lead you to the place He wants you to dive deeper and meditate on. The Spirit will guide you, but you must be intentional and ask God to speak to your heart, open your eyes, and give you the grace, patience and persistence to chew on a passage for as long as it takes.

> *Oh, how I love your law! It is my meditation all the day. Your commandment makes me wiser than my enemies for it is ever with me. I have more understanding than all my teachers for your testimonies are my meditation.*
> *—Psalm 119:97–99 (ESV)*

Have you ever just fallen in love with a passage of Scripture? I forgot earlier to mention the season I spent in Ps 119. Actually, I've had a few seasons in Ps 119. I love the insight, boldness, and confidence of the above passage: "I have more understanding than all my teachers for your testimonies are my meditation." Boy, have I lived this verse out. I've served with people much older than me, but they were so spiritually immature it was just plain sad. Because I made an intentional choice to devote myself to God and His word (including meditating on it), I would often see the right thing to do long before those with a lot more grey hair than I have.

Maybe you've experienced this before? A time where due to a God-given conviction, vision, passion, or insight which was placed in your heart, you just knew what to do in a given situation, even in times of crisis. If you haven't already, I encourage you to get Brother Lawrence's book, *The Practice of the Presence of God*. I imagine Brother Lawrence was one cool cat. Always calm under pressure and operating out of an abiding and deep connection with his Creator. God's word is the leader's lifeline and the wise and strange leader will choose to meditate on it day and night.

"Everything that can be counted does not necessarily count; everything that counts cannot necessarily be counted."
—Albert Einstein

"The most serious mistakes are not being made as a result of wrong answers. The truly dangerous thing is asking the wrong question."
—Peter Drucker

"One of the great mistakes is to judge policies and programs by their intentions rather than their results."
—Milton Friedman

"The pure and simple truth is rarely pure and never simple."
—Oscar Wilde

"I know that half of my advertising dollars are wasted. . . I just don't know which half."
—John Wanamaker

"True genius resides in the capacity for evaluation of uncertain, hazardous, and conflicting information."
—Winston Churchill

"The only man who behaves sensibly is my tailor; he takes my measurements anew every time he sees me, while all the rest go on with their old measurements and expect me to fit them."
—George Bernard Shaw

Evaluation

Count the cost

We're three-fourths of the way through this book, and I thought I'd share something I consider to be obvious and understood, but I learned a long time ago to not assume anything. This chapter is on the act of evaluation. After all, if you don't stop to evaluate and assess what you're doing, how will you ever know what needs to change, adapt, subtract or be added?

Please know my heart. I don't want you to innovate for the sake of innovation alone. I want you to follow the Spirit's leading and join God where He is at work. Part of the equation is finding out where He's not at work. We all wish we could hear an audible voice from heaven telling us what to do next, but when this doesn't happen, we're left to step out in faith and lead. Leading, and especially leading through change, can happen with great confidence when you've done your homework and thoroughly evaluated and analyzed why, what, how, who and when you do something.

For which of you, desiring to build a tower, does not first sit

> *down and count the cost, whether he has enough to complete it? Otherwise, when he has laid a foundation and is not able to finish, all who see it begin to mock him, saying, 'This man began to build and was not able to finish.' Or what king, going out to encounter another king in war, will not sit down first and deliberate whether he is able with ten thousand to meet him who comes against him with twenty thousand? And if not, while the other is yet a great way off, he sends a delegation and asks for terms of peace.*
> *—Luke 14:28–32 (ESV)*

The why, what, how, who and when—the Bible calls it counting the cost. It's vital that leaders count the cost of what they are considering God is leading them to do. It's also crucial you evaluate how what you're currently doing is working for your organization. I mentioned finding out where God's not at work. I know some of you wish I would stop referring back to the Subtraction chapter, but for some of you, it's the whole reason God led you to pick up this book.

You must constantly evaluate what's working and what's not and drop anything which will keep you from your vision, mission, and isn't effective at reaching people. People are very busy these days. They don't need us to fill up their schedules. They need us to pick a select few things for them to dedicate their time, treasure, and talent to. What this may be in your setting will have to be determined through this process of evaluation.

I learned something fascinating in Scott Wilson's book *Steering through Chaos*. He shared something he had learned from Dr. Samuel Chand—a noted author and consultant who has helped thousands of Christian leaders. Dr. Chand shared with Scott a variation of something called a sigmoid curve.

Basically, every organization (including the Church), experiences natural cycles of growth and decline. Most leaders wait until they get to the decline part of their organization and then say, "Something needs to change or we'll die." They get into panic mode and must lead change in a time of low morale and momentum (very difficult).

What Dr. Chand and Scott suggest in the book is taking action and implementing change in the good times (when you're experiencing growth and everyone is happy). Scott calls this time between the envisioning of the new wave of change at a time of growth after a period of preparation "chaos" (thus the title of the book).

Again, this fascinates me, and I don't want to quote Scott too much. I'll simply encourage you to get his book and read it. But this concept intrigues me. What he teaches is the time of change is not when things are going bad and you know you must change or die, but to begin to implement change when things are booming and exploding with growth.

This is a crazy concept, but one worth discussing as a team and wrestling with. Please read Scott's entire book in order to have a better understanding of this whole concept. I'm only sharing the tip of the iceberg, and this is something I'm exploring at my own church currently. We are in a season of growth and high morale. According to Scott's book, now is the time to make a change.

I've served as a consultant to churches, organizations, and ministry companies for a number of years. One reason I love doing this is because God has given me the gift of asking tough questions. I'm able to see what's going on and then ask the necessary questions which will bring to head issues which need changing or fixing. Good leaders know how to ask the right questions, when to ask the questions, and who to ask the questions to.

"Then you will know the truth, and the truth will set you free."
—John 8:32 (NIV)

Scott Hodge, a friend and pastor of The Orchard in Aurora, IL, wrote about the necessity of asking questions in Scott Wilson's book Steering through Chaos (on p. 53). He said, "As difficult and challenging as asking questions can be, when a church or organization is facing a crisis or a need for change, asking the tough questions that no one wants to ask can be one of the healthiest and most freeing steps we can take." Scott went on to share some great questions they asked during their journey of transition at The Orchard. These questions are wonderful insights and good for all ministry leaders to ask.

They asked: "Who has God positioned us to reach? What are we currently doing that is making it difficult to reach people? What do we need to stop doing? What do we need to start doing? Is this event or ministry helping or hindering our efforts to reach people?" Scott encouraged leadership to "start by asking questions! It may be a painful process in the short term, but eventually, the answers will open your eyes to the truth. And once you know the truth, your church will be free to follow God."

Five Crucial Questions to Ask

So if, like me, you agree with Scott Hodge, that asking tough questions is essential to leadership, then let's look at the questions I alluded to earlier. To lead an effective evaluation process, you must ask why? What? How? Who? And When?

First: ***Why?*** Why are we doing a particular ministry or initiative? Why should we do a new ministry or initiative? This goes back to your vision, your mission, your commission, and your motivation. How God has uniquely shaped and called your organization will play into why you would ever do something. If you can't solidly answer why you're doing something—if it doesn't help accomplish your vision—don't do it.

Second: *What?* What do we need to stop doing? What do we need to start doing? Please know sometimes, you can't start doing something until you stop doing something you're already doing. If you wrestle with this, go back and read the Subtraction chapter. You have to ask both what questions. You can't just keep adding stuff. You'll go crazy, be ineffective, spread thin, and not in the center of God's will.

Third: *How?* How you do something is huge! This goes back to the posture I referred to early in this book of how we approach God. We should humbly approach God with a sincere question of how He wants us to go about doing something. This takes patience, intentionality, and a hunger for wisdom. We know God gives wisdom to all who ask (James 1:5), but you need to have the humility and presence of mind to ask.

Fourth: *Who?* Who should be a part of what we do going forward is a sensitive and delicate question. One part of evaluation is evaluation of personnel. It's all about having the right people on the bus. The whole subtraction concept is sometimes used to find out who needs to leave the team in order for you to move forward as an organization. Some people's positions outgrow them (I'm talking about paid and volunteer leaders). Maybe someone was called to start a ministry but is not the person to lead it going forward. Think about this hard.

You will have to make the tough who call in order to break through your next barrier of growth. Handle people slowly and prayerfully. Go back to the how question and if you need to let someone go, ask God how to go about it, and treat your people graciously who have served your organization. I know some pastors who have had to let a staff member go but called up another church and gave them a huge recommendation and said they'd be a great fit for them.

Finally: *When?* When to let someone go, when to end an existing ministry, and when to start a new ministry—all these must be prayerfully and strategically considered. You don't rush through things like this. Timing is everything—just ask any famous home-run hitter.

When is a key question because it will keep you in step with the Holy Spirit. You don't want to rush or get ahead of God and you don't want to be behind. One of my mentors, Dr. John Swadley, taught me that there is a right way to make the right decision and a wrong way to make a right decision. Please chew and think on his words of wisdom. What is the right way to make the right decision? Like Dr. Chand's curve example, if you wait too long to implement change (when you're in decline and dying), you may never recover. If God is telling you to subtract, add, adapt, implement change or innovate, you must do it as He leads and in His timing.

I spoke at a conference once in Indianapolis, and I spoke briefly on this subject. Someone said, "This seems hard." We were talking about leading volunteers and how I've always expected a lot from my volunteers. I think it's a privilege and honor to serve God and not something to be taken lightly. I talked about the times I've had to fire volunteers. The person in my class asked how I went about something like this and I said, "Leadership is tough. It takes the gifting, calling, heart, courage, and vision of a leader."

I say this because God may call you to do something (meaning start, stop, change or adapt) which others think is crazy or strange. Many will question your heart and your motives. Scott Wilson addresses this "chaos" in his great book. Though this book is about strange leadership, I want to encourage you to rest in God's leading and calling if you've properly done your evaluation and make a decision out of this place of confidence. Not confidence in your idea but confidence in Christ, His Spirit's leading, and His provision every step of the way. Others might think you're strange (as they have many throughout history), but if you're in the center of God's will, you'll be exactly where God wants you and that's a great place to be.

"The ear of the leader must ring with the voices of the people."
—Woodrow Wilson

"The most basic of all human needs is the need to understand and be understood. The best way to understand people is to listen to them."
—Ralph Nichols

"One friend, one person who is truly understanding, who takes the trouble to listen to us as we consider a problem, can change our whole outlook on the world."
—Dr. E. H. Mayo

"Great ideas, it is said, come into the world as gently as doves. Perhaps, then, if we listen attentively, we shall hear amid the uproar of empires and nations a faint flutter of wings; the gentle stirring of life and hope."
—Albert Camus

"Man's inability to communicate is a result of his failure to listen effectively."
—Carl Rogers

"Of all the skills of leadership, listening is the most valuable—and one of the least understood. Most captains of industry listen only sometimes, and they remain ordinary leaders. But a few, the great ones, never stop listening. That's how they get word before anyone else of unseen problems and opportunities."
—Peter Nulty, "National Business Hall of Fame," Fortune magazine

Auscultation

Can you hear me?

Auscultation—now there's a fancy word for you. Auscultation is usually used as a medical term and means the act of listening either directly or through a stethoscope or other instrument to sounds within the body as a method of diagnosis. The title of this chapter actually came about by what I'd like to share with you—listening.

I knew I wanted to do a chapter on listening, which was the original premise of this whole book. I don't know if you noticed or not, but each chapter is a different -ion. I needed to come up with a word which meant listening but ended with an -ion, so I asked my followers on Twitter and Facebook. I got a number of great responses. The two I liked best were "paying attention" and "auscultation," which as I've already said means "the act of listening." Once I read the definition I knew my friends had hit a home run. A few different people actually suggested this word for my chapter on listening.

This chapter and concept are crucial to you and your capacity as a leader. Simply put, leaders are listeners. A few chapters back in the Illumination chapter, we learned in order to lead you must be led. Part of the being led is to listen—listen to the Spirit (Inquisition, Revelation,

Illumination and Meditation), listen to culture (Observation), listen through technology (Globalization), listen to the pain (Conversation), listen to the need (Compassion), and listen to the young and old (the next chapter on Instruction).

Many people have written books on the art of leadership. I'd like to suggest the art of listening is crucial to not only being an effective leader, but essential to being a Spirit-led leader, which is what I keep encouraging you to be. I was sharing this concept and the early premise of this book with my friend, Leonard Sweet, and he said something I wrote down: "Leadership isn't about vision. Close your eyes. It's about listening. Open your ears." You might want to write this down too, friend. Leadership is about listening. Open your ears!

As I've said before, our ultimate model is Jesus Christ, which is why I reread *Lead Like Jesus* by Ken Blanchard and Phil Hodges while I was writing this book. Jesus was perfect and therefore led perfectly. Throughout the four gospels, we see several accounts of Christ listening and responding. In the Old Testament, we see God listening to Abraham (who pleaded with him in Genesis 18), Moses in various passages, Rachel (Gen 30) and even the people of Nineveh, which led Him to change His mind (Jonah 3:10). I'm sure there are several more examples, but you get the point. God listens and so should we. Even now, Christ sits at the right hand of the Father, interceding on our behalf. Praise God! He listens to us and invites us to cast our anxieties on Him (1 Peter 5:7).

There are a number of ways in which the innovative leader listens. We've covered pretty consistently the concept of listening to the Spirit, which is paramount for all leaders to grasp and practice. In the Observation chapter, we discussed being a student of culture. In the Conversation chapter, we discussed listening to the pain and to others. In the Compassion chapter, we discussed listening to the need and responding accordingly. In the next chapter on Instruction, we'll look at why it's important to listen to peers as well as those younger and older than you. You can learn from all types of people. In this chapter, let's take a closer look at listening through technology—a concept my friend,

Tony Steward (former online community pastor at Life.Church), taught me several years ago.

When I first got into Twitter, I was real picky about who I followed. I had a lot of people following me, but I was following very few back. I was hanging out with Tony one summer and noticed he was following more people than were following him. I asked him about this and he told me he was "listening through technology." I was fascinated by this concept and thus began following more and more people as well as a diverse group of various areas like ministry and pastors, celebrities, tech gurus, culture gurus, musicians and artists, Christian and non-Christian—you name it. I started following them.

Through this intentional and strategic decision, I started to hear from various voices and began to feel more connected and relevant. Let's be real. What's missing from many good intentioned leaders and ministries is relevance—there's a disconnection from the leader and the world around him or her. I listen to know. I listen to understand. I listen because I care. I listen because I want to learn, grow, love, and because I'm extremely teachable.

I hope this is your goal, too. I'm amazed at the number of leaders who say they have a "heart for the lost," but don't know any. Do we really expect to connect with those far from God if we don't seek to understand them? I'm not saying you have to agree with them—just get to know them, respect their background, family history, experience, and the pain and needs they bring to the table.

If you haven't noticed yet, for a book on innovation, I talk very little about technology. Too many people think innovation and technology are synonymous. My hope is to share a biblical view of innovation and refer very little to technology. Out of the forty chapters in this book, I'm basically talking about the tool and function of technology in this and the Globalization chapters. Don't get me wrong—I love technology and use it daily. I just don't want leaders, who say they are caring for the poor, to think they're not being innovative because they don't have an Internet campus. Having a ministry which feeds and cares for the poor is just as innovative as your church having an Internet campus.

When I was on staff at Bent Tree in Dallas, TX, I met weekly with a fifteen-year-old high school student to mentor him. This young man was big into technology and especially Facebook. I saw this as an opportunity to teach this concept of listening through technology, so we began to talk about how God could use his being on Facebook to minister to his peers. I talked to him about this whole "listening" concept and encouraged him to view a Facebook status update as an opportunity to listen, and when appropriate reach out and encourage.

For example, I told him if he saw one of his friends update their status to something like, "Life sucks" or "I hate my parents" or "I'm so depressed" (which kids do—they're very transparent online), he had a divine opportunity to reach out in love and respond. I encouraged him to respond with a private message asking something like, "Is there anything that I can pray about for you?" or if he if knew prayer might turn them off, just something like, "I'm here for you if you want to talk." I recently ran into this young man years later, and he's now on staff at Bent Tree. There's another lesson there, but I don't have time to touch on it. I'll simply say my book *Church Leadership Essentials* has a chapter on mentoring.

> *Everyone should be quick to listen, slow to speak, and slow to become angry...*
> *—James 1:19 (NIV)*

What may God be up to?

One of the books which shaped me years ago was Charles Spurgeon's book on the Holy Spirit entitled *Spurgeon on the Holy Spirit*. In the book, Spurgeon shares how whenever somebody talks about God or something spiritual, the Spirit is active and at work behind-the-scenes. If a lost person asks you to pray for him or her, hear me (and Spurgeon) clearly: this is God at work! The enemy would never lead someone to come to you (a Christ-follower) and ask them about God, prayer, or anything spiritual.

How does this translate into our busy, digital worlds? If you ever see anyone update their Facebook or Twitter status to something like, "If you believe in God, please say a prayer for me" or "I'm stressed. If you're a praying person, please remember me" or "I have so many questions for God"—you get the picture. This is the very essence of listening through technology. Seize opportunities to be Christ to people who you connect with both in person and online.

When the beauty of what Spurgeon teaches about the Spirit's work and how He's been drawing someone to Himself for a long time blends with what Blackaby teaches about joining God where He's at work—watch out! The God-factor of technology is it has no limits, meaning we can pray for, encourage, discuss deep matters of faith, and lead to Christ people in our own town, in another state or across the globe. I have struck up great conversations with atheists, Jewish people, witches and Muslim people who were nowhere near where I lived. Technology is an amazing tool and gift and should be seen as such. I believe God has given us tools like Facebook and Twitter to be used for His glory and His fame.

On Thanksgiving of 2008, I had a great Twitter exchange with a non-Christian. Like I said earlier, I intentionally follow a wide variety of people. One of the people I followed was a well-known and popular tech guru. This woman had thousands of followers and was seen as an expert in her field. For some strange reason, she followed me back, which if you know how Twitter works, means I could send her a Direct Message (or private message). I was scanning through tweets on Thanksgiving and noticed a tweet from this woman which said something along the lines of "Looks like I'll be spending Thanksgiving in the ER." Since I have this concept ingrained in me and am intentional about listening through my online use, I saw this as an opportunity.

I sent her a direct (private) message so no one else would see our conversation. I first sent her a message, saying, "Sorry to hear you're at the ER. What happened?" She responded back to me that she had had a heart issue since she was a child and her heart was acting up. I thought about it, prayed about it, and knew the consequences (she could block me, ignore me or unfollow me, which meant I couldn't send her a private message anymore) but felt led to send her a message which read, "Would you mind if I prayed for you?" There was a delay between responses which seemed like forever, but she messaged me back and said, "That would be nice. Thank you." I told her I'd be praying for her and to let me know if she needed anything.

I didn't try to evangelize her or witness to her. God wasn't prompting me to. I simply let her know I was a Christian, and I'd be honored to pray for her. She ended up spending the entire Thanksgiving weekend in the hospital and got out on Monday. When this tech guru got back in the swing of things on Monday, she sent out a public Twitter message which said "I'd like to thank the few friends who actually took the time to check on me. Thanks to @So-and-so, @So-and-so, @GregAtkinson, and @ So-and-so." I knew we had a connection and that she will always remember a Christ-follower cared for her, prayed for her, and didn't preach at her.

Here's where the Spurgeon principle comes back around. One day, this person could go through another tough time and message me and say something like, "You're a Christian, right? What do you think about—?" I don't know if this will ever happen, but the possibility exists because of this concept of listening through technology mixed with me taking the initiative to reach out to her. This is what I've been learning from my friend, Clarke Cayton, about prevenient grace. I'm fascinated (as was John Wesley) with what I'm learning about the subject of prevenient grace.

This is a simple concept or principle but will change your life if you'll let it sink in. How do you view your use of Twitter, Facebook, blogs, and other online tools? Do you see them as opportunities to be the hands and feet of Christ to someone in need? Again, much like most of what I'm sharing with you, this won't happen by accident. You must be strategic and intentional in your use of technology and make an effort to see beyond a status update to a deeper need. People will often let you know when they're stressed, exhausted, frustrated, depressed, and hurting. There's something about typing in front of a screen. My friend,

Cynthia Ware, says it provides a "false sense of intimacy and security."

I was speaking to Church leaders in Atlanta, Georgia one time and some of the team from Catalyst was in the audience, including my friend, LV Hanson. LV shared how when his dad was dying of cancer he sent out an e-mail to a group of people who signed up to hear his thoughts and how he was processing this trying time in his life. I remember that in the e-mail, LV shared his hurt, his frustrations, his questions, and his wrestling with God over his dad's death. When he was sharing this at the meeting in Atlanta, he said, "I said things in that e-mail that I would never say to anyone face-to-face." I stopped him and said, "Did you hear what you just said? You shared things through the use of technology that you wouldn't even share with someone right in front of you!" He said, "Wow. I guess you're right."

This is the world we're living in now, and one reason of which Internet campuses and social media are seeing such great success right now. People are more open to chat with someone or vent online than they are face-to-face. Like it or not, this is a reality of the culture we live in. If you accept it and prepare for it, God can use you to reach out through digital hands and feet.

Dear friends: Lead with your ears, follow up with your tongue.
—James 1:19 (MSG)

I thought I'd close this chapter with the verse I shared earlier from James 1—this time as told in The Message. Meditate on these words: Lead with your ears. Follow up with your tongue.

The way I see it, James tells us to be extremely intentional. Whether the translation is to "be quick to listen" or to "lead with your ears," it won't happen by accident. I have to practice being "quick to listen" every day of my life. If you will join me in this and view all of life (including technology) as a chance to listen and see what God is up to, you might just stumble across something strange, new and innovative.

"We should never pretend to know what we don't know, we should not feel ashamed to ask and learn from people below, and we should listen carefully to the views of the cadres at the lowest levels. Be a pupil before you become a teacher; learn from the cadres at the lower levels before you issue orders."
—Mao Tse-tung

"It must be remembered that the purpose of education is not to fill the minds of students with facts . . . it is to teach them to think, if that is possible, and always to think for themselves."
—Robert Hutchins

"Education is a progressive discovery of our own ignorance."
—Will Durant

"Learning is a treasure that will follow its owner everywhere."
—Chinese Proverb

"Upon the subject of education, not presuming to dictate any plan or system respecting it, I can only say that I view it as the most important subject which we as a people may be engaged in."
—Abraham Lincoln

Instruction

Follow me

In the last chapter on Auscultation, we learned leaders are listeners. In this chapter on Instruction we are going to learn leaders are lifelong learners. I don't think this concept has to be lengthy or really needs much explanation. I simply want to bring up two key concepts I've referred to frequently: One is you must be intentional about learning from others. And two, you must approach this way innovation can happen with a posture of humility and a teachable spirit. I'd like to discuss two types of instruction one can receive (I'm sure there are more): mentoring and therapy.

> *Follow my example, as I follow the example of Christ.*
> *—1 Corinthians 11:1 (NIV)*

> *Timothy, my son, I give you this instruction in keeping with the prophecies once made about you, so that by following them you may fight the good fight, holding on to faith and a good*

conscience.

—1 Timothy 1:18–19 (NIV)

Paul was a mentor to Timothy (and Titus). The discipline and joy of mentoring is what I'd like to share about in this chapter on instruction. I believe we can learn from anybody. I especially believe we can learn a ton from people who we respect and form an intentional relationship with.

What I'd like to offer up to you as a source of education, inspiration, encouragement, wisdom, and knowledge could lead to a breakthrough in ministry (innovation) are three types of mentoring: Being mentored by someone older than you, being mentored by someone younger than you (reverse mentoring) and peer-to-peer mentoring (when iron sharpens iron).

As iron sharpens iron, so one man sharpens another.

—Proverbs 27:17 (NIV)

Allow me to share what I know of mentoring. Remember I'm only thirty-eight and have a lot yet to learn, but here's what I've experienced so far: Many great, wise, well-respected leaders who I look up to have mentors. I've heard mega-church pastors (who you would think have it all figured out) mention in their sermon their mentor or their therapist. I, personally, have several mentors in my life.

Wherever I live and serve, I find someone whom I'll approach (again, you have to be intentional—this won't happen by accident) and ask to mentor me. I will admit I've been nervous every time and had a fear of rejection, but almost all are honored to be asked and happy to share what they've learned. Only a handful over the years have said no.

So, locally, I have mentors I meet with regularly and

allow them to pour into me. Again, it's the posture in which I approach them. At the time of writing this chapter, I was living in Georgia and met with Lee Ross every week where we discussed leadership, ministry, and strategic planning. Lee is a senior pastor but also used to work for the Georgia Baptist Convention where he created and led workshops on strategic planning. Lee also used to work with Ken Blanchard and developed the *Lead like Jesus* curriculum and taught me leadership principles based on the model of Jesus' leadership as well as situational leadership as taught by Ken Blanchard. Presently, I live and work near Charlotte, NC, and meet regularly with a few different mentors.

I also have several long-distance mentors. These are people in ministry I greatly respect and have asked if I can pick their brain from time to time. Besides staying in touch with old mentors of cities where I used to live, I have these long-distance mentors who I communicate with via e-mail, text, phone, and Twitter. I'll ask them about their church, their organizational chart, books they're reading, books they suggest I read, and other questions which come up and I'm curious about. These are busy men who are gracious and have taken time out of their busy schedule to answer my questions, and I pray God will bless them tremendously. I, personally, do this for other leaders around the world and think God has opened these doors because I pour into others and He returns the favor.

Besides these formal and regular relationships, I have always been intentional about meeting with leaders when I have the occasion to pick their brain, ask questions, and learn from them. I started this when I was eighteen years old and serving my first church. I called up the worship pastors (Rob Flint and Alan Hendricks) at the local large church in town and asked them if I could meet with them. I was serving a church of sixty people.

They were serving a church of nine-hundred. God bless them, they agreed to meet with me and we had several meetings over the course of my years in Charleston, SC. Also, when I go to a conference, I look to see who else is speaking, and I'll e-mail them and ask if we can grab coffee while we're at the conference. I cannot tell you how many times I've done this.

> *An innovative leader is teachable and has a passion for learning, stretching, and growing.*
> *—@GregAtkinson*

I also believe in the power of reverse mentoring. I have several younger leaders who I spend time with, mentor, and pour myself into: from a high school student to college students to twenties in ministry. What I've found over and over again is I learn from them. They keep me young, focused, and in tune with the culture. I have had many ideas and decisions shaped by spending time with leaders younger than me. I hope you have to. If not, try it. It's humbling and exciting at the same time.

The third way I mentioned is peer-to-peer mentoring. This is the iron sharpening iron of which the Bible encourages us to make happen. I have a large network of friends and peers in ministry, roughly around my same age and amount of experience that I am friends first with but also bounce ideas off of. They come to me to ask questions, and I go to them. No doubt many leaders across the country who may read this can recall a time when I contacted them and said, "Hey what do you think about—?" or "I need your advice on—?"

One peer-to-peer relationship I enjoyed during my time in Dallas was a weekly meeting with Paul Watson. We met weekly for prayer, Bible study, and to talk about what was going on in our lives. Currently, I have several local pastors that I meet with regularly for peer-to-peer relationships.

Find someone who you can grow and share with—it could be a lifesaver for your ministry. Later this month, I'm flying to Austin to spend a few days with pastors all about my same age and learn from one another. I'm telling you: you got to give this a shot!

Lastly, I want to talk about something which is just now being seen as a valid, proper, and accepted form of instruction and this is therapy or counseling. I give thanks to friends like DJ Chuang, Rhett Smith and Anne Jackson for their passion, honesty, writing, and encouragement for ministers to experience regular times of counseling and therapy.

I'll never forget about many years ago, hearing Rob Bell (I'm not saying I agree with Rob Bell's theology or views of Scripture) speak at a pastors' conference. He was being interviewed by Ed Young, Jr. and in passing, he referred to meeting with his therapist, and there was an audible laugh from the crowd. Rob looked straight out at the audience and said, "That's right. I go to therapy." I wanted to stand up and applaud him.

I've blogged about this before, but honestly, I think it is pride which keeps most pastors from submitting themselves for counseling and therapy. Most leaders and especially pastors are used to being the ones doing the counseling and feel they need to act as if they've got it all together. I can think of nothing more stressful, important, and physically, mentally, emotionally, and spiritually draining than pastoring. It's exhausting, and the reason most people who start out in ministry don't finish is due largely in part to things, which may have been avoided if they simply had someone to talk to, confide in, and confess to.

The latest statistic I saw on ChurchLeaders.com said 1,700

pastors leave the ministry each month. You read that right.

Moving on. . . .

I am proud to say I go to see a counselor every other week, and I usually send out a Twitter message when I'm leaving his office saying something like, "Leaving therapist. I thank God for him."

Here's the real, raw deal: as senior pastor of a church, you feel stuck and trapped. You can't go to those who report to you and vent. You can't confess struggles and temptations to employees. They don't need or want to hear what you're struggling with. The dangerous thing—and this is what fires me up—is the enemy knows this and he desires to keep you feeling trapped and isolated. He will try his best to wear you down, and when you're at your weakest, he will make his move and strike. The devil likes to kick people when they're down.

When you get sick enough, tired enough, careless enough, and prideful enough, he will come at you with full force, and you'll end up being another statistic. Hear my heart: it doesn't have to be this way. Take my words and my testimony seriously. If you don't believe me, ask DJ Chuang, Rhett Smith or Anne Jackson.

Ask somebody and don't let anything or anyone in the world keep you from seeking out help. There's no shame in going to see a counselor—it's therapeutic and great for your health and longevity in ministry. Just trust me on this, and give it a try.

To wrap this principle up, it all comes down to being intentional (you must seek out mentoring relationships and therapy) and being humble and teachable enough to understand the value of this concept. It's the posture in which you approach learning. As I said at the beginning, we are lifelong learners. May you never stop learning and growing.

I've heard pastors in their sixties and seventies talk about their mentors and books they're reading. This is exactly how I want to be when I'm older. I pray the same for you. When you submit yourself to these types of relationships—mentoring, reverse mentoring, peer-to-peer mentoring and therapy—you'll be amazed at the potential you have to go to another level in your leadership and the ideas, dreams, plans, and innovations of the future will be made possible.

"One of the great mistakes is to judge policies and programs by their intentions rather than their results."
—Milton Friedman

"True genius resides in the capacity for evaluation of uncertain, hazardous, and conflicting information."
—Winston Churchill

"Success isn't about doing things right—it's about doing the right things well."
—David MacNicol

"We read to know we are not alone."
—C.S. Lewis

"You're the same today as you'll be in five years except for the people you meet and the books you read."
—Charlie "Tremendous" Jones

"When you sell a man a book you don't sell him just 12 ounces of paper and ink and glue–you sell him a whole new life."
—Christopher Morley

"No matter how busy you may think you are, you must find time for reading, or surrender yourself to self-chosen ignorance."
—Confucius

Information

What have you read lately?

This chapter is brief and to the point. An informed leader is an equipped and wise leader. In the last two chapters, we learned leaders are listeners and leaders are lifelong learners. In this chapter, we'll discuss a number of things; one of which is leaders are readers. Reading is more than a habit; it's a discipline, which, like most things I've suggested, takes intentionality and strategy. My wife and I have a little tension between us about books.

She's into fiction and I'm purely a nonfiction guy. She reads as a way to pass time and escape. I read to grow and learn. I'm very purposeful and picky about what I read. I read around six to eight books a month. However, sincc turning 38, God has opened my heart to read fiction and shown me that He can speak to me through it as well, so I have *The Lord of the Rings* trilogy of books on deck!

When a leader has a teachable spirit and a thirst for knowledge, he or she will find the time to read a wide variety of books besides the Bible. I read ministry books, pastoral leadership books, Harvard

Business School books, management and strategy books, worship books, books on innovation and several mainstream business and leadership books to feed and fuel myself with ideas and inspiration.

But this concept of information leading to innovation goes beyond reading. It includes research, preparation, assessment, and evaluation. I've had the privilege of coaching church planters across the country and I can vouch for how much research a church planter does prelaunch. They do demographic studies and surveys and spend countless hours online googling and studying their city and community.

They have a genuine desire to familiarize themselves with the people they're trying to reach and the environment and culture in which they are going to have to be in. Again, they're thinking like missionaries and approaching their new ministry as a missionary would a new people group.

Maybe you're not a church planter, but you're getting ready to start a new program, initiative or ministry in your church. You've hopefully done your homework and know whom you're targeting and what you're trying to accomplish. Maybe you've talked with some other churches who have tried something similar and got feedback from them. Regardless, you should be as knowledgeable as possible before you launch. I'm all for taking risks (like we've already discussed), but they should be calculated risks and educated guesses.

> *"Suppose one of you wants to build a tower. Will he not first sit down and estimate the cost to see if he has enough money to complete it? For if he lays the foundation and is not able to finish it, everyone who sees it will ridicule him, saying, 'This fellow began to build and was not able to finish.'*
> *—Luke 14:28–30 (NIV)*

Good preparation and good information (what the Bible calls "counting the cost") is just wise leadership and stewardship of your resources.

Jesus spent thirty years preparing for three years of ministry, which turned the world upside-down. Paul went away for three years to study and prepare. I'm sure many of you reading this went to Bible college and/or seminary.

Some of you went to graduate school and have advanced degrees. Some of you may not have been able to continue your education for various reasons but have filled yourself with knowledge and information from books, conferences, mentors, and a ton of sweat. I seriously doubt any of you reading this are lazy. I imagine you take pride in your work and I simply want to encourage you to "count the cost" and prepare as best you can before leading through change.

A practical example of this is a church who is exploring the possibility of launching a new campus, going multisite, merging, or planting a daughter church. There is a tremendous amount of studying, planning, preparation, research, and conferring with other churches who have taken this leap which must take place before moving forward. If you don't "count the cost" and practice this information principle, the result could be disastrous. Planting a church or launching another campus is a beautiful thing and a true innovation in ministry, but you have to do your homework before embarking on such an adventure. Change always comes with a cost as we discussed in the Decision chapter.

How do you know what to change? This is where assessment and evaluation come in. Good leaders ask the right questions. Peter Drucker said, "The most serious mistakes are not being made as a result of wrong answers. The truly dangerous thing is asking the wrong question." You need to approach the evaluation of your work and ministry with prayerful eyes and ears, a sensitive spirit and a supernatural wisdom. Andy Stanley in describing his book *7 Practices of Effective Ministry* said the book "is not so much about what to do as it is about what to ask." Knowing what to ask is vital.

Leaders that have the gift of leadership are good with questions. This is why I love consulting with churches, organizations and companies. God has gifted me to be able to ask tough, focused, penetrating, and probing questions. I take no credit for it. It is the Holy Spirit moving through me who brings these questions to mind. Maybe you're gifted like this too.

If you or someone in your organization has this gift and is good at asking the right questions, let him or her lead the charge. If none of you are good at this, and it will take a great deal of humility and soul searching to admit, bring someone from the outside in. It doesn't have to be a paid consultant. It could be a volunteer business person or executive in your church. It could be a local pastor who is gifted at this sort of thing and can ask you the tough questions. Whatever you need to do to generate the questions needed for the evaluation of your organization, do it, and do it regularly.

Once you've done your homework, gathered information, and known your goals, you must constantly evaluate how you're doing. Depending on what you're evaluating, the frequency varies. For your weekly worship service and Sunday experience, I hope you evaluate this weekly. For other programs and ministries in the church, maybe monthly or quarterly. For big areas like overall vision, future expansion, and building projects, you can have an annual retreat where you review the past year and look ahead to the future—based on the information and research you've gathered, prepared with the knowledge and study of your assessment of your organization's current situation, and armed with the right questions.

When you recognize a weak or unhealthy area in your

organization, this is an opportunity for growth and change and will inevitably lead to a new innovation. Remember innovation is about bringing positive change. If you take seriously this concept of gathering information, you will eventually come across something which needs to change and witness the birth of innovation.

"I want to put a ding in the universe."
—Steve Jobs

"My heart, which is so full to overflowing, has often been solaced and refreshed by music when sick and weary."
—Martin Luther

"In life you need either inspiration or desperation."
—Tony Robbins

"There never was a great soul that did not have some divine inspiration."
—Marcus T. Cicero

"Without inspiration, the best powers of the mind remain dormant; there is a fuel in us, which needs to be ignited with sparks."
—Johann Gottfried Von Herder

"Whatever the mind of man can conceive and believe, it can achieve."
—Napoleon Hill

"Do one thing every day that scares you."
—Eleanor Roosevelt

Inspiration

What puts wind in your sails?

Obviously, I'm greatly inspired by Christ, His finished work on the cross and Scripture, which we've discussed and we'll talk more about later, but you know what else inspires me? Good design. I happen to be friends with a few professional designers, and I have a huge respect for their natural gifting mixed with their skill and sharp eye. What most designers have in common is this concept of simplicity, which we touched on in the Subtraction chapter.

In this chapter, we're going to discuss a number of ways one can be inspired, which hopefully will result in you being led to do something new and innovative. I don't know about you, but I'm challenged, stretched, encouraged, and inspired by the example of another. One way we can be inspired is by observing and learning from other companies and organizations.

I mentioned good design. Apple is a company who inspires me frequently. Their intentional strategy to be simple, clean, and lead through design is something I receive a great deal of inspiration from and use to fuel my own thinking and leadership. I look to several companies like Apple, including IKEA, Nike, Starbucks, and BMW for models of inspiration.

One book which was a great inspiration and education for me is entitled *Do You Matter?: How Great Design Will Make People Love Your Company*. In the book, the authors list the previously mentioned companies as examples of innovation and intentional design and user experience. Actually, it was their intentionality and strategy for design and the user experience which drove them to create products, cars, and environments which resulted in their being known as innovative.

Another way I'm often inspired is by watching other organizations and nonprofits. I'm passionate about social justice/ compassion and fighting homelessness, poverty, and slavery. There are a number of organizations who are blazing new trails in innovation by using social media for good. They and their leaders inspire me. Organizations I'm a part of, support, and suggest you get to know are ones like Samaritan's Purse, Advent Conspiracy, Catalyst, Fermi Project, Food for the Hungry, International Justice Mission, Just One, Not For Sale, One, ROOV, Rick Warren's PEACE Plan, the Shema Movement, and World Vision—of which I've been a sponsor for over eighteen years. Their drive, determination, and passion for their cause inspire me.

As I mentioned in the Observation chapter, I watch and visit a lot of churches. Other churches inspire me. Please hear me loud and clear: I have traveled North America telling people over and over to "innovate, don't imitate." I'm not talking about imitating another church and taking their innovation and trying it out on your people. No, I'm talking about digging deeper and learning about the heart, vision, mission, passion, principles, and thought processes which went into their decision to do something new and innovative. I process through this, digest it, meditate on it, and again allow this to fuel me on in my own ministry and community.

You'll never hear me say to copy another church, but I do think there are wonderful churches all around the world that can encourage, challenge, stretch, and inspire us. Mind you, I'm not just talking about the big boys—the giga-churches who make the largest church list or the fastest growing list or the most innovative list. Yes, I keep my eye on them for obvious reasons, but I'm also very intentional to watch church plants and new movements who are doing some extremely innovative things in order to reach their community.

> *You can learn from churches of all shapes, sizes, and denominations.*
> *—@GregAtkinson*

Conferences have also been a tremendous source of inspiration for me. Fortunately, I speak at a lot of conferences, so I get to attend my fair share. I'm not one of those speakers who just shows up for my class and then hides out or leaves right after I'm done (sorry if that's you). No, I teach my class in the given time slot and then I go to other speakers' classes when I'm free. I try to learn as much as I can while I'm there. Again, I'm putting myself in a posture to learn—I'm intentionally teachable—and I believe what the other speakers have to share is just as important and insightful as what I might be there to share.

Besides the conferences I'm speaking at, I also try to just attend a few conferences each year. This is a real pleasure and treat for me as I have no pressure, schedule or responsibilities, I can simply be an attendee and learn, grow, worship, and fellowship. Speaking of inspiration, @inprogress just tweeted fellowship inspires her (I asked people on Twitter what inspired them). I would agree. As we discussed in the Conversation chapter, I believe God uses fellowship and our conversations with friends to encourage and inspire us.

Along those lines, another thing which inspires is being around people smarter, wiser, more gifted, and better skilled. My friend, Brian Davis, said excellence inspires him. I agree. I remember as a worship pastor in Washington DC, I would bring in "ringers" from time to time to play with our church's praise band. I had two professional musicians I would pay (the rest of my band was volunteer) an honorarium to come in and sit in with the band. One was a female violinist, who made her living playing violin, and one was a male saxophone player, who made his living playing the sax. I wish you could have seen the difference in my "normal," "ordinary" band of volunteers when these professionals came to play. Oh my! Everyone was on their toes, taking notes, and bringing their A-game. They rose to the level of the most skilled player (not quite as high, but they played beyond what they typically would). They were inspired, challenged, and stretched to be in the company of greatness and let it drive them to be a better musician.

I'm constantly calling, texting, e-mailing and meeting with people way smarter than me. This goes back to teachability and the posture I approach people with, but I am intentional about picking the brain of someone who has more experience than me or has been around longer than me. If they live in the same region as me, I'll offer to buy them breakfast, lunch, coffee or dessert, and drive to meet with them. My wife will often ask why I'm going to drive two hours to have lunch with someone and then drive back home, and I'll reply, "It's an investment"—a calculated and intentional investment in myself which I make to grow. You can do the same thing where you live.

Books inspire me. When I decided I wanted to write a book, I met with Greg Ligon, who is a friend, but also over the book division of Leadership Network. The first question he asked me was, "Why a book?" You know, why not a blog or an e-book? I instantly shot back, "Because I'm a reader and I love books!" I take great pride in my library—probably too much pride. Lord, forgive me. When someone walks into my office they usually remark on the number of books on the shelf and say something like, "Have you read all these?" I always reply with, "If it's on the shelf, I've read it. If I'm in the process of reading it or it's on deck, it's at home by my chair or bed."

Because I believe being teachable is the key to being an effective and innovative leader (remember: leaders are readers, and leaders are life-long learners), I am constantly reading. Of course, this is in addition to my Bible reading, but like you, I believe God can speak through other writing as well. I'm constantly being sent books to review, so finding new books is never a challenge. I get them in the mail every week. What I have to be intentional about is going back and reading the classics like C. S. Lewis, A. W. Tozer, Charles Spurgeon, Watchman Nee, and Brother Lawrence to name a few.

As I said in the Revelation chapter, nature inspires me. @inprogress agrees. When I get outdoors and among God's creation I am full of inspiration and new ideas just start to flow.

What energizes me

Two other things which inspire me that I could write on for days are movies and music. How can you see the world in which Michael Bay created in *Transformers,* James Cameron created in *Avatar*, and Christopher Nolan created in *Inception* and not be inspired? Ask anyone who knows me or has met me in person: I live for movies. You know what? God speaks to me through movies. Not every single movie, but more often than not.

Just today, I saw a movie (I had to take a break from writing) which had the theme of redemption all through it. There are so many spiritual conversations which can occur after a good movie. In all seriousness, "if I had a dollar for every time" God spoke to me through a movie, gave me an idea for my blog, writing, church or marriage, I would be a very rich man. Don't just plop down in a theater seat and unplug your brain, ask God to speak to you and look for spiritual themes—they're scattered all throughout most movies.

The other way I mentioned I get inspired is through music. It's been said, "Music is what feelings sound like." I grew up a musician, and my college degree is actually in music. I spent the first eleven years of my ministry career as a worship pastor, so music is extremely special and moving to me. You want to know something funny about me? I rarely cry. Actually, that's not entirely true. God has broken me enough times in my life that I now cry more easily and He has a hold of my heart. The truth is you could cut my leg off with a chainsaw and you wouldn't see me shed a tear. Pain doesn't do it. (Trust me—I had major back surgery).

Only God, spiritually moving things, including powerful movies and music, and of course the death, pain or suffering of a friend or loved one make me cry. I can't tell you how many times I've choked up, shed tears, or even cried like a baby while in a dark movie theater or listening to a powerful worship song. I've had times when I tried to describe a scene in a movie to someone and I get all choked up and can't get it out. There are some worship songs I simply cannot sing. The words resonate so deeply and my spirit connects so powerfully; if I try to open my mouth and make a sound, I just start crying.

An example of this is Chris Tomlin's song *Famous One*. I can't make it through the chorus without crying or choking up. Maybe because I struggle (like a lot of leaders) with pride, and I secretly hope to be famous? I don't know, but when I sing of Jesus as the famous One, my heart beats through my chest, and I can't help but cry. I also can't make it through New Life Worship's Great I Am without choking up or crying.

One season of life, we had many things going on, including my wife having some serious health issues with her kidneys, and I was in-between jobs. During that season, the song *Desert Song* by Brooke Fraser was what we cried through and held on to. The bridge, "All of my life, in every season, You are still God. I have a reason to sing. I have a reason to worship," messes me up. I share these stories because I don't think I'm alone here. Movies and music are God's gifts to us, and they move us. They motivate us. They inspire us.

Another way we get inspired is through a life or a testimony. Stories inspire. I've had the pleasure of producing several video testimonies over the years. It's always very moving to hear of what God has done in another person's life, family, and marriage. When someone shares their salvation story or a story of God delivering them from addiction, or healing them from a painful experience, hurt or disease, or rescuing their marriage—this moves me, and it resonates with a deep truth. Our God is alive and well and still at work in peoples' lives. We serve a living God and each story shines a light on this fact.

Last year, I got to go to Donald Miller's Storyline Conference, which is all about living a better story. I encourage you to check it out. Just tonight—on the eve before I turn my completed manuscript in for this book—I met with a couple that is divorced, got right with God and each other, and this Friday night I will remarry them. This fires me up and that, my friends, is a great story that inspires! The beautiful and wonderful thing is I have seen many stories of divorced couples getting remarried the last several years. God is so good! The picture below is of the couple I remarried and their son is smiling huge in the middle holding the "re." That's inspiration for why we do what we do and I get choked up every time I look at this picture.

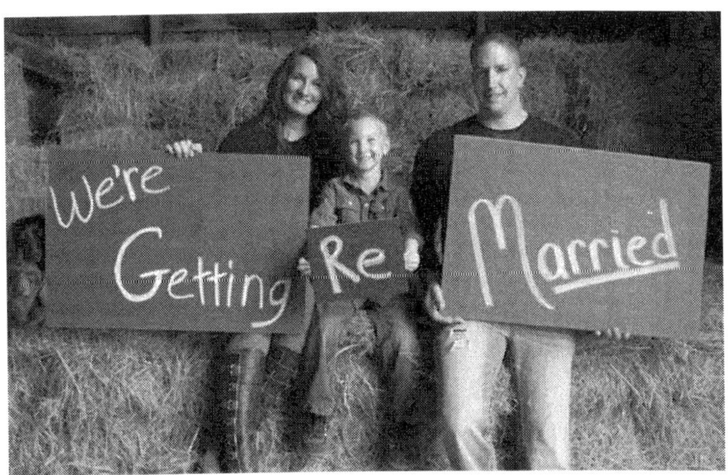

> *We continually remember before our God and Father your work produced by faith, your labor prompted by love, and your endurance inspired by hope in our Lord Jesus Christ.*
> *—1 Thessalonians 1:3 (NIV)*

Ultimately, we as Christians and Christian leaders are inspired by Jesus Christ. Even the examples I gave earlier of nature, movies, music, and stories are all connected to our love and relationship with Christ. It's His creation which moves me. It's a spiritual theme in a movie which grabs me. It's a true lyric in a worship song which stirs me. It's the testimony or story of a life transformed by Jesus Christ which motivates, encourages, and inspires me and you. Divine inspiration flows from Christ through the Holy Spirit, and it is fuel for the innovative leader. Check out the following passage of Scripture:

> *For the sake of His body, which is the Church. I have become its servant by the commission God gave me to present to you the word of God in its fullness—the mystery that has been kept hidden for ages and generations but is now disclosed to the saints. To them, God has chosen to make known among the Gentiles the glorious riches of this mystery, which is Christ in you, the hope of glory. We proclaim Him, admonishing, and teaching everyone with all wisdom, so that we may present everyone perfect in Christ. To this end I labor, struggling with all His energy, which so powerfully works in me.*
> *—Colossians 1:24b–29 (NIV)*

To be an effective leader, a lasting leader, a Spirit-led leader, and thus an innovative leader, you must have "His energy" working powerfully in you. Jesus gave us our commission, Jesus is our motivation, and He also must be our supreme inspiration. When Christ is preeminent in our lives and ministries, we will be filled to overflowing with inspiration for the tasks ahead of us. Make no mistake: ministry is tough. Living the Christian life is no field of flowers, but if we fuel ourselves with a variety of inspiration (Christ being chief here); we are more likely to make it long-term in our chosen career path and lead an innovative organization.

"The spirit of God, His presence, and His gifts are not simply desirable in our Christian congregations; they are absolutely imperative!"
—A. W. Tozer

"Organizations are living systems, not machines, because they are made up of people. As innovators in a living system, we must learn to think more like gardeners than mechanics. When we view the organization as a living system, our perspective becomes one of how to provide the right environment or context for the organization to fulfill its purpose."
—Andrew Papageorge, in Go Innovate!

"For even if the whole world believed in resurrection, little would change until we began to practice it. We can believe in CPR, but people will remain dead until someone breathes new life into them. And we can tell the world that there is life after death, but the world really seems to be wondering if there is life before death."
—Shane Claiborne

"Our God invites us into a creative partnership with him."
—Alan Hirsch and Michael Frost, The Shaping of Things to Come

Intersection

When it all comes together!

Have you ever had a magical moment happen to you? Some would say that all the stars aligned. I would suggest that we are dead in the center of God's will. There have been times in my life when I was so in tune with God, I literally felt and thought what He was feeling and thinking. I've had times when God told me to pray for someone and then later found out why as they confirmed that God truly must have been leading me to pray for them. This intersection is what we're going to briefly look at.

Henry Blackaby teaches us that we can discern God's will through Scripture, prayer, the Holy Spirit, people, and circumstances. When all these line up—watch out! Scott Wilson wrote about operating out of a God-given vision and said, "Most often this precise calling is found at the intersection of the pastor's spiritual gifts and passions, the demographics of the area, and the needs of the people in that community." (*Steering Through Chaos*, p. 45)

As I've stated, innovation is the act of doing or introducing something new. When you are trying to discern what new thing God is up to, it's vital that you head straight for this intersection.

I would combine the intersection that Blackaby talks of—Scripture, prayer, the Holy Spirit, people, and circumstances with the intersection that Scott Wilson talks of—your spiritual gifts and passions, the demographics of the area and the needs of the people in that community. Take into account all these factors and you will be sitting right smack dab in the middle of the leadership and innovation intersection.

> *We have different gifts, according to the grace given to each of us. If your gift is prophesying, then prophesy in accordance with your faith; if it is serving, then serve; if it is teaching, then teach; if it is to encourage, then give encouragement; if it is giving, then give generously; if it is to lead, do it diligently; if it is to show mercy, do it cheerfully.*
> *—Romans 12:6–8 (NIV)*

I like how Scott points to your spiritual gifts. I think gift-based ministry is revolutionary and sadly missing from many churches. Your weaknesses are an opportunity for someone else (who has that same thing as a strength) to shine. When you act out of what drives you and resonates with your God-given spiritual gifts, you will find more joy and fulfillment, not to mention success. When a person's passion, mission, and imagination intersect with a church's vision and God's purpose and plans, it's a beautiful thing. This chapter is intentionally brief because the concept is simple and doesn't need to be thoroughly explained. Seek to know God's heart, get in the center of His will (you'll know this when the intersection lines up) and then lead from that place of confidence. Even if you are looked at as strange and mocked or questioned, you should have a solid vision for how you are to lead and rely on that. So, if you find yourself at this perfect intersection, have faith, be bold and confident, and move forward in obedience to the leading of the Holy Spirit.

"Four steps to achievement: Plan purposefully. Prepare prayerfully. Proceed positively. Pursue persistently."
—William A. Ward

"Take time to deliberate, but when the time for action has arrived, stop thinking and go in."
—Napoleon Bonaparte

"Every improvement or innovation begins with an idea. But an idea is only a possibility—a small beginning that must be nurtured, developed, engineered, tinkered with, championed, tested, implemented and checked . . . ideas have no value until they are implemented."
—Alan Robinson and Dean Schroeder, in Ideas Are Free

"The immature mind hops from one thing to another; the mature mind seeks to follow through."
—Harry A. Overstreet

"Setting a goal is not the main thing. It is deciding how you will go about achieving it and staying with that plan."
—Tom Landry

"Vision without action is merely a dream. Action without vision just passes the time. Vision with action can change the world!"
—Joel Arthur Barker

"Successful leaders have the courage to take action while others hesitate."
—John C. Maxwell

"Vision is not enough, it must be combined with venture. It is not enough to stare up the steps, we must step up the stairs."
—Vaclav Havel

"You miss 100% of the shots you don't take."
—Wayne Gretzky

Execution

"What's missing isn't the ideas . . . it's the will to execute them." Seth Godin's quote above and Wayne Gretzky's quote about "You miss 100% of the shots you don't take" pack a powerful punch. Throughout this book, I've shared principles, concepts, and ideas that can spark innovation. As Seth says, the ideas aren't what's missing— "it's the will to execute them." Just as we talked about how crucial evaluation is in the Information chapter, it's all for nothing without execution. All forty chapters are pointless if you don't practice this concept of execution. In each chapter so far, I've shared ways that innovation can happen. In this chapter, I'm sharing how innovation won't happen—if you do nothing. Some of you know what you need to do; you just need to do it.

> *Therefore, to him who knows to do good and does not do it, to him it is sin.*
> *—James 4:17 (NKJV)*

Strong words from James. I don't need to add anything to them. I'll let God's word speak for itself. Moving on, it's been fifteen chapters since we talked about the subtraction principle.

Some of you may have been glad to get that chapter over with and ready to move on to something "easier" or more fun. I'm afraid I'm going to have to bring that chapter back up.

For some of you, the most innovative thing you can do as an organization is to kill some things, clean up your programs, ministries and projects, and narrow your focus. I'm writing this chapter to encourage you to execute and act upon that tension you feel in your spirit.

For some of you, maybe another chapter resonated more with you and where you're at and headed as an organization. Maybe you have a vision, a mission, motivation, dedication, or a call to compassion? Maybe you're ready to explore and experiment or start a revolution? This chapter is here to give you a little extra push in the right direction and say the hard, simple truth: none of these good intentions will matter if you never pull the trigger.

> *Execution is a crucial part of innovation, change, and growth.*
> *—@GregAtkinson*

Why didn't I make this the last chapter in the book? Because I've saved the best for last! The chapters from here on out get better and better. The last four chapters are ones that get me fired up, and I most enjoy speaking on when I teach about innovation. You're coming down the homestretch in this book and getting closer and closer to my heart. Before we can move forward, though, you must wrestle with and choose (remember the Decision chapter) to act on what you feel God is calling you to do or what He may speak to you in the remaining chapters.

Move on

In Deuteronomy chapter 1, the Israelites were in the land of Moab. Moses explained the Lord's instructions to the people. Let's look at what he tells them:

The Command to Leave Sinai

"When we were at Mount Sinai, the Lord our God said to us, ' You have stayed at this mountain long enough. It is time to break camp and move on. Go to the hill country of the Amorites and to all the neighboring regions—the Jordan Valley, the hill country, the western foothills, the Negev, and the coastal plain. Go to the land of the Canaanites and to Lebanon, and all the way to the great Euphrates River. Look, I am giving all this land to you! Go in and occupy it, for it is the land the Lord swore to give to your ancestors Abraham, Isaac, and Jacob, and to all their descendants.'"
—Deuteronomy 1:6–8 (NLT)

God said they had done one thing "long enough," and it was now time to "move on." God had something new and greater for them, but they had to listen, obey, stop what they were doing, and act. This is the execution principle. Dr. Maxell Maltz said, "Often, the difference between a successful person and a failure is not one has better abilities or ideas but the courage that one has to bet on one's ideas, to take a calculated risk—and to act." Having an idea, discovering you need to change and stumbling across an innovation are all great, but worthless if you never act on it.

The innovative leader is a courageous leader. Thankfully, we know that perfect love drives out all fear.
—1 John 4:18.

The strange and innovative leader cares more about pleasing God than pleasing man.
—@GregAtkinson

The innovative leader is obedient to God's will and will follow wherever He leads. I am fully aware that following God is not always easy and will probably cost you something. I've stated that throughout this book.

Bryant Nielson in his article on *Courageous Leadership* suggested some benefits of leading courageously. "First, you'll create momentum, both within your own team and the organization as a whole. The more you act on your beliefs, ideas, and strategies, you'll find that you begin to align your movement in your work, community, or family with your own personal values. By having a courageous leader, your team will begin to feel morale grow, will feel more comfortable with their own ability to be innovative, and will communicate with each other—and you more readily."

Whenever I teach on leadership at conferences, I find myself constantly saying, "Leadership is not easy." It's my go-to answer when someone says, "Yeah, but that sounds hard." I just read this tweet today from @RealEricGeiger: "If you want to make everyone happy, don't be a leader. Go sell ice cream." Ha! I love Eric.

Most leaders would give anything to boost morale and create momentum in their organization. If there were a way to bottle it, the product would be flying off the shelves. Bold and confident leadership (rooted in the peace that you're being obedient to Christ) will do just that. Your team will not only become excited and passionate about their work and service, but as their confidence in you grows, their confidence in their own calling and gifting also grows.

They, following your cue as the leader, start to see themselves as a crucial piece to the puzzle and a vital member of the body of Christ. When they see you willing to stick your neck out, fail, risk, and lead through tough and sometimes uncharted waters, their respect for you deepens, and you end up with an army ready to follow you into battle and fight alongside you.

Dev Patnaik, in his article, *The Fundamentals of Innovation*, said, "Innovation is about growth, and growth takes empathy, creativity, and execution. Empathy, on an organizational scale, is a shared intuition for what people outside the company really need and value. Creativity is the ability to come up with new ideas for products, services, and businesses that are different and distinct.

And execution is the art of getting things done. Companies that innovate sustainably over time don't choose to focus on empathy to the exclusion of creativity or execution. They're great at all three. After all, you can't be a great runner with just a good right leg or left leg. Execution isn't a trade-off for creativity, and neither is it a trade-off for empathy. Two out of three won't cut it. Great companies focus on all three." Wow, that's good stuff!

Execution works hand in hand with your vision, mission, and ideation as an organization. It's a crucial piece of the puzzle. It seems James was pretty passionate about this execution principle. We all know that "faith without works is dead" (James 2:17). Let's look at this passage in a different light—*The Message*:

> *Dear friends, do you think you'll get anywhere in this if you learn all the right words but never do anything? Does merely talking about faith indicate that a person really has it? For instance, you come upon an old friend dressed in rags and half-starved and say, "Good morning, friend! Be clothed in Christ! Be filled with the Holy Spirit!" and walk off without providing so much as a coat or a cup of soup—where does that get you? Isn't it obvious that God-talk without God-acts is outrageous nonsense?*
> *—James 2:14–17 (MSG)*

Boy, do I love reading Scripture in *The Message*. "God-talk without God-acts is outrageous nonsense!" Your team may be tired of hearing your talk, your sermons and your theories. They may be waiting to see if you'll back that talk up with action. Not only your team, but your congregation and community may be sitting back waiting to see if you really believe what you're reading and preaching (God's living and active word).

Please hear my heart: I don't want you to do anything that you're not supposed to do. Being bold and brave just for the sake of saying, "Go big or go home" can be stupid, reckless and dangerous. My heart is about the obedience factor and that if and when you feel God leading you to try something new, you'll have the follow through and execution to do it. This concept must be taken to heart and applied to everything we've discussed so far and are getting ready to discover in the remaining chapters. God be with you as you lead and serve Him.

"Your present circumstances don't determine where you can go; they merely determine where you start."
—Nido Qubein

"To hell with circumstances; I create opportunities."
—Bruce Lee

"Nothing gives one person so much advantage over another as to remain always cool and unruffled under all circumstances."
—Thomas Jefferson

"You must take personal responsibility. You cannot change the circumstances, the seasons, or the wind, but you can change yourself. That is something you have charge of."
—Jim Rohn

"The ideal man bears the accidents of life with dignity and grace, making the best of circumstances."
—Aristotle

"The flower that blooms in adversity is the rarest and most beautiful of all."
—Walt Disney Company, **Mulan**

Situation

The cool church with the DJ

I was speaking to Church leaders in Washington, DC, and we took a break to have lunch. I was sitting with several pastors from the DC region and we were discussing the special challenges of ministry. One pastor from Columbia, Maryland, began to tell me the story of their church and its unique situation.

In his community, he was not able to find any musicians. He said there was one other church in the area, and they had a band, but he was simply not able to find anyone to start a band for his church. He did, however, have a friend who happened to be a DJ. So, without players for his church's band, they used what they did have and became known as the cool church with a DJ.

They weren't trying to be cool, edgy, innovative or futuristic, they were just working with what they had—a DJ. At this time, I was traveling and speaking on four ways that innovation happened. I stopped him and said, "You just showed me a fifth way innovation happens!" He asked what and I told him, "It's through your situation." I then continued to share his story as I went on to future cities and held local forums with Church leaders.

The more I chewed on this reality, the more I realized what a real breakthrough of innovation that one's situation truly is. I began to hear of more and more people who are doing innovative things due to their situation. In Craig Groeschel's book *It*, he talks about innovation happening due to limitation. This is generally the same principle, just different terminology. Craig said that it was in times that they were limited that amazing innovations often happen. I agree.

I was once at a great conference where the host church had a very innovative and creative worship space. I won't name the church because my intent is not to make their architect or design company look bad, but the reality is they had a big mistake happen in their design and build and when it was time to get ready for their first service, they realized they had a problem. They have a very modern room with stadium seating, but unique to them are flat platforms that go up and around their stadium seating.

When the church went to go put out chairs on these flat platforms, they realized they had a problem as people couldn't see due to people on the same level being right in front of them. After tossing around ideas, they decided to turn a negative into a positive and purchased bistro table and stools. They turned their flat platforms into a cool and innovative seating area with stools, bistro tables, chairs and shorter tables (in front of the bistro tables and stools).

As you can imagine, this coffee shop vibe is very popular and these seats fill up fast. I was at the church three days in a row and never got to sit there because the seats were claimed quickly. Like the DJ church, people see these coffee shop-type seating areas and think it was planned intentionally. In reality, the church faced a challenge and answered with a creative solution—and I like it! Craig Groeschel's church, Life.Church, is known as a multisite machine and of their twenty-five campuses (plus an online campus and many strategic partners), only one has a "live" preacher. Do you know the story of how Life.Church first used video for their teaching?

Craig had preached their Saturday night service and planned on preaching again Sunday, but his wife went into labor at 4:00 on Sunday morning, and Craig had to be at the hospital. They didn't have anyone else prepared to speak and didn't know what to do. Someone had the idea of using the video from Saturday night on Sunday morning. They did that with a little fear and an awareness of the risk they were taking, and nobody minded. They stumbled across an amazing truth and innovation for their church due to their situation.

Now spread out across five states and seen daily around the globe on their Internet campus, they are reaching far more people than they could have ever dreamed. Are they doing this because in some brainstorming or strategic planning meeting ten years ago someone laid out this grand plan? No. Their situation led to them being forced into taking a risk and this risk just so happened to be a breakthrough for their church and its future. Sometimes, things that seem bad or negative at the time can lead to something greater that God has in store for you—just look at the life of Joseph (Gen 37–45). Joseph went from one bad situation to another, but eventually ended up in a place that he could have never dreamed. Actually, I guess he did dream it. Ha!

Some of you may have heard of Seacoast Church, which has several campuses and is a true pioneer in the area of multisite campuses. What you may not realize is how they came to be multisite. It was due to their situation. Back in the 90's, I lived and served in Charleston, South Carolina. I would attend Seacoast on Saturday night to worship for myself and then lead worship at my church on Sunday morning. I can remember driving down the road in Mt. Pleasant, SC and seeing the giant signs planted in the ground on this huge piece of land that read, "Future Home of Seacoast Church". I remember hearing of their plans for a massive worship center and new facility they had planned to build to hold their growing church.

I've had the blessing of hearing Seacoast's senior pastor, Greg Surratt, share the story of how they ended up multisite. One night, he went to present the plans of their new building project to the city, and it got voted down. The dream and the amazing plans of this new facility to hold their growing congregation seemed dead. I've heard Greg share of how frustrated and pained he was that night when he returned home. He wrestled with God and couldn't believe that this was His will. What came out of their situation? The idea of starting another venue and sending it a video feed. Ten physical campuses later plus an online campus, and you see that God used their situation to lead them to a true innovation. They are now able to reach far more people, across two states than they ever could if they had built one mega worship center on that piece of land that I saw with the signs.

Biblical innovation due to situation

> *In those days, when the number of disciples was increasing, the Hellenistic Jews among them complained against the Hebraic Jews because their widows were being overlooked [situation] in the daily distribution of food. So the Twelve gathered all the disciples together and said, "It would not be right for us to neglect the ministry of the word of God in order to wait on tables. Brothers and sisters, choose seven men from among you who are known to be full of the Spirit and wisdom. We will turn this responsibility over to them [innovation] and will give our attention to prayer and the ministry of the word." This proposal pleased the whole group. They chose Stephen, a man full of faith and of the Holy Spirit; also Philip, Procorus, Nicanor, Timon, Parmenas, and Nicolas from Antioch, a convert to Judaism. They presented these men to the apostles,*

who prayed and laid their hands on them.
So the word of God spread. The number of disciples in Jerusalem increased rapidly, and a large number of priests became obedient to the faith.
—Acts 6:1–7 (NIV)

Here in Acts 6, we see a situation (their widows were being overlooked in the daily distribution of food) and an innovation that came out of it—the choosing of the seven. It's important to note that in verse 7, it reads, "So the word of God spread." Their situation pushed them into trying and doing something new, but this in actuality allowed God to use them more effectively and thus the "word of God spread" and "the number of disciples in Jerusalem increased rapidly . . . ."

Here's the beauty of this principle: it's a win-win. It may not be much fun when you're in the early stages of going through something like this, but when your situation leads to an innovation, unexpected things happen. In the apostles' case, when they allowed their situation to move them to make changes, both the widows' needs were met, and the word of God was spread and disciples increased. It was a win-win. They could have kept going like they were and the widows would have been neglected and the Gospel would have suffered. They answered their challenge and situation with a new form of ministry and all benefited from their decision.

Ken Blanchard is famous for his teaching on situational leadership. His book *Leadership and the One Minute Manager: Increasing Effectiveness through Situational Leadership* is a number one New York Times Bestseller. When I lived in Georgia, I used to meet weekly with one of my mentors who is a nationally certified trainer of these principles and was formerly on staff with Ken Blanchard. We met weekly to discuss the principles of situational leadership.

Blanchard's teaching is that different leaders and employees need different styles of leadership and management; basically, you don't lead all people the same way. I think, we, as church leaders need to look at a bigger picture of situational leadership. Meaning this is my situation, so God, what are you pushing us toward or away from?

As a leader, one of your key jobs is to be constantly asking the right questions. What are we going to need to try to remedy our situation? The widows are not being taken care of. What can we do to see that they are ministered to and that we keep the main thing the main thing? These are the questions and situation that the apostles wrestled with and it led to a breakthrough in how we structure and design ministry roles in the Church.

As you know, I was greatly impacted by Henry Blackaby's book *Experiencing God*. In his work, Blackaby says that we can learn God's will through a series of things, like Scripture, prayer, the Holy Spirit, people and circumstances. This Situation chapter best relates to what Blackaby was talking about circumstances being used by God to show us what He's up to.

The thing about circumstances or the situation you may find yourself in is that you can't change your circumstances. Craig Groeschel couldn't stop his wife from going into labor. Greg Surratt couldn't fight the city that had rejected his building plan. But they each chose to try something new, something different, something unusual, something risky to remedy their situation, and the world is a better place because they did. Alan Hirsch and Michael Frost said something profound: "The question that must drive us is the question of whether we can join with God in his mission—in whatever place we find ourselves." (*The Shaping of Things to Come* p.161)

When you feel trapped, stuck, challenged, or pushed into a corner, watch out! God might be ready to take you in a totally different direction for His glory. My prayer for you is that you wouldn't let your situation stop you from your mission as a local body of Christ, but that you'd prayerfully consider other ways to accomplish your mission that take into account your situation and lead you to new ways of doing ministry.

"We live, in fact, in a world starved for solitude, silence, and private: and therefore starved for meditation and true friendship."
—C. S. Lewis, The Weight of Glory

"Every person needs to take one day away. A day in which one consciously separates the past from the future. Jobs, family, employers, and friends can exist one day without any one of us, and if our egos permit us to confess, they could exist eternally in our absence. Each person deserves a day away in which no problems are confronted, no solutions searched for. Each of us needs to withdraw from the cares which will not withdraw from us."
—Maya Angelou, Wouldn't Take Nothing for My Journey Now

"Most people are so busy knocking themselves out trying to do everything they think they should do, they never get around to what they want to do."
—Kathleen Winsor

"There is more to life than increasing its speed."
—Mahatma Gandhi

"When we get too caught up in the busyness of the world, we lose connection with one another and ourselves"
—Jack Kornfield

"Doing nothing is better than being busy doing nothing"
—Lao Tzu

"Everything needs a break."
—Toba Beta

Vacation

I've got to get away!

When I originally wrote this chapter on vacation, I wrote from a hotel room. It was a Saturday afternoon and I was in Dallas, GA. I went to attend West Ridge Church and spend the day with Tony Morgan.

I decided to leave a day early and allow God to speak to me on the drive there and in the quiet of my hotel room.

As I've stated before, this book has evolved from the first time I spoke on innovation. One day, I was teaching on the subject of innovation (at that time, there were fourteen ways that it could happen) at a conference in California and a woman came up to me after my class and said, "What about vacation?" Immediately, her suggestion resonated with me. Not only did I know this principle to be true, I had written about it several times in the past.

I had blogged on this subject and I also wrote an article for *Relevant* magazine years ago entitled *Noise*, where I talked about a time that I went on vacation with my family in the middle of Nowhere, Arkansas. We didn't have any Internet connection or cell phone reception. It was just me, God, and my journal. I filled my journal with pages and pages of ideas, insights, inspirations, dreams, and words from God. Because I had gotten away from the routine of life and the "noise" of our digital world, I could clearly hear God's whisper.

In my article entitled *Noise*, I said, "With all the new movies, X-box games, iPods, podcasts, blogs, and an endless web to search, we must work harder than ever to find that alone and quiet time with our Creator. With all the noise and many cool distractions around us, we must fight for intimate time with God in that 'secret place.' My encouragement to you today (whatever year you're reading this in) is to fight for that intimate time with God. This will not happen by accident. You must withdraw. Detox. Get away. Unplug. It takes a great deal of intentionality. You know who was intentional about doing that? Jesus. I once heard Bob Goff say, "Exhaustion is creativity's biggest enemy. 'Come away to a quiet place and rest'—Jesus."

> *Immediately, Jesus made his disciples get into the boat and go on ahead of him to Bethsaida, while he dismissed the crowd. After leaving them, he went up on a mountainside to pray.*
> *—Mark 6:45–46 (NIV)*

> *Jesus, knowing that they intended to come and make him king by force, withdrew again to a mountain by himself.*
> *—John 6:15 (NIV)*

> **The Twelve Apostles**
> *One of those days Jesus went out to a mountainside to pray, and spent the night praying to God. When morning came, he called his disciples to him and chose twelve of them, whom he also designated apostles...*
> *—Luke 6:12–16 (NIV)*

Now if the Son of God made it a point to get away for times of refreshing, prayer and alone time with His Father, how much more should we? Did you notice how intentional Jesus was to get away alone and pray? In Luke 6, we see a huge innovation (new thing) and decision for Jesus—the choosing of His twelve disciples. Before Christ made that decision, he "spent the night praying to God." If you're facing a major decision in your life, ministry and leadership, possibly on the brink of trying something for the first time—do you get away?

St. John Chrysostom answered the question: Why did Jesus go into the mountains to pray?

> *"To teach us, that loneliness and retirement is good, when we are to pray to God. With this view, you see, He is continually withdrawing into the wilderness, and there often spends the whole night in prayer, teaching us earnestly to seek such quietness in our prayers, as the time and place may confer. For the wilderness is the mother of quiet; it is a calm and a harbor, delivering us from all turmoils."*
> *—Chrysostom, Homily L. Matt. XIV. 23, 24*

Daniel Brown, a pastor in Truro, Nova Scotia posted a sermon online where he shared his thoughts on why Jesus went to the mountains to pray. His sermon stated three very important reasons: One, to be alone; two, to commune with God; and three, to model prayer for us. If Jesus needed to "be alone," "commune with God," and this was how He modeled prayer for us, then I think this is a timeless principle that we should all practice. The Bible tells us that occasionally Jesus would get away from the pressures and busyness of ministry to pray and have some alone time.

I can only imagine how busy you are. Maybe you're a church planter trying to get your church launched and off the ground. Maybe you're in a decline and struggling to bring life and health back to your dying organization. Maybe your ministry is booming, growing and expanding, and you're doing all you can to keep up with the pace of it. Whatever your situation, this discipline will be vital to your personal health, longevity, passion, energy, and clarity of vision and the mission that God's called you to. If you're so busy that you can't fathom taking time to get away and go on vacation, a vacation may be just what the doctor (Great Physician) ordered.

In 2013, I had a sabbatical and the gift of a month away from my church. No calls, no texts, no church emails—zero contact from anyone (even my staff). I felt so relaxed, stress-free and energized to return and give it all I've got. And yes, I came up with many new ideas during my time away. The main innovation or new thing, that I came away with was setting healthy boundaries and protecting my family time. I know that it is God first, family second and my career (even though I'm a pastor) third. I saw that clearly and built up my resolve during my sabbatical or time away from work.

This principle of God speaking to us applies in a number of ways. Yes, there's a need for us to just plain get away. Take time to go on a vacation. Leave your actual home, job and city, and drive or fly. I can't tell you how many times God has spoken to me on flights or while driving a long distance. Many times, I will use the voice recorder on my iPhone to capture thoughts or ideas that God is speaking to me while I'm driving. On family trips, I have constantly asked my wife to write down a thought or idea in my journal for me. Usually, my wife is reading and my kids are in the back watching a DVD, so I'm just driving and thinking and praying. Driving and thinking and praying. Eventually, God shows up, and I just start spouting out thoughts to my wife, and she writes them down for me, so I don't wreck.

Retreats can take you to a whole new level

I also think there's something to Jesus retreating to the mountains. I find that God (as I mentioned in the Revelation chapter) often speaks when we're close to His creation. When I'm at the beach, on a hike, fishing or gazing at one of God's amazing mountains, I'm usually awestruck and filled with inspiration and worship. When our family goes camping, we love to look up into the night sky and see the thousands of stars spread out across the dark canvas. Each time we do that, we remark to our kids how we had to leave the city and get out in the country to be able to see that many stars. You see, you won't be able to see everything that's happening around you (those stars are always there, you just can't see them with the city lights) until you take the time to break away from the norm.

Team leaders, bosses, and pastors, this is why going on a staff retreat can be so healthy for your team. I was recently talking with a pastor that was remarking how he desperately wanted to get away with his team and just enjoy a retreat, time of fellowship, prayer, and planning but that he felt guilty and didn't know what to say if a church member asked why they were going away to a condo on the beach. He felt guilty and decided to stay in town, at their church, and hoped that they'd get some time together on-site.

Friends, don't apologize for going on a retreat. If someone asks, tell them there's a strategic, intentional, and biblical reason and that for the sake of the health and longevity of your team, you're going away. Maybe one of you just needed to read that and be free of any false guilt and shame of daring to take your ministry team on a retreat.

I go on at least two retreats every year, one with my staff and one with our church's senior leadership team. And sometimes I get away with other pastor friends for times of refreshing.

I asked Larry Osborne (pastor of North Coast Church) about this and he said, "I've had numerous 'zero-based' planning retreats in which we've as much as possible asked the question, 'What would we do if we were starting all over again from scratch? What would stop—and what would we start? That has helped us immensely in terms of staying open and hungry to innovation." Have you ever taken your team on a "zero-based" planning retreat? Can you imagine the possibilities of change and innovation that could come out of a retreat that asked those specific questions?

The other beauty of retreats is you get to really know the people you're doing life with. Bill Hybels often talks about chemistry and staff relationships. Chemistry is built up over time and relationships grow exponentially when you get away and dream with one another. Throw the football around, play some horseshoe, go horseback riding, sit around the campfire and like one staff retreat I went on: we watched episodes of *The Office* together.

Laughing together goes a long way toward team health and remember, health creates the right environment for growth. If you want your team to grow spiritually and professionally, you must strive for team health.

When I was on staff at Bent Tree, I had an amazing boss, Scott Dyer. I remember one especially busy and stressful season we were in as a church getting ready to move into our brand new 3,300-seat worship center and all the craziness that was going on preparing for our first services in the new space. Right in the midst of one of the craziest weeks in my life (the week leading up to the first service in the new building), Scott told us to carve out an afternoon with nothing planned. He would not tell us what we were going to do, but he said we'd love it. We did. I think he would have blindfolded us if he could, but he put his team in cars and we headed off to the unknown. Scott knew where we were going, and everyone else just followed him.

Eventually, we came pulling up in the parking lot of our local IMAX movie theater. We got out, thinking, Cool—we're going to see a movie. Scott had a big ol' smile on his face. This wasn't just any movie; this was U2 in 3D on an IMAX screen. He hurried us inside, bought us all the popcorn, candy, and soda we wanted and then ushered us into the theater. We sat there, relaxed and happy, for over two hours, blown away by the creativity, musicianship, technology, and innovation that went into the making of U2-3D. He gave us posters from the movie to remember the special time we had (which was still hanging up in my office a year later) and the most important thing he, as a leader, did was to give us a mental and stress break.

We returned that afternoon rejuvenated, happy, inspired, and motivated to give our best to the busy weekend ahead. In hindsight, it was a genius move. Scott knew he would have a healthier team if we took a three-hour break and did something fun, than if we just worked straight through. Not only that, he was rewarding us. Rewarding us for all our hard work and that goes a long way toward building community and trust on a team. In addition, the inspiration (which we talked about earlier) from the spectacular display of music, cinema, tech and stage design spurred us on to want to do amazing things in our new space. The time away actually led to new innovations as a worship team and staff.

Remember the Sabbath day, to keep it holy.

Another part of this principle is the concept of observing the Sabbath. Let me ask you: Do you have a day off? To some of you, that may seem silly and unthinkable, but believe me, I've come across pastors that worked seven days a week. No wonder nothing new and innovative is coming out of you; you're too busy. Daniel Brown reminded me that the Sabbath "was made for us as an opportunity to slow down, to rest, to relax, to set a boundary that says we as people cannot keep up this kind of pace."

Let's dive deeper and this might be more painful. Do you observe "dark days"? A dark day is what I experienced when I wrote my article Noise. I'm grateful for my friends Tony Steward and Rhett Smith that have advocated this concept as well. What I'm talking about is a dark day from technology—a day where you don't go on Twitter, Facebook, blogs, etc. Some of you might have been feeling good when I asked if you had a day off. You might respond, "Sure.

I have off every Friday and Saturday." But if I were to dig deeper, I might find that your laptop and your cell phone are with you almost 24/7. In the Fall of 2013, I went "dark" on all social media for a month—Facebook, Twitter, Instagram, Foursquare, even my blog—you name it, I went dark and it was marvelous!

When I travel and speak on the use of Twitter for ministry, I always encourage the listeners to set boundaries and observe regular dark days where they don't do Twitter at all. Listen—if you try this and have a tough time doing this, you know you have a problem. If I said, "Let's make tomorrow a dark day for you" and you found your hands shaking in withdrawal and by noon had picked back up your phone and checked Twitter or Facebook, there's an issue. For some of you, you may need to chew on this for a bit and take it to God as a matter of prayer.

Be still

> *Be still before the Lord and wait patiently for him...*
> *—Psalm 37:7 (NIV)*
> *"Be still, and know that I am God; I will be exalted among the nations, I will be exalted in the earth."*
> *—Psalm 46:10 (NIV)*

One final thought on this whole issue is that silence is the opposite of noise. Being still is the opposite of being busy. You must be intentional and deliberate to sit still before your God and strive to have times of silence in your lives. Maybe for you, it's your morning commute. Why not try turning off the radio and just having some quiet and personal time with you and your Creator. Maybe it's late at night before you go to bed.

Whenever you can, my exhortation to you is to fight for those times of silence and stillness before God. This concept of vacation, rest, respite, and getting away is deep. I'm not just talking about taking an annual vacation or a staff retreat, I'm going as far as to talk about your days off and time away from technology. It's a comprehensive proposal, but one that if you take seriously will lead you to a place of health where God can release new ideas and innovations into your life.

Be still.

"There's a way to do it better—find it."
—Thomas A. Edison

"That person who irritates you most has the potential to cause you to grow the most in character."
—Rick Warren

"I've come to believe that all my past failures and frustrations were actually laying the foundation for the understandings that have created the new level of living I now enjoy."
—Tony Robbins

"Laughter and tears are both responses to frustration and exhaustion. I myself prefer to laugh, since there is less cleaning up to do afterward."
—Kurt Vonnegut

"Frustration, although quite painful at times, is a very positive and essential part of success."
—Bo Bennett

"Eagles come in all shapes and sizes, but you will recognize them chiefly by their attitudes."
—E. F. Schumacher

"There is no greater agony than bearing an untold story inside you."
—Maya Angelou

Frustration

I've had all's I can stand, and I can't stands no more!
Have you ever been just plain fed up with something? Have you been sick of the same ole, same ole thing? Have you ever wondered or said aloud, "Do we have to do it like we've always done it?" It happens to all of us at some point in our life and I believe that many times it's a God-thing that God is using to drive you to new heights in your life and ministry.

In February of 2009, I was speaking at the Church Solutions Conference in Phoenix. In between my classes, I got to pop my head into a class being taught by Larry Osborne (lead pastor at North Coast Church). He was speaking on the subject of innovation and he said, "Innovation often comes out of frustration. It's the frustrated staff member or pastor, asking, "Why does it have to be done this way?"

When I heard that, it deeply resonated with my spirit, and I knew I had found another way that innovation can come about. Ever since then, as I continued traveling and speaking on ways that innovation can happen, I've added frustration to my list. What I've seen is many people nodding their head in agreement and the look on people's face that told me they, too, resonated with this principle. Maybe you can relate too.

> *David asked the soldiers standing nearby, "What will a man get for killing this Philistine and ending his defiance of Israel? Who is this pagan Philistine anyway, that he is allowed to defy the armies of the living God?" . . . "Don't be ridiculous!" Saul replied. "There's no way you can fight this Philistine and possibly win! You're only a boy, and he's been a man of war since his youth."*
>
> *But David persisted. "I have been taking care of my father's sheep and goats," he said. "When a lion or a bear comes to steal a lamb from the flock, I go after it with a club and rescue the lamb from its mouth. If the animal turns on me, I catch it by the jaw and club it to death. I have done this to both lions and bears, and I'll do it to this pagan Philistine, too, for he has defied the armies of the living God! The Lord who rescued me from the claws of the lion and the bear will rescue me from this Philistine!"*
> *—1 Samuel 17:26, 33–37 (NLT)*

Have you ever been just plain ticked off about something? David was. With great boldness, frustration, and a declaration that basically said, "Who does this giant think he is?" David put his life on the line to make sure no one dishonored the Living God. He was frustrated that someone had the gall to defy the armies of the Living God and he let his frustration drive him to action. When was the last time your frustration drove you to action?

Bill Hybels (founding pastor of Willow Creek Community Church) encourages: "Figure out what you can't stand. Channel your holy discontent energy into helping to fix what's broken in this life." (*Holy Discontent: Fueling the Fire That Ignites Personal Vision*, p. 149)

James W. Miller (author of God Scent) in his review of Hybels's book Holy Discontent remarks, "Hybels uses the line from the Popeye cartoon to communicate the concept: "I've had all I can stands, and I can't stands no more!'"

Turn that negative into a positive

There is in any given person's life something that makes them desire change. For Hybels, he could not stand stale churches that failed to communicate the gospel effectively. "We are not wholly content in this world, because this world is not yet what God wants it to be. By stoking our own awareness of and frustration with that given problem that most gets under our skin, we can find our calling and build a ministry." Is there something that frustrates you? An old-school system that you cannot stand? A ministry that should have been subtracted or terminated years ago? If so, there is a way to turn that discontent into a holy passion that can change things for the better.

I don't presume to know what nerve this chapter gets on in your own personal life. I'm just praying that the Holy Spirit brings to mind something that is making you bang your head up against a wall right now. When you consider your life, your work, your passion, and calling, where is the thing that like Popeye pushes you to cry out, "I've had all I can stands, and I can't stands no more!" My guess is something comes to your mind right away. You don't have to think about it too long to know what it is that you desire to see change in your organization.

TD Jakes likes to say, "Your misery is your ministry." Think about it. The very thing that drives you crazy in your ministry situation may be the very reason God has you there. He could be waiting for you to get fed up with the same ole, same ole and leading you to break out of your rut and try something new.

Darren DeLaune, in a sermon titled *Going Vertical* that he gave at New Life Church in Conway, AR, on July 19 and 20, 2008, said the following: "The only way out of a rut is through change. Think about this . . . Many times, we are faced with challenges or pressures. You go to the doctor and he says, 'Lose fifty pounds and quit smoking or you're going to die!' Your boss says, 'Improve your performance or you're fired!' Your teacher says, 'Get an A on this test or you fail the class!'—that's pressure. Pressure at times can be a tremendous motivator while it lasts. The problem is, once the pressure subsides, we go back to our normal ways. What I am talking about today is not pressure but letting God change you!" I agree with Darren.

What I'm proposing is a God-given frustration or holy discontent that drives you to change the way you do ministry, business and/or life. For some of you, you may need to let God deal with you first and then allow Him to use you to bring about a much-needed change in the way things are done where you serve. Now if you'll grant me a little grace and boldness for a moment, I'd like to address the senior pastor who is not the one frustrated. You oversee a frustrated team member and quite honestly, he gets on your nerves. You may perceive him to be negative and controversial. Maybe he or she questions the way you do things, the decisions you make, or the validity of a certain program. Could it be (maybe not, but bear with me)—could it be that God has placed that person in your midst and as a part of your team to dream up a new way of doing ministry (innovation) that is born out of that team member's personal frustration? Let me put this another way: For all you CEOs, presidents and senior pastors, please don't think that you're the only one who is allowed to be frustrated about something. Frustration can start at the top, yes, but it can also grow from the bottom.

There may be a very gifted and talented person in your organization that is literally or figuratively hitting his or her head up against a wall. Maybe they've reached a roof or ceiling in your organization that is keeping them from growing and being fulfilled in their work. If they are not allowed to burst through that ceiling and break out of a rut, they're going to go work somewhere else. You might say, "Good. Let him go." But I would strongly caution you to create cultures that encourage innovation, growth, and change, which at the same time will attract quality team members.

Gary Hamel at the 2009 Willow Creek Leadership Summit, in his keynote said, "Listen to the renegades on your church staff. Don't fire them." Read that again. Remember, good leaders surround themselves with people more gifted and smarter than themselves. This is why I am a huge fan of President George W. Bush—because he hired and surrounded himself with people like Condoleezza Rice, and Dr. Rice is one of the most brilliant people I've ever heard speak. Rice is a faculty member of the Stanford Graduate School of Business and a director of its Global Center for Business and the Economy—now that's smart and President Bush wasn't intimidated by her genius—he embraced it and used it to his administration's advantage.

Nobody, especially God, expects you to have the answer for every situation. That's not the way the Body of Christ was designed. God intentionally made it so that you (an eye) will have to rely on a foot, a hand, and other crucial parts it takes just to move.

Young Eagles

In November of 2009, I spoke at the National Outreach Convention in San Diego. One of my four classes was a panel (called "A Panel of Innovators") where I sat with some pretty phenomenal leaders like Greg Ligon, Dave Ferguson, Larry Osborne, Hugh Halter, Greg Surratt, and Dino Rizzo. I'll never forget Larry Osborne talking about this very thing. He calls these young, talented leaders in your organization, "young eagles," and he said, "Young eagles have to fly, and if they can't fly in your place, they'll fly somewhere else. It's what they do."

Larry shared about his early days as a youth pastor. He said he would have "stayed at that church in that role probably five to seven more years" if he was truly allowed to lead and make decisions. He went on to say, "In their minds, they thought they'd taken this twenty-three-year-old kid into leadership. They had no clue that you can only sit at the kids table so long."

Man, have I been that guy before—the "young eagle" sitting at the kids table. I've had God-given frustrations that led to God-given ideas, inspirations, and insights and seen them shot down time and time again. I'm just now at a season in my ministry career where I'm not the youngest on staff, but I remember years and years of always being the youngest pastor on a church staff and not being allowed to soar as a "young eagle." And Larry is right. I didn't stay much longer after being shot down enough.

Was I being disrespectful or having trouble submitting to authority? Not at all. Once a decision had been made (from the top), I got on board and made sure we executed it, but it only takes so many times of not being heard or listened to, to get you looking elsewhere and open to a move. Young eagles are often called and recruited by other like-minded and innovative organizations, and if they can't fly in yours, they'll leave or God forbid, you'll kill the dreamer in someone and turn them into a robot. Who wants a robot? I sure don't.

I remember Andy Stanley years ago speaking at the Catalyst Conference in Atlanta, said, "The toughest challenge for most senior pastors is learning how to lead leaders." It takes a great deal of humility, respect, and wisdom to lead strong leaders and that includes listening to their frustrations and allowing them to lead and act out of their holy discontent.

Andy Stanley also said, "If you are consumed with the tension between what is and what could be, if you find yourself emotionally involved . . . frustrated . . . brokenhearted . . . maybe even angry . . . about the way things are, and if you believe God is behind your anguish, then chances are you are on the brink of something divine. Something too important to walk away from." (*Visioneering* p.271)

Here's what I'm suggesting: Life and ministry are deeper and more complex than meets the eye. Are there times when frustration is shown in anger, disrespect, and outright sin? Yes. But many times frustration is appropriate and the outcome of God at work. My encouragement is to make your (or your team member's) frustration a matter of prayer.

Once our staff read *The Four Obsessions of an Extraordinary Executive: A Leadership Fable* by Patrick Lencioni. In that book, Lencioni talks about a team having spirited, lively, and passionate debate about something and then everyone getting along afterwards and coming to an agreement that all can get behind. Does your team or team leader allow passionate debate? Do you as a leader get upset when a staff member or peer debates or argues with you? Could it be that they are frustrated and God could use them and your discussion to lead to new and wonderful things in your life and ministry? Just pray about this and really chew on this topic, friends.

I'm suggesting you delve. Delve is defined as "to carry on intensive and thorough research for data, information, or the like; investigate." You need to delve deeper into your frustration, your board's frustration, your staff 's frustration and your volunteer's frustration. Don't dismiss it as negativity or disrespect. Prayerfully consider the frustration and look for where God may be up to something. You might just be on the verge of a breakthrough of innovation in your ministry.

"God whispers to us in our pleasures, speaks in our conscience, but shouts in our pains: it is His megaphone to rouse a deaf world."
—The Problem of Pain, C.S. Lewis

"In life you need either inspiration or desperation."
—Tony Robbins

"The enemy of innovation is success."
—Ben Arment

"The greatest inspiration is often born of desperation."
—Comer Cotrell

"If God wants you to do something, he'll make it possible for you to do it, but the grace he provides comes only with the task and cannot be stockpiled beforehand. We are dependent on him from hour to hour, and the greater our awareness of this fact, the less likely we are to faint or fail in a crisis."
—Louis Cassels

"Every now and again, our Lord lets us see what we would be like if it were not for Himself; it is a justification of what He said, "Without Me you can do nothing." That is why the bedrock of Christianity is personal, passionate devotion to the Lord Jesus."
—Oswald Chambers, My Utmost for His Highest

Desperation

A dependency upon the Holy Spirit

What do you think of when you think of being desperate? One of the ways that the dictionary defines being desperate is "having an urgent need, desire, etc." (Desperate for attention.) When I talk about being desperate, this is what I'm referring to: being desperate for God, for His presence, for His power—desperate for Him to show up.

I saved this way that innovation happens for last because it's my favorite. If you get this, you get the whole thing. If you can grasp onto this concept and live it out, you will be a changed person. The way I usually refer to desperation is a kind of desperation that leads to a dependency upon the Holy Spirit. A desperation that leads to a dependency upon the Holy Spirit—that's the key to not only the innovative life but the Christian life.

> *Those who know your name will trust in you, for You, Lord, have never forsaken those who seek You.*
> *—Psalm 9:10 (NIV)*

As an adolescent, I struggled with trying to gain my independence.

I wanted so badly to be a man and not to be told what to do. As an adult, I'm learning to be dependent upon God and to constantly be aware of my need for Him—my Savior, protector, provision, my guide, my portion, my forgiver, and leader. The list could go on and on. Whether new in our faith or seasoned and mature believers, we should be filled with a sense of desperation that leads to a dependency on the Holy Spirit.

A few years ago, the time had come for my son, Tommy, to learn to ride his bike without training wheels. Our whole family went to a local elementary school parking lot after I had taken the training wheels off. My other two children, both girls, started to ride their bikes; the younger with training wheels and the older without training wheels. I focused on Tommy and being a help and encourager to him.

I'll never forget how God used that moment to speak directly to my heart. My son had started to get the hang of things pretty quick. I would keep one hand on the handle bars and one on his back or shoulders. He picked it up fast, so soon, I was just running alongside him with one hand on the back of his shirt, and he was steering and pedaling all on his own. At one point, after he was really feeling confident, he said words that stopped me in my tracks.

With a sweet innocence and excitement about what he was getting ready to do, he said, "Daddy, hold me while I get started and then let me go." Immediately, God spoke to my heart. Those words, "Daddy, hold me while I get started and then let me go," pierced my heart as I could hear my Abba Father, saying, "That's what I hear all the time"—from ministers and leaders.

I don't know why, but this struck a chord in my spirit. Here's where my mind and heart went: I'm a dreamer, a visionary, a builder, and have sort of an entrepreneurial spirit about me. What cut me deep is how many times I cry out to God to help me in the beginning of something and then after a while I lose that sense of dependency and say "I've got it. You can let go now."

Now I know that I can only take this analogy so far. I know that I can't hold on to my son forever—that he's got to be able to ride that bike by himself eventually (which he is doing now). It was the desperation, fear, and urgency that I heard in my son's voice as he called out to me that grabbed my attention.

So often when a new ministry, new service, new campus, new (you fill in the blank) is starting, we are so desperate and dependent upon God to lead, guide, and direct us—it's natural. We sincerely need Him and will often fast, pray, and intentionally seek His leading for every step we take. The problem is once that ministry grows and has some success that sense of urgency and desperation seems to fade away. Without really realizing it, we say, "I've got it now, God. You can let go of me. I'll be fine."

I don't know whom I'm speaking to. Maybe a church planter. Maybe a nonprofit that's in the early stages. Maybe someone who's been serving somewhere for a long time and has become comfortable. Hear my heart: Let's never stop crying out to God and longing for His presence and His hand to guide and hold us. I hope I never again (because I have before) get to a place where I say to God, "I've got it now. You can let go." I pray that for you as well.

> *"I am the vine; you are the branches. If a man remains in me and I in him, he will bear much fruit; apart from me you can do nothing."*
> *—John 15:5 (NIV)*

I would like to shout that verse right at you, my friend, Mr. or Ms. Ambitious, passionate, driven, innovative leader. Apart from Christ, you will never be truly innovative, unusually creative, and eternally effective. My friend, Mark Batterson wrote, "There is a pattern that I see repeated throughout Scripture: Sometimes, God won't intervene until something is humanly impossible." He goes on to say, "Maybe God allows the odds to be stacked against us so He can reveal more of His glory." (*In a Pit with a Lion on a Snowy Day* p. 23)

I remember writing about innovation for the Catalyst newsletter about two years ago and one of the comments was from someone that didn't seem to get this. His comment was, "Innovation isn't always doing something new . . . in fact, if we're truly honest with ourselves, most of the stuff, the majority of the stuff we do, is just copycat. Seriously, how much stuff that we do today is really innovative as per your definition?"

I remember thinking, what a shame. What a shame that you would put God in a box and say nothing new can happen or be done anymore; now, we just copy others and that's the extent of our creativity. Sadly, a lot of church leaders I know do equate innovation with copying other churches. If an "innovative church" does a certain campaign or sermon series, other churches copy it and think they are innovative. What the person who commented on my article and many other church leaders don't realize is this principle from John 15—that "apart from me you can do nothing." Keep on walking independently, unaware of your desperate need for Christ and the leading of His Holy Spirit and you will always think copying is the best you can do. Start leading lives with a sense of desperation that leads to a dependency upon the Holy Spirit and you'll be amazed at the things that God leads you to accomplish, the places He will call you to go, and the initiatives

He will guide you to start.

The Big Three

When I teach on this subject of desperation, I share about three ways that I see desperation in the Church. The first way that I see a sense of desperation is with church plants (new works). For a while, I coached church planters through the ARC, a church planting organization. I got to attend the church planter's initiation and first training, their assessment process, and their one-week intensive basic training.

As I interacted with church planters in person at these events or on the phone through my coaching, I picked up on their sense of desperation. They were so nervous, so full of excitement mixed with fear; that it made them extremely teachable, which is key to growth and opens the gates for innovation to occur. Teachability is something that comes pretty naturally to church planters. I just recently returned from a church planters conference, and I again was reminded of just how hungry and teachable they are. I'm not just talking about hungry to grow and survive, but a hunger for God and His hand on their ministry.

As Shawn Lovejoy, senior pastor at Mountain Lake Church and cofounder of ChurchPlanters.com, said at the Velocity Conference in 2010, "Church planting is hard business. If you can do anything else, do it." The good news is that with great organizations out there, such as ARC, NewThing Network, The Launch Network, ChurchPlanters.com, NewChurches.com, NAMB, Acts 29, Stadia, The Orchard Group, and Exponential and coaches, consultants and writers, such as Ed Stetzer, Nelson Searcy, and Stephen Gray, there is plenty of help and guidance for church planters.

Ed Stetzer told me that "68 percent of church plants survive after four years," which is an encouraging number compared to some of the urban legends I've heard of church planting statistics. Still, church planting is an extremely difficult task and not something to be taken lightly. I've heard it called the "extreme sport" of pastoring.

Because everything in church planting is so new and there are so many firsts, it is like my son, Tommy, saying, "Daddy, hold me." Church planters are very dependent upon the Holy Spirit. You could say they lead, serve, and act out of a sense of desperation that leads to a dependency on the Holy Spirit.

Dead and Declining Churches

The second way that I see desperation in the Church is through older, established, and dead or declining churches. I used to teach on two ways that I saw desperation in the Church and a nice older man came up to me after I was speaking to Church leaders in Dallas, TX, and gently suggested I consider older, declining churches. He said, "Just as church plants are in 'survival mode,' older churches are also in survival mode. They're trying not to close the doors and become extinct." God used that older man to speak straight to my heart, and his words resonated with my spirit. I knew what he was saying was true.

Please don't misunderstand what I'm saying. I'm not making a blanket statement about older churches in general (First Baptist Name Your City, First United Methodist, First Pres, etc.). I'm talking specifically about established churches that are in decline, which sadly, most churches in the US are in plateau or decline. Many of these churches started out with a burning vision, passion, mission, and other things I've shared in this book. Like the church in Ephesus in Rev 2, they have somehow forsaken their "first love."

This goes back to the decision we talked about in the second chapter. You have to decide to grow, decide to try new things and dare to follow God wherever He leads. This takes great faith, courage, obedience and a tremendous amount of intentionality. Andy Stanley says, "Vision leaks." We all if we're not careful will drift off course and find ourselves in maintenance mode, too scared to try anything new. It's the old we've-always-done-it this-way mindset.

For this second group of the Church that I watch, somewhere along the way, they wake up, they get mad, they have a God-moment, they have revival—something occurs, and they return to their dependency upon the Holy Spirit. Maybe it's a pastor, deacon, or elder with a burden. Something leads them to attempt to be vibrant and full of life again. They start seeking God like they used to and this sense of desperation comes about. I'm watching it happen right now with the local First Baptist Church in my very own city. Only God can revive a dead church, but you must be desperate for Him.

I remember several years ago hearing TD Jakes preach and him, saying, "Some of you need to fight. Don't give up." When the leadership of a declining church wakes up to the reality that if something doesn't change soon they are going to close their doors forever, they start to become desperate again, and it's a beautiful thing.

If you don't believe God can turn around a dead church, you haven't met our Redeemer who raises the dead. As a matter of fact, raising the dead is kind of His specialty—He's actually pretty famous for it. I don't care how old your church is, how many people are attending and how far behind budget you are; to say your church couldn't turn around would be to say that God is not big enough. He is and you can see new life and ideas again. Thom Rainer has written extensively on this and covers it far greater than I ever could.

Turnaround examples

I served on staff at Bent Tree in Carrollton, TX, which is a thriving church. When pastor Pete Briscoe came there, it was a declining church of around two hundred people. Now, years later, it is a church of around five thousand and well known for their global missions work and many strategic partners. In 2013, they branched out and went multisite to increase their reach in the DFW Metroplex.

When Matt Chandler felt called to go to Highland Village Baptist Church, it was a dead church of about 150 people. Now, years later, The Village is one of the fastest growing churches in Dallas with over 10,000 people attending at three regional campuses.

My friend, Scott Hodge, is senior pastor of The Orchard in Aurora, IL. The Orchard is now 90 years old. Scott took over the church where his dad was pastor for 24 years. They had been declining and Scott's dad, Larry Hodge, felt God's leading to ask Scott to join him in turning around the church. Together, they led the church through significant change. Larry has since gone on to Heaven, but Scott is now at the helm and pastors a growing, healthy church that has gone from 250 people at the beginning of the transition to over 1,500.

Brad Powell came to Temple Baptist Church (now NorthRidge)

in Plymouth, MI, in 1990. Temple Baptist had seen better days. In 1969, they were one of American's ten largest churches. Brad came there with 1,000 people attending—less than one-fourth of what the church's attendance had been—they had lost nearly 90 percent of its membership in the 10 years prior to Powell's arrival. Now the church is healthy, vibrant and runs over 10,000 people.

Clayton Coates was led away from Saddleback Church to become senior pastor of First Baptist Church Coppell (Texas), now GracePoint Church. He walked into a declining situation with recent attendance well under 170 on Sundays. The church now has a new staff, new by-laws and constitution, has acquired an adjacent property, transformed the overlook and feel of the entire property, planted a church in Kagwada, South Sudan, doubled the number of small groups and is averaging around 450 in weekend attendance, while seeing highs in the 800s. The story is young, but Clayton and the staff are focused as they honor the past, rejoice in the present, and move with great faith into the future.

Bruce Fosdick is pastor of The Rock of Southwest in Denver, CO. They were a declining church of 80 people and now they are a church of over 1,200 with 3 daughter churches.

Ike Reighard has served at Piedmont Church since January 2006 (as interim pastor) and became the Lead Pastor in February 2007. When Ike first started at Piedmont, they were running about 200. Through challenging messages for people to exchange ordinary living for an extraordinary life through Jesus and an intentional focus on serving the community, Piedmont has grown to present attendance of 800.

After 2 pastors and 5 years of slowly declining attendance, and on the verge of dying, Real Life Christian Church in Chesapeake, VA, asked their veteran youth pastor to consider taking the lead pastor position. When Doug Forehand stepped in as the lead pastor, the church was running less than 200 people in attendance weekly and was about $60,000.00 in the hole. During his first sixteen months, the church restored its waning building project, giving increased by 110 percent, they increased from one to two services, and attendance jumped to over 550 practically overnight when they moved into their new building.

Michael Robison came to Grace Church in Kingsport, TN, in 2008. This church had crumbled from 1,100 to just over 100 due to the previous pastor's infidelity as well as some other leaders in the church. In the next 20 months, they replanted, restructured and started to grow. Their demographic changed from forty- five plus years to twenty-five plus years of age. They built a new 23,000-square-foot building with cash and have grown to over 500 in weekly attendance. Now preparing to launch a second campus and a new mission compound/church in Haiti, they are a story of God's divine grace and provision.

Please know that none of these leaders take credit. They give God all the glory, but I'd guess they did some things right. These are just a few stories that I knew of off the top of my head. I know there is a ton more just like this. Yes, most churches in the US are in plateau or decline, but we must never forget that if God so chooses, He can bring the dead back to life. He's looking for obedient men and women of God that he can whisper to. Energetic, reverent, and sensitive leaders (Philip 2:12) that have a sense of desperation that leads them to a dependency on the Holy Spirit.

The Persecuted Church

The third way I see desperation in the Church is through the persecuted Church. The underground Church. These heroes of the faith are in true survival mode. Where the church plant is in survival mode to make it as a church and the older, declining church is survival mode to keep from closing their doors, the persecuted church is in survival for their very lives. They are beaten, imprisoned, tortured, and even killed. They have a special place in my heart, and I sincerely believe we have a ton to learn from them.

I have often said that I'd love to get our big-name pastors from America in a room with one no-name pastor of a church overseas. I'd love to be a fly on the wall as he shares how he's seen God move and why he believes his church has been growing. For some mysterious, divine reason, the church that is persecuted seems to grow like wildfire—it's like God breathes on them and the fire is so contagious it spreads rapidly regardless of the consequences many of the leaders face.

I was once visiting Saddleback Church and was in the Green Room backstage before the service and got to meet their guest speaker for the day, Brother Yun. He is a living legend—someone that I was honored and humbled to shake his hand and be in the company of. His story is an unimaginable one that led to him miraculously walking out of a maximum-security prison in China. I encourage you to get the book, *The Heavenly Man*, and read his story.

What would a pastor of an underground church have to say to a keynote speaker, author, and popular blogger/pastor in the US? I believe (and I've been around a few of these heroes) he would share of his lifeline to God through prayer. How they live, lead, and move out of a sense of desperation that leads to a dependency upon the Holy Spirit. I believe they would share how they relate to and equate fasting with what we in America equate technology. Read that again.

I believe that the way some pastors I've been around view technology (Twitter, Facebook, lighting, haze, sound systems, HD video, eye candy screens, environmental projection, Internet campuses, and on and on) is similar to how some overseas pastors view Scripture, prayer and fasting. I know that stings, but it needs to be said. I've been around pastors and been brought in to consult with churches and church leaders that talked more about video switchers and moving lights than God the Father, Jesus, the Holy Spirit, prayer, Scripture, and fasting combined. There are churches that have what Craig Groeschel calls *It* that don't have good lighting or amazing video intro bumpers before the message.

The Bible exhorts us to "pray without ceasing" (1 Thess 5:17). These are words that I fear many pastors don't take seriously. How dependent are you on God? Are the words of Acts 17:28, "For in him we live and move and have our being," true for you? Is there desperation and dependence in America? Absolutely.

Though I believe we have much to learn from our overseas brothers and sisters, I have seen vibrant houses of prayer here in the US. Most of us know the story of Jim Cymbala and Brooklyn Tabernacle. If not, I encourage you to pick up the book *Fresh Wind, Fresh Fire*.

Praying Pastors

In my time working with ARC, I got to be around and sit under the teaching of Chris Hodges and Rick Bezet. Chris Hodges is the founding pastor of Church of the Highlands in Birmingham, AL. Rick Bezet is the founding pastor of New Life Church in Conway, AR. Interestingly enough, they were the first two ARC church plants. Besides that, they both share a common distinction: in 2008, Church of the Highlands was listed as Outreach magazine's fastest growing church in the United States. In 2009, New Life Church was listed as the fastest growing church in the US. Why is this special to me? Because I know these guys and the one thing that I see that they have in common is their dependency upon the Holy Spirit.

Remember, Chris Hodges said, "You can't delegate prayer." His church does a week of prayer and fasting every January and a week of prayer and feasting every August. Each day, over those two months they meet from 6:00 a.m. to 7:00 a.m. for prayer and seeking God. I got to attend one time in August of 2009. Rick Bezet does something similar at his church. There are several churches that have adopted this and do a prayer and fasting month each year. I bring these two guys up together because so many see their churches make the number one spot on the fastest growing church list and don't make the correlation. If we're not careful, we'll find ourselves thinking I bet they have great facilities or I bet they use technology well. There's nothing wrong with either of these things, but we need to give credit to where credit's due: God and God alone.

These churches are exploding because they've tapped into that pipeline. They operate out of a sense of desperation that leads to a dependency upon the Holy Spirit. Do you want to know Chris Hodges's secret? The reason his church has been blessed? I'm sure there are several reasons, but I'm sure he wouldn't mind me sharing with you my favorite reason because it will drive you back to God and on your knees.

Every Saturday morning since Chris launched Church of the Highlands, his core people gather together to pray and cry out to God to move the next day. They don't gather to pray for Aunt Susie or Uncle Ed (hear my heart)—they gather to pray for one thing and one thing only: for God to show up and move in their midst when they gather on Sunday for corporate worship. Chris has done this his entire ministry. When he was a youth minister and met on Wednesday nights, he would gather people to pray the night before. Chris would make a good underground pastor—he's got the prayer thing in his DNA and the DNA of his church. His church has an active and comprehensive prayer ministry led by two amazing staff leaders and a large volunteer team.

I bring these guys up not to shine the light on them or their churches, but to shine the light on Christ and the work of the Holy Spirit when we connect with Him through prayer and operate, plan, lead, and minister with an awareness of our need for Him. Please, please don't look at external things like buildings, multisite campuses, coffee shops, great music and technology as the formula for a fast-growing, innovative church. I'm trying my best to save you a lot of heartache, frustration, burnout, and confusion by pointing you to this key way that innovation can happen. Again, if you get this, you get it all. Grasp this concept of dependency and you can do anything! All things are possible with God (Matt 19:26).

I've shared several other ways that innovation can happen, but honestly, this is the main premise. Rely on Christ, live a life dependent on the Holy Spirit, and leave the innovative stuff up to Him. Since God is the one doing a new thing (Isa 43:19), we just need to remain close, faithful, sensitive, and reverent before Him. When He moves and acts and does something new, if we move and act with Him (Henry Blackaby's principle of joining God where He's at work), we'll naturally or rather, supernaturally, be innovative. Get it?

"The cross and the Confederate flag cannot co-exist. One will set the other on fire."
–Russell Moore

"Racial reconciliation rests upon this basis: you have never seen a mere mortal."
–Thabiti Anyabwile

"Once you have been reconciled to God, you have no problem with being reconciled with others."
–Fred Luter

"Our lack of unity and oneness is a direct contradiction of our missiological goal: disciples of all nations."
–Kevin Smith

"God is not asking blacks to be white or whites to be black, but for both to be biblical."
–Tony Evans

"Our goal is not just to get black people and white people in the same room; Jay-Z can do that. We want blacks and whites in the same family."
–Trip Lee

"Racial reconciliation isn't just a good idea because it's politically correct. The message of the gospel is at stake."
–Afshin Ziafat

"Racial indiscrimination should be driven by an indiscriminate gospel."
–Danny Akin

Bonus Chapter

***Reconciliation* by Dr. Derwin L. Gray**

What was the first major church dispute? Was it over Calvinism, Arminianism, or Molinism? Was it over speaking in tongues, prophecy, or healing? Maybe it was over worship music styles? Those Jews just couldn't stand those Greek worship leaders wearing tight, skinny leg jeans.

A Third Race of Humans is Born Out of the True Human: Jesus

The first major church dispute was over how fast multi-ethnic churches were growing outside of Jerusalem. These (ethnically) racially diverse congregations were blowing up the mental and cultural circuits of the Jewish believers in Jerusalem.

Ethnocentrism gives way to Christocentrism.

These 1st Century, multi-ethnic churches (Jew and Gentile) were filled with uncircumcised Gentiles (Africans, Arabs, Greeks, Syrians, Asians, Romans, Persians, and more). See Colossians 3:11, Ephesians 2:14-16, Galatians 3:24 and the rest of the Bible.

Sure, the Council at Jerusalem in Acts 15 was about circumcision and food, but it was also about race (ethnicity). The Gospel of grace is so glorious; a new humanity is birthed and humanity is reconciled to God and to each other (2 Cor. 5:14-21).

Before Jesus, there were two ethnic groups on earth: Jew and Gentile. After Jesus' resurrection, a new ethnic group made up of Jews and Gentiles was birthed. This new ethnic group is called the Church; the one "new man." Ethnocentrism gives way to Christocentrism.

For He Himself is our peace, who has made us both one and has broken down in his flesh the dividing wall of hostility by abolishing the law of commandments expressed in ordinances, that he might create in himself one new man in place of the two, so making peace, and might reconcile us both to God in one body through the cross, thereby killing the hostility. Ephesians 2:14-16 ESV

Theologian Christopher J.H. Wright in his marvelous book, *The Mission of God,* page 191, insightfully writes:

> *"If only all the theological disputes in Christian history had been caused by successful mission and rapid church growth. Undoubtedly the first dispute was. The first major council of the church (Acts 15) was convened to consider a knot of problems caused by the success of cross-cultural church planting efforts. These had been initiated by the church of Antioch and carried out among the predominately Gentile and ethnically diverse peoples of the Roman provinces that made up what we now call Turkey. Paul and Barnabas, who had been entrusted with this initiative, were not the first to cross the barrier from Jew to Gentile with the good news of Jesus Christ. Philip (Act 8) and Peter (Acts 10) had already done that. They were, however, the first to establish whole communities of believers from mixed Jewish and Gentile backgrounds—that is, to plant multiethnic churches."*

Be Like Paul

As a church planter of a multi-ethnic, local church, it is so beautiful to see ethnically diverse people loving Jesus and each other as one voice glorifying God.

Are you concerned with multi-ethnic church planting? You should be. The Apostle was—and it's God's heart.

Whether you are a church planter, pastor, or other Christ-follower, I hope you will seriously grapple with the words of my good friend and doctoral advisor, New Testament scholar Scot McKnight. In his book *A Community Called Atonement: Living Theology*, he shares some powerful and sobering thoughts about how the gospel that the apostle Paul preached produced local churches that were much different than ours are today in America.

He writes, "About 90 percent of American churches have developed in such a way that about 90 percent of the people in those churches are of the same color. Which is to say that only about 10 percent of churches are integrated. Why might this be so? Michael Emerson and Christian Smith, in their prophetic book *Divided by Faith*, conclude with this: 'The processes that generate church growth, internal strength, and vitality in a religious marketplace also internally homogenize and externally divide people. Conversely, the processes intended to promote the inclusion of different peoples also tend to weaken the internal identity, strength, and vitality of volunteer organizations.' In other words, 'The gospel we preach shapes the kind of churches we create. The kind of church we have shapes the gospel we preach.'"

The gospel we preach shapes the kind of churches we create. The kind of church we have shapes the gospel we preach.

The gospel Paul preached

The gospel that is preached in America produces homogeneous churches. But the gospel Paul preached in the first-century, Greco-Roman world produced multiethnic, multiclass churches. Reflect on these texts (emphasis added):

> *"There is neither **Jew nor Greek**, there is neither **slave nor free**, there is no **male and female**, for you are all **one in Christ Jesus**" (Gal. 3:28, ESV).*

> *"Here there is not **Greek and Jew**, circumcised and uncircumcised, **barbarian, Scythian, slave, free**; but Christ is all, **and in all**" (Col. 3:11, ESV).*

> *"I am under obligation both to **Greeks** and to **barbarians** . . . For I am not ashamed of the gospel, for it is the power of God for salvation to everyone who believes, to the **Jew** first and also to the **Greek**" (Rom. 1:14, 1:16, ESV).*

> *"To win **Jews and Gentiles**, Paul says, "I have become **all things to all people** so that by all possible means I might save some. I do all this for the sake of the gospel, that I may share in its blessings" (1 Cor. 9:22b, ESV).*

Paul planted and built multiethnic churches for the "sake of the gospel" because at the heart of the gospel that Paul preached was reconciliation between God and man and between man and man. Man was separated from God; thus man was separated from one another. The gospel unites all.

According to another leading New Testament scholar, N.T. Wright in Paul and the Faithfulness of God, "The reconciliation of Jew and Greek, particularly, was obviously near the heart of Paul's aim . . . Paul wanted to see as the result of all his labours cross-culturally united worship."

Intrinsic to Paul's gospel was a barrier-breaking, hostility-destroying power that brought ethnically diverse people together in Christ and created a species of humanity that was no longer defined by its tribe or ethnicity, but by Christ. Marinate on Paul's God-inspired words of Ephesians 2:14-16: "For he himself is our peace, who has made us both one and has broken down in his flesh the dividing wall of hostility by abolishing the law of commandments expressed in ordinances, that he might create in himself one new man in place of the two, so making peace, and might reconcile us both to God in one body through the cross, thereby killing the hostility" (ESV).

According to Paul:

1. Jesus is the peace that brings ethnically diverse people together.
2. Jesus breaks down walls that divide ethnically different people.
3. Jesus creates a new man or new human species. Before Jesus, only Jews and non-Jews existed. After Jesus, a new group of people was created in him, called the church.
4. Through the cross, individual sins are forgiven, different ethnic groups are reconciled, and hostility between people has been killed.

As Paul writes in these verses, these four gospel realities are complete. God's people just need to walk in the "good works" Jesus has prepared beforehand for us to walk in (Eph. 2:8-10).

Final Thoughts

Whether you are pastor, church planter or Christ-follower, ask yourself this question: Is the gospel I'm hearing and believing in accordance with Paul's passion to see the local church be ethnically diverse?

"Art is a collaboration between God and the artist, and the less the artist does the better."
—Andre Gide

"I love strange choices. I'm always interested in people who depart from what is expected of them and go into new territory."
—Cate Blanchett

"Write to be understood, speak to be heard, read to grow."
—Lawrence Clark Powell

"Because God has made us for Himself, our hearts are restless until they rest in Him."
—Augustine of Hippo

"The irony is that while God doesn't need us but still wants us, we desperately need God but don't really want Him most of the time."
—Francis Chan

"Is prayer your steering wheel or your spare tire?"
—Corrie ten Boom

"I am fallen, flawed and imperfect. Yet drenched in the grace and mercy that is found in Jesus Christ, there is strength."
—Adam Young

Conclusion

Forget everything I said

I was consulting with a church and I urged the pastor to change something (do something new and different). What I urged him to do is a widely-accepted thing in most modern churches and something I've asked many people to do. This pastor I was speaking to used to be a consultant too and knew where I was coming from. I'll never forget his words to me. He said, "I know you're saying what I would say to a church and I get your reasoning, but I haven't had the Spirit tell me to do that yet. When the Spirit releases me, I'll make the change, but I'm not going to do it without the Spirit's leading."

As this pastor that I greatly respect said those words, it resonated deeply with me and I said, "That is what my book is about: Spirit-led leadership. I totally agree with you and don't want you to do one of my ideas over what God is leading you to do."

I share this with you in this concluding chapter because it's at the very heart of what I've tried to weave throughout this book. Being a strange leader is about more than doing new or different things; it's about being Spirit-led. From the introduction, I tipped my hand and said that "God tells us in Isaiah 43:19 that it is God Who is doing new things. He's the Chief Innovator.

Henry Blackaby teaches that "when you recognize where God is working, you can join in what He is doing." (*Experiencing God* p. 70) That to me, friends, is at the very core of being innovative— to be so in tune with God that His dreams become your dreams.

> *"This is God's Message, the God who made earth, made it livable and lasting, known everywhere as God: 'Call to me and I will answer you. I'll tell you marvelous and wondrous things that you could never figure out on your own.'*
> *—Jeremiah 33:2–3 (MSG)*

Did you catch that? Call to God, rely on Him, desperately seek Him, and He'll tell and show you "things you could never figure out on your own." That's the beauty of this whole innovation thing and my urging you to be Spirit-led. You don't have to think of everything! Isn't that a relief? You don't have to struggle to be innovative. God, Himself, will show you things that you couldn't even imagine or dream up.

Genesis 6:9 teaches us that Noah "was a righteous man, blameless in his time; Noah walked with God." What did Noah do? Only one of the most innovative and unprecedented acts in all of human history. He built an ark to protect himself, his family, and many animals from a flood before it had ever rained—that's innovative (doing something new) and at the time, it was strange.

The question is: Whose idea was it?

Let that sink in for a moment. Did Noah come to God with a plan to build a boat and ask him to bless it or did God speak to Noah and guide Him because he was a man that "walked with God"? When it comes right down to it, we really can't take credit for innovative ideas. They are truly gifts from God that should lead us to worship.

The Genius of the Holy Spirit

Dave Browning said, "The success of CTK is a credit to the genius of the Holy Spirit. We have been given a different conceptual framework with which to work, and we are thankful." It's all about participation with the Holy Spirit. Dave Browning described the CTK story as a divine-human partnership. He said, "We couldn't do it without God, but God has also chosen not to do it without us. And we have worked hard to cooperate with God" (*Deliberate Simplicity* p. 12). Amen—that's strange leadership and could be said of all of us who strive to follow hard after God.

> *What we've learned is this: God does not respond to what we do; we respond to what God does. We've finally figured it out. Our lives get in step with God and all others by letting him set the pace, not by proudly or anxiously trying to run the parade.*
> *—Romans 3:27b–28 (MSG)*

> *Dave Gibbons at the 2010 Exponential Conference said, "Respond to the Holy Spirit's movement in you, your capacity, calling, and context." That's what this whole book is about and the thread woven through each chapter—we respond to the Holy Spirit's movement. And remember God is always at work around us.*

> *"God is always doing 10,000 things in your life, and you may only be aware of 3 of them."*
> *—John Piper*

From the introduction to the first chapter on Salvation through the last chapter on Desperation, we've looked at forty different -ions. One -ion that I intentionally didn't write on is "imitation." I cringe when I hear other church leaders tell people (especially when they're speaking at a conference) that innovation is imitating what someone else is doing. No! —that's copying.

Innovation is the act of doing or introducing something new.

If you're going to copy someone, copy God. Follow His leading. That's the point of this entire book.

My encouragement to you, friend, is to reread this book sometime with new eyes and an overall understanding that I desire each chapter to be covered by the Spirit's leading and truly desire you to lead wherever and however God leads you and your church and that has nothing to do with what the "cool" church down the street is doing. Churches that are known for being innovative didn't get there by copying others—they're original in their approach to ministry, outreach, and service and the world has noticed.

Think of David and King Saul's armor. If David had tried to be like Saul and wear his armor instead of being himself, David would have died. He had to go at it his own way, using his own weapons and approach to battle. When you get back from a conference, read a book (even this one), or see in a magazine something innovative and new that another church or church leader did that had success, don't be fooled into trying on their armor. What worked for them may be a disaster for you.

Now I realize that sometimes, we, as Church leaders do use ideas, products, processes or concepts from other churches and lots of times, it works out fine and fits our church's culture. All I'm saying is don't call that being innovative. Admit you're copying another church's approach and leave it at that.

What I long to see are the special moments in your church's history when you come up with something totally brand new and truly innovative and do a real "first" for you and your ministry—that's strange leadership and that's what people will point to and say, "That's an innovative church."

If you remember anything, remember to be intentional.

As we come down the home stretch, I want to bring back the whole concept of intentionality that you've read throughout this book.

Strange leaders are intentional and strategic. Even something as basic and vital as praying together as the leadership of your ministry and being Spirit-led is something that will take an enormous amount of intentionality. Please remember we work "hard" to partner with the "genius of the Holy Spirit"—and that takes intentionality, friends.

I'd also like to remind you of the whole concept of listening. First and foremost, listening to the Holy Spirit and then listening as we covered in this book to the people, pain, need, culture, and through technology. Leaders are listeners. Strange leaders are intentional listeners. When your intentionality intertwines with your listening, that's the intersection of where God can meet you and show up in mighty ways in your ministry.

Lastly, I want to remind you to be brave and take courage. Being a strange leader is not easy or glamorous. You may make a tough decision sometime and will be talked about and not be the most popular person for a season. Many innovative leaders that I mentioned throughout this book have been shunned by their denomination, made fun of behind closed doors, and attacked pretty harshly on blogs and websites. Strange leaders have battle wounds and take some pretty hard hits.

Eric Geiger once tweeted: "If you want to make everyone happy, don't be a leader. Go sell ice cream." At the Exponential Conference in 2010, Bill Hybels said, "The only way to avoid criticism is to do nothing significant with your life." Hybels is a strange leader, and he gets it. He knows that choices he and his team make will often lead to criticism and he's okay with that. Are you okay with that? Remember: be brave and take courage.

Here's that intersection again. Was David brave and courageous when he fought Goliath? Absolutely, but he was an original and went about it in an unconventional way. He didn't try to be like Saul or other warriors, he blazed a new trail and due to his sticking with his gut feeling and conviction of the Holy Spirit, he was successful.

"Most men lead lives of quiet desperation and go to the grave with the song still in them."
—Henry David Thoreau,
Civil Disobedience and Other Essays

Sometime, somewhere along the way in your leadership journey, someone is going to suggest a way of doing something that has worked in the past and seems logical, but the Holy Spirit of God may be telling you to depart from the conventional way of thinking and leading and do something that's never been done before.

When you suggest a new direction, or cast a new vision, you may very well be called strange and crazy. Take heart friends: If you're in the will of God and listening to His still, small voice, you're exactly where you need to be and all of heaven waits in wonder to see what God is going to do through you. Be bold, be brave, be sensitive, be desperate for God and lastly, be strange. The kingdom needs more strange leaders. Will you be one?

Bibliography/Works Cited

Angelou, Maya. *Wouldn't take nothing for my journey now.* New York: Random House, 1993.

Atkinson, Greg. *Church Leadership Essentials.* Nashville: Rainer Publishing, 2013.

Barna, George. *Revolution.* Wheaton, Ill.: Tyndale House Publishers, 2005.

Batterson, Mark. "*Postmodern Wells: Creating A Third Place* by Mark Batterson." Q: Ideas for the Common Good. http:// www. qideas.org/essays/postmodern-wells-creating-a-third- place.aspx (accessed October 21, 2013).

Batterson, Mark. *In a pit with a lion on a snowy day.* Sisters, Or.: Multnomah Publishers, 2006.

Beach, Nancy. *An hour on Sunday: creating moments of transformation and wonder.*

Grand Rapids, Mich.: Zondervan, 2004.

Bennis, Warren G., and Patricia Ward Biederman. *Organizing genius: the secrets of creative collaboration.* Reading, Mass.: Addison-Wesley, 1997.

Blackaby, Henry, and Richard Blackaby. *Experiencing God.* Revised and Expanded ed. Nashville: B&H Publishing Group, 2008.

Blackaby, Henry T., Richard Blackaby, and Claude V. King. *7 truths from Experiencing God.* Nashville, Tenn. LifeWay Press, 2007.

Blanchard, Kenneth, and Phil Hodges. *Lead Like Jesus: Lessons from the Greatest Leadership Role Model of All Time*. 2005. Reprint, Nashville: Thomas Nelson Inc, 2007.

Blanchard, Kenneth H., and Spencer Johnson. *The one minute manager.* New York: Morrow, 1982.

Blanchard, Kenneth H., Patricia Zigarmi, and Drea Zigarmi. *Leadership and the one minute manager: increasing effectiveness through situational leadership*. New York: Morrow, 1985.

Brown, Robert E. Jonathan Edwards and the Bible. Bloomington: Indiana University Press, 2002.

Browning, David. *Deliberate simplicity: how the church does more by doing less*. Grand Rapids, Mich.: Zondervan, 2009.

Brunner, Robert. *Do You Matter? How Great Design Will Make People Love Your Company.*

Upper Saddle River: FT Press, 2008.

Card, Michael. *Scribbling in the sand: Christ and creativity.* Downers Grove, Ill.: InterVarsity Press, 2002.

Chambers, Oswald. *My utmost for His highest.* Uhlrichsville, Ohio: Barbour & Co., 1997.

Chandler, Matt, and Jared C. Wilson. *The explicit Gospel.* Wheaton, Ill.: Crossway, 2012.

Chester, Tim. *Unreached: Growing churches in working-class and deprived areas*. Nottingham: Inter-Varsity Press, 2012.

Claiborne, Shane. *The irresistible revolution: living as an ordinary radical*. Grand Rapids, Mich.: Zondervan, 2006.

Claiborne, Shane, and Chris Haw. *Jesus for president: politics for ordinary radicals*. Grand Rapids, Mich.: Zondervan, 2008.

Cloud, Henry, and John Sims Townsend. *Boundaries*. Grand Rapids, Mich.: Zondervan, 2004.

Cole, Neil. *Cultivating a life for God.* Carol Stream, IL: ChurchSmart Resources, 1999.

Cordeiro, Wayne. *Tuan dui shi feng xing wang jiao hui = Doing church as a team: the miracle of teamwork and how it transforms churches*. Chu ban. ed. Taibei xian Zhonghe shi: Gan lan, 2011.

Covey, Stephen R. *The 7 habits of highly effective people: restoring the character ethic*. [Rev. ed. New York: Free Press, 2004.

Cymbala, Jim, and Dean Merrill. *Fresh wind, fresh fire: what happens when God's spirit invades the heart of his people*. Grand Rapids, Mich.: Zondervan, 1997.

Eisenstein, Elizabeth L. *The printing press as an agent of change: communications and cultural transformations in early modern Europe*. Cambridge [Eng.: Cambridge University Press, 1979.

Floyd, Ronnie. "Pastors.com ~ Rick Warren's Online Community for Pastors and Church Leaders."Pastors.com ~ Rick Warren's Online Community for Pastors and Church Leaders. http://pastors.com (accessed October 21, 2013).

Frost, Michael, and Alan Hirsch. *The shaping of things to come: innovation and mission for the 21st-century church*. Peabody, Mass.: Hendrickson Publishers, 2003.

Gibbons, Dave. *The monkey and the fish: liquid leadership for a third-culture church*. Grand Rapids, Mich.: Zondervan, 2009.

Godin, Seth. *Meatball sundae*. London: Piatkus, 2008.

Godin, Seth. *Tribes: we need you to lead us*. New York: Portfolio, 2008.

Groeschel, Craig. *It*. Grand Rapids, Mich.: Zondervan, 2008.

Hamel, Gary, and Gary Getz. "*Funding Growth in an Age of Austerity*." Harvard Business Review 77, no. July/August (2004): 83.

Hattaway, Paul. *The heavenly man: the remarkable true story of Chinese Christian Brother Yun*. London: Monarch Books, 2002.

Hirsch, Alan, and Dave Ferguson. *On the verge: a journey into the apostolic future of the church.*
Grand Rapids, Mich.: Zondervan, 2011.

Hybels, Bill. *Courageous leadership*. Grand Rapids, Mich.: Zondervan, 2002.

Hybels, Bill. *Holy discontent: fueling the fire that ignites personal vision.* Grand Rapids, Mich.: Zondervan, 2007.

Johnson, Spencer. *Who moved my cheese?: an a-mazing way to deal with change in your work and in your life.*
New York: Putnam, 1998.

Lawrence, Brother. *The practice of the presence of God, being conversations and letters of Nicholas Herman of Lorraine,* Brother Lawrence. Westwood, N.J., Revell, 1958.

Lencioni, Patrick. *The four obsessions of an extraordinary executive: a leadership fable*. San Francisco: Jossey-Bass, 2000.

Lewis, C. S. *The weight of glory and other addresses.*
New York: Macmillan, 1949.

Lewis, C. S. *Reflections on the Psalms.*
[1st American ed. New York: Harcourt, Brace, 1958.

Lewis, C. S. *The problem of pain.*
New York, NY: HarperOne, 2001.

Little, Steven S. The *milkshake moment: overcoming stupid systems, pointless policies, and muddled management to realize real growth*. Hoboken, N.J.: John Wiley & Sons, 2008.

Outreach, January 1, 2008.

Maraboli, Steve. *Unapologetically you: reflections on life and the human experience.* Port Washington, N.Y.: A Better Today, 2013.

Marketing Group, Miniwatts. "*World Internet Users Statistics Usage and World Population Stats.*" *Internet World Stats– Usage and Population Statistics.* http://internetworldstats. com/stats.htm (accessed October 21, 2013).

Morgan, Tony, and Tim Stevens. *Simply strategic volunteers: empowering people for ministry.* Loveland, Colo.: Group, 2005.

Mulan. Theater viewing. Directed by Tony Bancroft. Burbank, Calif.: Walt Disney Home Video:, 1998.

Murray, Andrew. *With Christ in the school of prayer.* Springdale, PA: Whitaker House, 1981.

Nielson, Bryant. "*Foundations of Leadership II–Courageous Leadership.*" EzineArticles.com. http://ezinearticles. com/?expert=Bryant_Nielson (accessed October 21, 2013).

Patnaik, Dev. "*The Fundamentals of Innovation–Businessweek.*" Businessweek–Business News, Stock market & Financial Advice. http://www.businessweek.com/innovate/content/ feb2010/ id2010028_823268.htm (accessed October 22, 2013).

Rainer, Thom S., and Eric Geiger. *Simple church: returning to God's process for making disciples.*
Nashville, Tenn.: Broadman Press, 2006.

Rizzo, Dino. S*ervolution: starting a church revolution through* *serving*. Grand Rapids, Mich.: Zondervan, 2009.

Robinson, Alan and Dean M. Schroeder. *Ideas are free: how the idea revolution is liberating people and transforming organizations.* San Francisco, CA: Berrett-Koehler, 2004.

Robinson, Alan and Dean M. Schroeder. *Ideas are free: how the idea revolution is liberating people and transforming organizations.* San Francisco, CA: Berrett-Koehler, 2004.

Seaver, Bill. "*MicroExplosion Media–Social Media Marketing Strategy and Consulting.*" MicroExplosion Media– Social Media Marketing Strategy and Consulting. http:// microexplosion.com/ (accessed October 21, 2013).

Shelley, Marshall. "*The Good to Great Pastor.*" Leadership Journal, April 1, 2006.

Spurgeon, C. H. *Spurgeon on the Holy Spirit.* New Kensington, PA: Whitaker House, 2000.

Stanley, Andy. "*Inside North Point: Practically Speaking.*" Inside North Point: Practically Speaking. http://practicallyspeaking. org (accessed October 21, 2013).

Stanley, Andy. *Visioneering*. Sisters, Or.: Multnomah Publishers, 1999.

Stanley, Andy, Reggie Joiner, and Lane Jones. *7 practices of effective ministry*. Sisters, Or.: Multnomah Publishers, 2004.

Stanley, Andy. *The principle of the path: how to get from where*

you are to where you want to be.
Nashville, Tenn.: Thomas Nelson, 2008.

Stanley, Andy. *Deep & wide: creating churches unchurched people love to attend.* Grand Rapids, Mich.: Zondervan, 2012.

Stevens, Tim, and Tony Morgan. *Simply strategic stuff: help for leaders drowning in the details of running a church.*
Loveland, CO: Group, 2004.

Stevens, Tim, Tony Morgan, and Ed. Young. *Simply strategic growth: attracting a crowd to your church.*
Loveland, Colo.: Group Pub., 2005.

Swanson, Eric, and Rick Rusaw. *The externally focused quest becoming the best church for the community.*
San Francisco, Calif.: Jossey Bass Wiley, 2010.

Tchividjian, Tullian. *Jesus + nothing = everything.*
Wheaton, Ill.: Crossway, 2011.

Thoreau, Henry David. *Civil disobedience, and other essays.*
New York: Dover Publications, 1993.

Walsh, John. *The art of storytelling: easy steps to presenting an unforgettable story.* Chicago: Moody Publishers, 2003.

Waltz, Mark L. *First impressions: creating wow experiences in your church.* Loveland, Colo.: Group Pub., 2005.

Wang, Yue. "*More People Have Cell Phones Than Toilets, U.N. Study Shows* | TIME.com." NewsFeed | Breaking news and updates from Time.com. News pictures, video,Twitter trends. TIME.com.

http://newsfeed.time.com/2013/03/25/more-people-have-cell-phones-than-toilets-u-n-study-shows/ (accessed October 21, 2013).

Warren, Richard. *The purpose-driven life: what on earth am I here for?* Grand Rapids, Mich.: Zondervan, 2002.

Willard, Dallas. *Hearing God: developing a conversational relationship with God.* Downers Grove, Ill.: InterVarsity Press, 1999.

Wilson, Scott. *Steering through chaos: mapping a clear direction for your church in the midst of transition and change.* Grand Rapids, Mich.: Zondervan, 2010.

Wood, Shawn. *Wasabi gospel: the startling message of Jesus.* Nashville, TN: Abingdon Press, 2009.

Zalta, Edward N. *Stanford encyclopedia of philosophy.* Stanford, Calif.: Metaphysics Research Lab, Center for the Study of Language and Information, Stanford University., 2002.

Zevin, Gabrielle. *Memoirs of a teenage amnesiac.* New York: Farrar Straus Giroux, 2007.

Chicago formatting by BibMe.org.

Are you a leader in a Christian organization?

Is your church, ministry, or business lacking innovation? Perhaps you're experienced in trying new things and moving in new ways, but you haven't ever tried anything strange. Truly innovative leaders are often considered strange. Don't settle for everyday leadership; immerse yourself in *Strange Leadership*!

Greg gives 40 different ways the Bible teaches us to be strange leaders. Greg pulls from Scripture to illuminate these concepts and, from the words and writings of other leaders, to drive them home. *Strange Leadership* is practically an encyclopedia on the subject of innovation.

> *"Innovation is imperative in today's leadership culture.* ***Strange Leadership*** *reminds us all that innovation is about doing a whole new thing, that ultimately flows from God, the Chief Innovator. Thanks Greg for pointing us back to our true source for innovation and inspiration."*
> *-Brad Lomenick,*
> *Former President of Catalyst and author of The Catalyst Leader*

*"Because leadership in Jesus' upside-down Kingdom is so different and distinct from the world, it is **Strange Leadership**. In his book, Greg offers practical and helpful thoughts on leading others as one under the rule of God."*
-Eric Geiger,
Author and Vice President of LifeWay Christian Resources

*"**Strange Leadership** is an engrossing and enchanting collection of probes into the emerging field of innovation studies. It is filled with firecrackers, and sometimes even fireworks. "*
-Leonard Sweet, Best-selling author, professor (Drew University, George Fox University)

Greg Atkinson is a pastor, author, consultant and speaker who loves Jesus, the gospel, and the Church.

Made in the USA
Middletown, DE
10 February 2018